UNCANNY BODIES

UNCANNY BODIES

THE COMING OF SOUND FILM AND THE ORIGINS OF THE HORROR GENRE

Robert Spadoni

UNIVERSITY OF CALIFORNIA PRESS

BERKELEY   LOS ANGELES   LONDON

University of California Press, one of the most
distinguished university presses in the United States,
enriches lives around the world by advancing
scholarship in the humanities, social sciences, and
natural sciences. Its activities are supported by the UC
Press Foundation and by philanthropic contributions
from individuals and institutions. For more information, visit www.ucpress.edu.

University of California Press
Berkeley and Los Angeles, California

University of California Press, Ltd.
London, England

Library of Congress Cataloging-in-Publication Data
Spadoni, Robert.
    Uncanny bodies : the coming of sound film and
the origins of the horror genre / Robert Spadoni.
        p.   cm.
    Includes bibliographical references and index.
    ISBN 978-0-520-25121-2 (cloth : alk. paper)
    ISBN 978-0-520-25122-9 (pbk. : alk. paper)
    1. Horror films—United States—History and
criticism.   2. Sound motion pictures—United States—
History and criticism.   I. Title.
PN1995.9.H6S66   2007
791.43'6164—dc22   2006029088

Manufactured in the United States of America
16   15   14   13   12   11   10   09   08   07
10   9   8   7   6   5   4   3   2   1

The paper used in this publication meets the minimum
requirements of ANSI/NISO Z39.48-1992 (R 1997)
(Permanence of Paper).♾

For my parents,
Edward and Norma Spadoni

"O friend and companion of night, thou who rejoicest in the baying of dogs *(here a hideous howl bust forth)* and spilt blood *(here nameless sounds vied with morbid shriekings)*, who wanderest in the midst of shades among the tombs *(here a whistling sigh occurred)*, who longest for blood and bringest terror to mortals *(short, sharp cries from myriad throats)*, Gorgo *(repeated as response)*, Mormo *(repeated with ecstasy)*, thousand-faced moon *(sighs and flute notes)*, look favourably on our sacrifices!"

As the chant closed, a general shout went up, and hissing sounds nearly drowned the croaking of the cracked bass organ. Then a gasp as from many throats, and a babel of barked and bleated words—"Lilith, Great Lilith, behold the Bridegroom!" More cries, a clamour of rioting, and the sharp, clicking footfalls of a running figure. The footfalls approached, and Malone raised himself to his elbow to look.

The luminosity of the crypt, lately diminished, had now slightly increased; and in that devil-light there appeared the fleeing form of that which should not flee or feel or breathe— the glassy-eyed, gangrenous corpse of the corpulent old man, now needing no support, but animated by some infernal sorcery of the rite just closed.

H. P. Lovecraft, "The Horror at Red Hook," 1927

Contents

Acknowledgments

At the University of Chicago, the Program in Cinema and Media Studies and the Department of English Language and Literature provided generous funding support while I wrote this book. At Case Western Reserve University, the Department of English and the College of Arts and Sciences further funded the project, and my colleagues there gave me helpful feedback on pieces and versions of the manuscript. For their assistance with my research efforts, I am grateful to Barbara Hall and Janet Lorenz at the Margaret Herrick Library of the Academy of Motion Picture Arts and Sciences, Jan-Christopher Horak at Universal Studios Archives and Collections, Charles Silver and John Harris at the Museum of Modern Art Film Study Center, Karen Lund at the Library of Congress, Annette Marotta at the New York Public Library for the Performing Arts, Maureen Lasko at the University of Chicago Regenstein Library, the staff of the New York State Archives, Karan Sheldon at Northeast Historic Film, Kerryn Sherrod and Sarah Heiman at Turner Classic Movies, Daniel Edelson at *Variety*, Rakim Jihaad at Facets Multimedia, Frederick C. Wiebel Jr., and Claudine Adamec. Special thanks go to Ned Comstock at the Cinema-Television Library of the University of Southern California for helping me make the most of a hectic research visit, and to M. V. Carbon at the University of Chicago Film Study Center for helping me get image captures from film.

Donald Crafton and Yuri Tsivian provided thoughtful commentary on a version of the first chapter. David Levin, Barry Grant, Jeremy Butler, and Daniel Goldmark supplied much-needed advice at critical moments in the process. Early in my research, George Turner spoke to me one morning at the Academy of Motion Picture Arts and Sciences library and shared his love of classic horror movies and also some great stories about their making and first receptions. (He also gave me driving directions to Red Rock Canyon, where, "if you root around in the dirt a little, you can still find nails and bits of plaster from the *Mummy* set.") It was only after our conversation that I discovered his wonderful pieces on the films in *American Cinematographer.* I am glad for the chance to have met George before his unfortunate passing in 1999.

William Veeder read several early drafts and helped me clarify my writing and thinking. James Lastra shared his expertise in film sound and helped me nuance and sharpen my arguments. Kevin Heffernan offered many useful suggestions on how to improve the manuscript. Tom Gunning's faith, guidance, and insights, as well as the examples of his writing and teaching, have made this book and a great many other things possible. Mary Francis at the University of California Press believed in the project and shepherded it into production with expertise and patience. Laura Harger, Steven Baker, and Kalicia Pivirotto provided invaluable help as well. Two anonymous readers for the Press offered their terrific suggestions.

I also owe thanks to two departed friends. Kendra Morris talked me back into going to graduate school after I had talked myself out of it. I will miss her and always be grateful to her for helping me take the less certain path. James Fogarty and I watched Creature Double Features on many a Friday-night sleepover. My love of old horror movies began when his did. I will remember him and those special times when I think of these films.

Michael Simeon and the late Ilona Simeon offered their love and support in many forms, for which I am most grateful. My parents, Edward and Norma Spadoni, have encouraged me in my interests and pursuits from the beginning and have done a great deal to help me realize this book and other dreams as well. My children, Nora, Louise, and Matilda, good sports while their dad has been around less than he wanted to be, continue to give meaning to all my endeavors. Lastly, I am grateful to Diana Simeon for her love, inestimable support, superhuman endurance of what it took to get me here, and a life that makes it all worthwhile.

INTRODUCTION

It is the *between* that is tainted with strangeness.

Hélène Cixous, "Fiction and Its Phantoms: A Reading
of Freud's *Das Unheimliche* (The 'Uncanny')"

The two films that mark the dawn of the horror film as a Hollywood
genre, Tod Browning's *Dracula* and James Whale's *Frankenstein* (both
1931), make a curious pair. When I first saw them as a child, I was at
once awestruck by the creaky, majestic slowness of *Dracula* and disappointed to find in the film so little in the way of sensational action and
monster effects. No monsters locked in mortal combat tumble through
a laboratory about to be flooded with water from an exploded dam, as
in *Frankenstein Meets the Wolf Man* (Neill, 1943), and no vampire glides
on a coffin-barge over misty waters toward his next bride, as in *Son of
Dracula* (R. Siodmak, 1943). Instead, *Dracula* gives us a tuxedoed figure
who speaks with a thick Hungarian accent and spends a lot of time glaring. *Frankenstein* at least had a real monster, and yet this film, too, exuded an ancient quality that set it a world apart from the other horror
films I loved. In *Dracula* and *Frankenstein* we hear no "movie music,"
and this registered to me not as an absence but rather as a scratchy presence that suffused everything in the films with a tangible and delicious
weirdness. There was something quintessential about these horror movies
as horror movies. Their luminous gray worlds and yawning silences
transfixed me. This was before I knew anything about film history. To
me, all black-and-white films swam in the same ocean of undifferenti-
ated oldness (except for silent films, which came from another planet),

and if you had asked me, I would have told you that the first color film was *The Wizard of Oz.*

I have since learned that *Dracula,* released in February 1931, appeared three months before the end of Hollywood's transition from silent to sound cinema, a tumultuous three and a half years that began with the release of *The Jazz Singer* (Crosland) in October 1927 and ended in May 1931 with the close of the 1930–31 film release season.[1] The classic horror cycle, beginning with *Dracula* and followed, in November 1931, by *Frankenstein,* ended in 1936 with *Dracula's Daughter* (Hillyer). Here, then, are two time lines, one for the sound transition and one for the classic horror cycle, which overlap by one film—Browning's. This overlap has not been closely considered by historians of the horror genre, who have been more apt to point out that there were uncanny, horrific, and even full-blown horror movies before there was sound film, and that these hailed from places outside the United States, most notably Germany. To be sure, the cinematic heritage of horror—to say nothing of its sprawling prehistory in literature, theater, and other media—predates sound film, and as certainly, the fullest account of the genre's origins will encompass cinemas other than Hollywood. But we can just as surely note that with *Dracula* and *Frankenstein,* things changed. Film critics and marketers started referring explicitly to "horror pictures," and producers started making films with this appellation in mind. And initially, this was a phenomenon of the Hollywood cinema.

That the genre's inception fell directly on the heels of the coming of sound has been presumed to hold implications mainly for the way horror films sound. There have been asides about "things that go bump in the night" and acknowledgments that sound was needed before victims could be heard screaming. Such observations suggest that off-screen sound figures importantly in the genre and that screams, on-screen and off, represent an especially useful type of sound to horror filmmakers.[2] Unseen bumps and audible screams—while no one would deny that such sounds are ingredients of the horror film as we know it, to recognize as much is not the same thing as identifying the major influence of the coming of sound on the genre's initial formulation. This influence has been missed perhaps because it reveals itself more in the way the first sound horror films look than in the way they sound.

This book compares the first year of the classic horror cycle to a pattern of response that characterized general film reception during the immediately preceding sound transition years.[3] It envisions the emotional responses of viewers "radiating outward" from the sites of the first screenings of sound film, and these responses infiltrating the making and first screenings of *Dracula* and *Frankenstein,* two horror films that, by virtue of their massive influence, further transmitted the shock waves of the sound transition deep into the mature sound era.

By regarding horror film making and form as two things shaped, forcefully as well as in fine-grained ways, by film reception, I may seem to have my cart set before my horse. Most horror film histories take *Dracula* as the obvious starting place for asking questions about how film viewing has inflected the course of the genre's development; and most reception studies—of any sort of film—begin with one or more films and then branch out into the audience and the broader cultural space. These studies view reception as a process of diffusion that is never more concentrated than at the launch point of the film text itself. Such a trajectory, while it might seem a natural one for anyone interested in historical viewers' responses to films, has led too few analysts to ask how tracing out patterns of film reception can lead an investigation back into the production sphere and back to film texts.[4] In their preface to *The Classical Hollywood Cinema,* David Bordwell, Janet Staiger, and Kristin Thompson write that a reception history of Hollywood cinema, "as yet unwritten, would require another book, probably one as long as this."[5] I think it is a mistake to conceive of this work to be done as a separate book. We need to ask whether production history is necessarily incomplete without a consideration of how it has been shaped by film reception (versus seeing the force lines running primarily in the opposite direction). How can we see audience responses flowing back into production practices—and not just in the forms of box office numbers and this or that critic's call for filmmakers to do more or less of something?

As film viewers, Hollywood's first horror film makers encountered the same body of films that general audiences and professional critics did during the sound transition years. I will argue that this viewing experience predisposed these filmmakers to conceive of a new kind of film in a way that capitalized on impressions that synchronized sound film had recently made on the viewership at large. The one-film overlap between the sound transition and the classic horror cycle becomes, according to this view, a window of opportunity through which passed an influx of creative energies. Determining precisely what came through this window, again, involves looking at the first sound horror films more than it does listening to them. Also, my approach will entail examining the cinema of the sound transition, and specifically its reception, in some depth before getting to the classic horror cycle.

This book does not posit the sound transition as the sole determining factor in the early development of the genre—to the exclusion, say, of the effects of the Depression on film studios and audiences.[6] In his 1931 psychoanalytic study *On the Nightmare*, Ernest Jones writes that "none of the group of beliefs here dealt with is richer or more over-determined than that in the Vampire, nor is there one that has more numerous connections with other legends and superstitions."[7] In this book I consider but one "determination" of the first vampire film of Hollywood's sound era, although I claim that it was an important one. The sound transition acted as a kind of filter through which strained all the other materials and forces that coalesced into the first sound horror films Hollywood produced. Everything that came through that one-film window was colored by this filtering process.

Major inspiration for this book comes from two sources. The first is an essay by Tom Gunning titled "'Those Drawn with a Very Fine Camel's Hair Brush': The Origins of Film Genres," in which Gunning calls for genre analysts to look more closely at the formal distinctness and characteristic effects of film genres. He wants us to ask how this distinctness and these effects reflect the specificity of the film medium. Gunning borrows from the Russian Formalists the concept of the *ciné-genre,* which is the sum of all the expressive devices that are both native to cinema and characteristic of a given genre. Regarding a genre as a ciné-genre, Gunning reasons, should lead to fewer genre-film analyses that focus mainly on film *narratives,* and it should inspire us to pay closer attention to such formal characteristics of the films as editing, mise-en-scène, framing, and, most basically, the very textures of cinema as they are experienced by viewers and explored by genre film makers.[8]

Arguing for the new opportunities that such an approach would open up, Gunning writes that "while narrative-centered genre criticism inevitably approaches the specific devices of cinema as means of expressing semantic or syntactic elements, a genre criticism founded in the specificity of cinema might describe genres as ways of narrativizing and naturalizing primal fascinations present in cinematic form itself."[9] Near the close of his essay, Gunning speculates that horror films might be especially good candidates for the sort of approach he is proposing. He notes descriptions, written during the cinema's first years, of films as unreal-seeming, sometimes disturbingly so. The first films could seem, simultaneously, to elicit sensations of presence and absence, to bristle with movement and visual detail while, disconcertingly, lacking all color and sound.[10] Gunning wonders if horror films like those in Wes Craven's *Nightmare on Elm Street* series reawaken viewers to the at-once dreamlike and photorealistic qualities of the medium as they spin out their distinctly cinematic horror fictions. He finds "primal fascinations present in cinematic form itself," ones that registered especially intensely at the beginning of cinema history, getting tapped in distinctive ways by one ciné-genre.

The initially strong impressions of the ghostliness of film that Gunning describes correspond to sensations that I find characterizing some initial responses to sound film. I also find that narrowing the aperture of inquiry to the years immediately following sound's advent brings into focus a weblike array of interconnections between the reception of early sound films and the launch of the classic horror cycle. If my impetus to look for this network of similarities and relationships was Gunning's essay, the handbook for fleshing it out was Yuri Tsivian's *Early Cinema in Russia and Its Cultural Reception*.

Tsivian's book serves this purpose in a few ways, two of which make it a promising model for reception study in many areas and periods of film history. First, Tsivian sifts through reviews and other written discourses on the cinema and, from these, constructs convincing arguments about the responses of *general* viewers, most of whom of course never wrote down their impressions of the films they saw. Second, he closely examines *formal* aspects of films, both ones whose reception he considers and ones that, he argues, constitute sites at which evidence of the reception of earlier films can be collected. Tsivian thus describes a mechanism for looping processes of film reception back into the production sphere and into the most intimate contact with individual film texts.

Tsivian also makes possible the extended comparison that I draw between film reception during the early cinema and the early sound cinema periods. Four claims that he makes correspond to the four-part parallel that constitutes the backbone of my argument. First, viewers during the early cinema period (from 1895 until about 1910) were more aware than most later viewers would be of the artificial nature of cinema. Second, this awareness could shade perceptions of the worlds on view in the films. Third, these altered perceptions were absorbed by some films during the period. And fourth, "reception works like a diffusing lens: whatever comes into its field 'goes out of focus' and comes to look like something else rather than itself."[11] Each of these claims inspires a major turning point in the argument to come.

Most film histories take for granted that with the coming of sound, films instantly became more realistic. More of the "real world" now was being incorporated into the total sensory package. The first Vitaphone shorts thrilled audiences with their realism, and Al Jolson's electrifying human presence in *The Jazz Singer* kicked off, virtually by itself, the mass conversion to sound. The common assumption is, as Rudolph Arnheim writes, that "the felt presence of the events is enormously enhanced by the sound of voices and other noises."[12] Much initial commentary on sound films supports this view. However, evidence also suggests that a countercurrent of sensations ran underneath the exclamations of realism. In particular, something seemed to be wrong with the status of the human figure on sound film. This figure could seem ghostly—or uncanny—a perception founded on the return to the foreground of general viewer awareness of cinema's artificial nature.

By calling this impression *uncanny,* I mean to invoke Freud's famous 1919 essay on the subject—although I am quite selective in my application of his ideas. In his essay, Freud catalogs impressions that can trigger sensations of the uncanny, two of which he borrows from a 1906 essay by Ernst Jentsch. These are momentarily perceiving an inanimate object to be alive and, conversely, momentarily perceiving a living thing to be inanimate.[13] These impressions correspond to the reception phenomenon that I find shaping the initial development of the horror genre.

A second idea in Freud's essay, and another one he borrows—this time from Schelling—is that the "'Unheimlich' is the name for everything that ought to have remained . . . secret and hidden but has come to light."[14] If the uncanny of early sound films marked a "return of the repressed," then what returned was the uncanny of early films.[15] Nicholas Royle writes that "the entire [film] 'industry' might be defined as a palliative working to repress the uncanniness of film."[16] If so, this work was overwhelmed during the sound transition, when the industry struggled against new and formidable obstacles to continue making films according to long-established norms and practices. The mechanical marvel that astonished and disturbed viewers at the start of cinema history astonished and disturbed them again thirty years later, and it continued to do so until Hollywood and its audiences learned to adjust to the new films.

The sensations of strangeness were temporary, but they lasted long enough to creep into some sound films. No films absorbed these perceptions more systematically and with more influential results than the first two films in the classic horror cycle. *Dracula* and *Frankenstein* earned impressive box-office returns, won critical acclaim, and "trapped" within their forms the uncanny reception energies of the early sound cinema. These films also set in motion an offshoot development: horror films featuring monsters that evoked not the uncanniness of the sound transition cinema but, thanks to the "diffusing lens" tendencies of film reception, the uncanniness of the recently extinguished silent cinema.

Two "primal fascinations," then, lurked like shadows behind the first sound horror films. True to their genre, *Dracula* and *Frankenstein* capitalize on what Noël Carroll describes as an innate human abhorrence of certain kinds of category transgression.[17] One transgression, recently and collectively witnessed by the makers and first viewers of these two horror films, concerned human figures in earlier sound films. These figures could seem both alive and dead at the same time. This sensation, although widespread, started to dissipate almost immediately, and it would trouble few viewings of Hollywood films once sound film production practices and reception patterns became stabilized. *Dracula* took advantage of this fading perception to appall its first audiences. *Frankenstein* carried the development forward by a leap. Together, the two films converted a fleeting reception phenomenon into the solid basis for an enduring genre practice.

The potentially disturbing sensations that sound film churned up would have to be neutralized before Hollywood could regain its footing as a robust and predictably profitable entertainment monolith within U.S. and world popular culture. They were the same sensations that had needed to dissipate decades earlier before the cinema could develop into a popular storytelling form. Both times, some filmmakers found ways to profit from the momentarily troubling side effects of new representational technology. A *Dracula* reviewer paid this dubious compliment to director Browning: "Of all the people of the cinema, only Tod Browning, specialist in the macabre, was properly equipped to direct this grotesque, fantastic, slightly unhealthy melodrama with proper forcefulness and conviction."[18] Another reviewer, writing about *Mystery of the Wax Museum* (Curtiz, 1933), noted that "after witnessing this unhealthy film, it is very agreeable to gaze upon a short subject dealing with the wonders of Yellowstone Park."[19] Sound film could display a scene of natural beauty or it could dredge up something dark and "unhealthy" out of the cinema's past and pour that into the frame instead. In 1931, the second of these possibilities was especially, vividly clear.

CHAPTER 1

THE UNCANNY BODY
OF EARLY SOUND FILM

There are uses of sound that produce a desirable effect;
on the other hand, there are uses that disgust people.

"Facts about Talking Pictures and Instruments—No. 4,"
Harrison's Reports, 8 September 1928

The coming of sound fueled a number of genre developments in Holly-wood cinema. One obvious example is the film musical. Less obvious is how the horror genre also dramatized and explored potentials that syn-chronized sound brought to Hollywood films. Where do we situate this outgrowth of the sound transition in relation to others of the period? We can start by noting that some genre developments were inspired by im-pressions, widespread at the time, that the coming of sound marked a huge forward leap in cinematic realism.

Signs of this impression appear everywhere in commentaries on the new films. Many noted that human figures in particular now seemed more ex-citingly present than before. Of a 1927 Fox Movietone short featuring George Bernard Shaw, *Photoplay* wrote that "it is the first time that Bernard Shaw ever has talked directly and face to face with the American public. What a voice and what a face! Although over seventy years old, Shaw is built like an athlete. He moves as gracefully as Jack Dempsey. And he has so much sex appeal that he leaves the gals limp."[1] Another commentator, considering sound films generally, wrote that "now, when a great singer opens his mouth in song we feel the thrill of his voice and his personality."[2] Alexander Bakshy, one of the most perceptive critics writ-ing about film at the time, agreed, noting that "the popularity of the talkies is not wholly a craze for novelty. Their success is much more due to the warmth and intimacy which has been given the picture by the human voice and which is so unmistakably missing in the silent picture as this comes from Hollywood."[3] How this new warmth and intimacy was to find immediate application within the character-centered narrative tradition of Hollywood cinema was suggested by the exhibitors' weekly *Harrison's Reports* when it explained the success of *The Jazz Singer:* "It was the talk that Al Jolson made here and there, and his singing of his 'Mammy' song, chiefly the singing of 'Mammy.' It was so successfully done that people were thrilled. The sight of Mr. Jolson singing to his mother, sitting in the orchestra, stirred the spectator's emotions as they were stirred by few pictures; it brought tears to the eyes of many spectators."[4]

If filmmakers could tug harder at viewers' heartstrings than before, they also could aspire to new heights of intellectual achievement. A journalist writing in 1928 gleefully predicted that now "the sparkling epigram, the well-turned phrase, even the cadences of Shakespeare will make their appeal."[5] Bakshy, although also critical of the period's stage-bound film adaptations of plays, felt that Hollywood definitely had something to learn from the theater's "relatively superior intellectual approach to the material of life."[6] Striving for these heights more ambitiously than most other Hollywood films of the period was *Strange Interlude* (Leonard, 1932), MGM's adaptation of Eugene O'Neill's play. In the play the characters speak their thoughts aloud to the audience; in the film their thoughts can be heard on the sound track while the characters' lips do not move. This technique, though it may remind viewers today of a television soap opera, impressed the film's first critics. *Screenland* called the film "restrained, highly intelligent, beautifully directed."[7] *Variety* called it "a natural for discourses on academic analyses of the contemporary 'art of the cinema.'"[8] *Film Daily* called it "a class picture finding the talking film in its highest form."[9]

With sound, then, came new opportunities to arouse the intellect, stir pathos, and elicit sensations of realism. Hollywood took advantage of these impressions by adding sounds to the same kinds of films that it was already making and also by developing some new kinds. One existing film type was the topical newsreel. Popular during the period, these shorts were constructed, as Donald Crafton notes, to maximize impressions of "being-there-ness."[10] A new film type, also popular and also energized by the perceived realism and immediacy of sound film, was the social problem film, especially the cycle of gangster films that began with *Little Caesar* (LeRoy) in 1930.

Social problem films led a trend that capitalized on impressions of sound films as open windows on the world. Not just the crisp reports of machine-gun fire or the slangy talk of the street persuaded viewers that these films held a special purchase on the real thing; also validating the producers' assertions was the resonance of these films with stories then in the news. A movie could be based on current events, or it might be built out of their very material. The *Motion Picture Herald* noted that *I Am a Fugitive from a Chain Gang* (LeRoy, 1932) was "written by a man who is himself still a fugitive from just such a chain gang as is here delineated. It is a tremendous selling point. That man wrote of his experiences and a motion picture has been woven from it."[11] Another critic jokingly reported that a prop used in *Scarface* (Hawks, 1932) was highly authentic: "The corpse flung from a taxi in one scene is no dummy but a remnant actually procured from some convenient morgue."[12] The same nouns and adjectives pepper the reviews of these films. *The Public Enemy* (Wellman, 1931) was "raw and brutal with that brutality flung to the front," "a grim and terrible document," and a film that "will get you, with its stark realism."[13] Also singled out was the films' *stylistic* leanness. Of *The Public Enemy*, one reviewer wrote that "there's no lace on this picture" and that "there doesn't appear to be a wasted foot of film. That means speed."[14] These films, then, were less like paintings or poems than like crime scene photographs or court transcripts. These were *documents* struck unfussily on newsprint, the output of a cinema freshly ventilated by the bracing effects of synchronized sound. The special capacity of the medium to render in fine detail the sordid realities of the present day earned the gangster cycle detractors as well as fans. One of the former complained in a letter to *Picture Play:* "I can't understand why people like these underworld pictures. It really hurts me to see one of my favorites in gangster films, because movies seem so real to me."[15]

Another spur to genre innovation during the period stemmed from a very different experience of sound film, one in which viewers now felt greatly distanced from the world outside the movie theater. To get a sense of this other experience of the medium, picture a horizontal scale for measuring the relative strength or weakness of the perceived realism and transparency of sound film, with perceptions growing stronger as we move to the right. Now bisect this scale with a vertical line and place the disembodied, "intellectual" appeal of *Strange Interlude*'s voice-overs at the top. The result is a simple grid for imagining some of the evocative

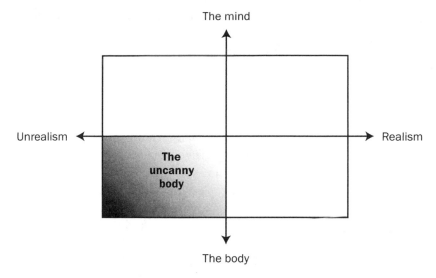

Figure 1

potentials of sound film (Fig. 1). On this grid, the bottom-left quadrant stakes out a zone of sensation in which the *unreal* and the *bodied* nature of sound film come across the most forcefully. This zone contains what I call *the uncanny body modality of early sound films.* Out of this zone the classic horror cycle emerged near the close of the sound transition period. We can gather some initial clues to the existence and source of this reception phenomenon from critics of the day who voiced their dissatisfaction, often in vague and grasping terms, with the touted realism of the first sound films.

THE SHRINKING OF PERSONALITY

> Synchronization of music and movement was perfect.
> It left nothing to be desired and created an illusion of
> reality—almost.
>
> **Ruth Russell,** "Voice Is Given to Shadows of Silver Screen,"
> *Chicago Daily Tribune,* 16 September 1926

Within the chorus of praise for the realism of the new films were indications that sound simultaneously was *getting in the way* of viewers' sensations of the figures speaking and singing on the screen. In 1929 Fitzhugh Green, in his book *The Film Finds Its Tongue,* recalled a 1926 sound film—one in the premiere program of Vitaphone shorts—in which Will Hays delivered a brief speech. Green wrote that Hays "seemed to be present, and yet he did not seem to be present."[16] In 1932 technical sound expert H. G. Knox remembered that "the early sound pictures required the exercise of considerable imagination to actually feel the actor's presence on the screen before you."[17] Of the partly talking film *Tenderloin* (Curtiz, 1928), *Variety* wrote that "another angle is whether the voice on the screen does not suggest something missing, with that missing element the physical self. This is undeniably felt."[18] And in what was perhaps the most in-depth articulation of this potentially troubling quality of the new films, Bakshy—who, as I noted, also championed the human warmth of the films—reflected on his dissatisfaction with recent films in which such stars as George Arliss and John Barrymore led the casts. In a piece titled "The Shrinking of Personality," he wrote:

> As I now try to recall my main impressions I am struck by a rather puzzling fact. None of the popular actors I saw stands out before me as a personality with whom I had a direct and all but physical contact. I know that on the stage some of these actors and others of equal gifts were and are able to escape the shell of the characters they represent and to fill the entire theater with their own beings, so that one feels as if one almost touched them. More phantom-like, but no less expansive and penetrating, were the personalities of the famous stars that radiated from the silent screen. . . . There can be no question of the success of the producers in establishing their screen stars not merely as favorites with the public, but as personalities that somehow . . . transcended their screen characters and came into a direct contact with the audience. The appeal of Chaplin, Fairbanks, Mary Pickford, Pola Negri, or Jannings in the old days of silent films had that quality of expansion.
>
> The situation with the talking pictures seems to be paradoxically different. The personal magnetism of the actor has lost its force. His entire personality has shrunk to something that is only a little more than the character he represents. This does not necessarily mean that his personality is completely submerged in the character. More often than not the reverse is actually the case, and the same George Arliss, for instance, will be seen in a number of characters that differ but little from one another. . . . But I doubt that his failure to loom as large from the speaking screen as he does from the stage, and as he probably would from the silent screen, is due to any lack of magnetism in his acting personality. The reason, I am inclined to think, lies rather in the curious effect that the addition of mechanical speech has had on the relationship between the screen actor and the audience.[19]

Bakshy goes on to blame the theatricality of the current cinema, specifically its strong reliance on stage techniques and sources, combined with the cinema's capacity to present scenes unfolding in "natural surroundings," for this effect of remoteness. While he definitely has a point, I believe we can discern a deeper source of the trouble than the decisions of any individual producers regarding this or that source or setting. A *Variety* reviewer of a 1927 program of Vitaphone shorts came much closer to grasping this deeper cause:

> An hour of mechanical sound production, together with its flicker accompaniment, is a pretty severe experience. There is something of colorless quality about the mechanical device that wears after so long a stretch, not because the reproduction is lacking in human quality, for it has extraordinary exactitude and human shading. It must be that the mere knowledge that the entertainment is a reproduction has the effect of erecting an altogether imaginary feeling of mechanical flatness such as one gets from a player piano.[20]

The root of the problem was, as this critic intuited, viewers' renewed awareness of the mechanical nature of cinema. This awareness stemmed from two sources: the temporary coarsening of film style that accompanied the transition to sound film production, and the initial sensational novelty appeal of synchronized sound films.

THE RETURN OF THE MEDIUM-SENSITIVE VIEWER

> It would doubtless seem strange if upon a screen a
> portrait (head) of a person were projected, and this
> picture slowly became of an animated character,
> opened its mouth and began to talk, accompanied by
> an ever-changing countenance, including the formation
> by the mouth as each peculiar sound is uttered.
> **Claude Friese-Greene**, 1889[21]

During the earliest years of cinema history, viewers were aware of qualities of films that most later viewers would tend not to notice. They were medium-sensitive viewers. I take this term from Yuri Tsivian's book *Early Cinema in Russia and Its Cultural Reception,* in which, following observations made by Eileen Bowser, Tsivian notes instances in which commentators during the early cinema period write vividly about such seemingly mundane events in films as a train or other object coming into the foreground, a bush trembling at a water's edge, waves breaking on sand and bursting into rivulets, and the faintest unsteadiness in a card player's fingers.[22] Viewers then also might notice elements of the cinematic discourse that later viewers would find unremarkable. These elements could include a close camera distance, a camera tracking forward or backward, the edges of the frame, the flatness of the image, and the monochrome color of the film.[23] Tsivian's observation of this phenomenon of early cinema reception is important for our study of early sound cinema reception because the coming of sound triggered the first major return of medium sensitivity to ordinary viewing in thirty years.

A number of practical and technical realities of production during the early sound period imprinted themselves on the finished films in ways that help to explain why viewers now were suddenly much more aware of films as manufactured objects. The addition of the recorded voice alone went a long way toward producing this result. Most obviously, there could be synchronization problems, which continued to occur in sound-on-disc film presentations until Warner Bros. phased out the technology in 1930—and later in theaters that continued to show sound-on-disc films.[24] Every synchronization mishap served to remind viewers that the bodies speaking on the screen constituted whole entities only tenuously, ones that had been pieced together in a movie studio and that could come apart quite easily once inside the movie theater. But even perfectly synchronized voices could heighten medium awareness in several ways.

To begin with, the voices could sound unnatural to viewers' ears. The technology was derided as "the cold, rasping Noisytone inventions."[25] *Harrison's Reports* reminded its readers: "You are well aware of the fact that the voice can under no circumstances be made to sound natural through a megaphone. And the horn is a megaphone."[26] At the end of 1930, Knox recalled "how queer some of the first talking pictures sounded. . . . Actors and actresses often sounded as though they were lisping and voices were quite unnatural."[27] A history of film published in 1931 noted that "by 1927, talkies had lost nearly all of their early squeaks and squawks and were delivering to audiences reliable reproductions of music and of the human voice."[28] Whether the problem was solved by 1927 or later depended as much on the acclimation of individual viewers to sound film as it did on the ongoing improvements in the technology itself. At any rate, locating a precise line of demarcation to characterize the before-and-after experience of most viewers is less important than is simply recognizing that, initially, the voice on sound film could strike a viewer as patently unreal.

Also making the speech seem unreal could be the slowness of its delivery. A reason for the slowness was a set of notions that preoccupied critics and industry professionals during the transition period concerning the so-called quality voice, which, Crafton notes, drew heavily on speech standards derived from the theater.[29] One result was that film dialogue was often articulated noticeably slowly and distinctly. Further, sound technicians seeking to record maximally intelligible dialogue could insist that actors enunciate carefully and deliberately. As Alexander Walker writes, "there was a heavy concentration on picking up ev-ery syl-lab-le, which led to retarded delivery."[30] Such plodding deliveries could make already muffled, hollow, and tinny speech sound even more unnatural.

Finally, the speech could seem unreal because viewers could tell that the sounds were not issuing from the lips moving on the screen. Mordaunt Hall at the *New York Times* was confident that with the arrival of the Vitaphone, this problem was now in the past: "Hitherto the efforts to couple pictures and sound have possessed weak points. In the earlier conceptions the voice appeared either to come from the top or the bottom of the screen, and although the lips of the character moved to the utterances it was not he or she who seemed to be doing the talking."[31] But this problem continued to crop up after 1926, in *Tenderloin,* for example, of which *Variety* wrote that "the voice, though issuing from the picture player, seems a thing apart, albeit synchronizing."[32] French film critic Alexandre Arnoux reported, after watching an early talkie in London, that "right at the start the general effect is rather disconcerting. Since the loudspeaker installed behind the screen never changes its locus of sound propagation, the voice always comes from the same spot no matter which character is speaking. The synchronization is perfect, of course, but it confuses and annoys the listener."[33] Rick Altman notes that some industry professionals believed that positioning several loudspeakers behind the screen and having an on-site operator fade the sound in four directions, to keep the voices close to the speaking mouths, was the only way to solve this problem.[34] It turned out that no such measure would be necessary, because this problem, which was largely a function of the newness of the technology to those who were supposed to be fooled by it, eventually solved itself. Once audiences got used to the loudspeaker-screen configuration, the bodies on the screen merged with the voices. Until then, even perfectly synchronized and acceptably natural-sounding speech could strike a viewer as a transparently mechanical contrivance.

Elements other than sound functioned to raise general awareness of the films as films. Synchronized speech in the first sound features came in distractingly discrete packages within the films. These were talking sequences abutted, usually at both ends, by silent sequences that had been scored with music. A transition from one type of sequence to the other could register as a sort of awkward mechanical gearshift in a film's mode of narrative presentation. All at once, dialogue titles gave way to synchronized speech; figures emoting and gesturing in the familiar silent-film acting style became figures keeping comparatively still so as not to make distracting sounds that could be picked up by the insufficiently discriminating microphone; the mobile frame of the silent film became the noticeably more restricted camera viewpoint of the early talkie; and flowing music yielded to a scratchy quiet that engulfed both the figures and their speech. Transitions out of as well as into a talking sequence could deliver a jolt. A reviewer of *The Jazz Singer* complained about "the abrupt blankness when the singing or dialogue stopped and the ordinary screening continued."[35] Another, writing about part-talkies generally, found that "the abrupt change of tempo when the words stop and the action resumes is a terrific strain on the credulity of the customers."[36] The edits that marked these transitions were more obtrusive than the edits in silent films. They could seem like raised seams along which disparate types of cinematic material came together. This problem, moreover, would persist after all-talking feature film production became the norm, for the first all-talking features also often clearly announced, via a perceptible change in the quality of the surrounding quiet, when a talk-free stretch of film was ending and a dialogue exchange was about to begin.[37]

Actors could exacerbate the general medium awareness for reasons other than their slow talking. Because of the difficulties associated with editing sound film, dialogue scenes now were being assembled out of fewer total shots.[38] This meant that actors needed to get their lines and blocking right for longer stretches, and this imperative, combined with the higher costs of filming retakes in the period, increased the likelihood of a slightly flubbed line here or a missed cue there making it into a finished film.[39] Viewers watching an actor making a mistake had little choice but to be reminded of the artificiality of the entire package. In all, the state of narrative absorption that had been (and would soon be again) intrinsic to the classical Hollywood viewing experience was partially disrupted as the augmented medium began to exhibit its materiality and the unsteadied practice to flaunt its techniques.[40]

Switching focus from the films to the viewers brings to light more reasons why general viewing during the period was shot through with uncommon medium sensitivity. For one thing, viewers were aware of a connotation of *synchronization* that the word no longer carries today. During the silent era, as James Lastra notes, the word in the context of moviegoing had referred primarily to live musical accompaniment.[41] *Synchro-*

nization in this context suggests something extratextual pieced onto the whole for effect rather than something intrinsic to the profilmic world that has been drawn out of it and captured on film or disc. Synchronized voices are understood to *accompany* moving lips rather than to issue from them. This connotation helps to explain instances in which the word is applied, during the early sound period, to describe sloppy postdubbing and even foreign speech that has been dubbed over English-speaking mouths.[42]

The sense of synchronization as something more provisional than essential accorded well with a viewer's impression of synchronized speech as a marvelous mechanical gimmick. The novelty of the technique guaranteed that even if there had been no discernable problems with the synchronization, the quality of the sound, or the disparity between the locations of the loudspeakers and the speaking mouths, viewers still would have experienced a heightened awareness of the artificial nature of cinema as a direct result of the sound. The editor of *Motion Picture News* noted in 1928: "There has not been, until now, any great, basic mechanical change in the motion picture. I am not speaking now from a scientific standpoint, nor am I overlooking the technical advances in picture making or projection or presentation. I am speaking only from a public viewpoint."[43]

The novelty of sound produced some unforeseen side effects, one of which appears to have been an increased awareness of the image as a flat entity. Sound, that is, reasserted the presence of the screen within the space of exhibition. It was a reassertion because, as Tsivian notes, the screen during the early cinema period had fascinated viewers.[44] Hints of the screen's restored visibility include this comment from 1926: "So remarkable is this synchronizing machine it seemed incredible the figures on the screen were only shadows."[45] This writer, in addition to indicating that the "synchronizing machine" is what is drawing her notice, conveys an impression of the figures on the screen as flat shadows. Hall likewise described a Vitaphone short featuring opera singer Giovanni Martinelli in which "the singer's tones appeared to echo in the body of the theatre as they tore from a shadow on the screen."[46] In 1922 a journalist covering a Phonofilm demonstration remarked that "each word was clearly audible as articulated by the moving lips of the moving picture."[47] Here the suggestion clearly is one of lips belonging to a picture and not to any person. Sensations of the image's flatness could, moreover, be heightened by the emerging practice of rendering dialogue comparatively loud and keeping it at a steady volume in order to make it easily comprehendible. A commentator wrote in early 1930 that speech so foregrounded, "while it may result in technically good recording, will cause all voices to seem to come from the same plane and thus destroy the effect of spatial depth, so necessary for dramatic effect."[48]

The novelty of sound also could induce viewers to register the unnaturalness of the sound more acutely. The novelty drew attention to qualities of film speech that soon would become submerged within the total filmgoing experience. Initially, viewers were unable to process synchronized speech as routinely and transparently as they had the silent film intertitle.[49] They might find the speech fascinating not for anything a speaker was saying but simply because the speaker could be heard saying anything at all. To viewers used to following a film narrative relatively distraction free, this sort of ravenous interest was something new. Viewers would soon be gauging, unimpeded, the characters' emotional states from the tones of their voices and listening, undistracted, to dialogue to gain information about what was happening in the stories; at first, however, synchronized speech could harbor fascinations that competed with these basic functions. A *New York Times* foreign correspondent implied in April 1930 that Parisians who could not understand English were turning out to see Hollywood talkies.[50] Clearly the virtues of synchronized speech as a conveyor and clarifier of story information were not foremost on these viewers' minds. A critic noted that the first all-talking film, *Lights of New York* (Foy, 1928), "would have been laughed off the stage had it been presented without benefit of Vitaphone"; he then added that "novelty, however, has a fascination all its own."[51] Another commentator recalled in 1931 that "in the early days of talking pictures both stories and actors were forgotten—every one went to the cinema for a voice."[52] Such comments suggest that early sound film viewers could be engaged less by the semantic content of a speech utterance than by the very fact of it. Viewers so engaged would be more inclined to notice the *textural* qualities of the speech, which, as I have noted, could seem to them obtrusively unnatural. Initially, then, synchronized speech carried a strong potential to impress viewers with its *strangeness* and its *materiality*, two qualities the speech would substantially lose once viewers grew accustomed to sound film and once the quality of the sound itself had sufficiently improved.

The increase in medium awareness meant that general reception during the period could be less predictable than in the years immediately preceding and following the transition. During this time of relative instability, synchronized speech could pin a viewer's attention on a speaking figure, as it did the *Photoplay* critic's on Shaw, or it could direct attention to the film as a visibly and audibly present object within the theater auditorium. Crafton's characterization of critical debates surrounding the voice during the early part of the transition is relevant: "It is as though the 'quality voice' was not part of the actor but part of the medium itself. The actor's job was to adjust his or her physiology to that mechanical paragon."[53] Until the voices took up permanent residence within the actors' bodies, sound film could strike a viewer as a dazzling reproduction of a preexisting unity or as merely an approximation and reassembly (however thrilling) of that unity. According to the latter view, cinema was less a window that had always been transparent—and now had been opened to let the sounds through—than it was a noisy attraction busily cranking out sensory delights before a house of astonished patrons.[54] This is our starting point for understanding the "shrinking of personality" and, beyond that, the uncanny body of early sound film.

THE COMPLEXION OF THE THING

In the key-cities, it would have "starved to death." But the novelty of having the screen shadows talk naturally changes the complexion of the thing.

"Motion and Sound," *Harrison's Reports*, 14 July 1928, referring to *Lights of New York*

Like the smallest movements that could rivet viewers when pictures first began to move, so the smallest sounds now could startle and excite viewers as moving pictures first began to make sounds. Fitzhugh Green recalled that Will Hays "advanced to the foreground and there was a little sound. It penetrated through people's minds that they had '*heard*' him clear his throat."[55] A review of the same program noted that "when Mischa Elman played there was not only the delicate pizacatti [*sic*] as the violinist plucked the strings, but the brush-sound of his bow as it moved legato over them." *Photoplay* wrote that when Shaw walks forward, "you hear his footsteps—scrunch, scrunch—on the path." And reportedly Sam Warner was thunderstruck when he found that he could hear the pianist in a Vitaphone demonstration film unbuttoning his gloves.[56]

There also were indications that sound resensitized viewers to the visual image. A sound technician wrote in August 1928 that "a review of the present talkies suggests an exaggeration of lip gymnastics. This is unnecessary, because of the intimate detail characteristic of motion picture photography, as compared to the legitimate stage declamation."[57] But were actors now really exercising their lips to a greater degree or were viewers now just more sensitive to these movements? Another commentator, without mentioning sound film, wrote the same month that "an actor whose face is slightly disfigured or disproportioned, so slightly that no abnormality is noticed in real life, becomes a marked man in a large, high-lighted close-up."[58] Another, who did explicitly link sound to his sense of the current enhanced potential of faces—especially ones viewed in close-ups—to appear grotesque, explained why acting expressivity must now be toned down:

> How can a dramatic episode be under-acted? This would surely not do for the legitimate stage, so how could it suffice for the talking picture?
> The answer to the question lies in the size of the screen. Even if we sit in the orchestra stalls of an ordinary theatre we can rarely detect whether the leading lady has a dimple. On the screen, however, we sometimes get a close-up of a star, where not only her dimple, if she has one, is visible, but the very pores of her skin. In fact, there are very few things one could avoid seeing when the features are magnified to 10 ft.
> Add to this huge physiognomy sobs which are only too often stentorian, and is it a wonder that the exhibition becomes so grotesque that the audience can remain polite no longer, but burst into laughter? These super-close-ups should never be used for sound pictures, especially if any strong emotion is being portrayed.[59]

This comment, which resembles ones that Tsivian finds from the early cinema period—expressions of shock and disgust at the graphic ugliness and gigantism of close-up faces—suggests that faces in early sound films could appear strangely energized when they were mouthing synchronized speech.[60]

Such changes in the appearance of objects in profilmic space could be compounded by another by-product of medium-sensitive viewing. Audiences also now—and just as Tsivian finds them doing during the early cinema period—were projecting elements of the cinematic discourse onto the diegetic or story worlds in the films.[61] We see this happening in mild form above, where a close camera view yields a "huge physiognomy."[62] Tsivian's examples of this act of projection in early cinema viewing include interpreting a shot in which the camera is moving toward a figure's head as one in which the head is moving toward the camera (or growing larger in size), and perceiving the edges of the frame as bounding a mysterious, unseen zone with the power to suck objects, persons, and even physical space into itself.[63] Tsivian is careful to stress that, very quickly, viewers learned to distinguish discursive elements from diegetic ones. Still, he maintains, throughout the early cinema period, films could elicit sensations of motion and transformation, even in viewers who knew better, and these sensations could turn watching the (to our eyes) most mundane film into a strange and even vertiginous experience.[64]

Sometimes early-film viewers projected onto the diegesis elements they perceived to be *missing* from the cinematic discourse. And so a crowd filmed with a silent camera became a crowd bustling with activity but making no sounds at all. The central text in Tsivian's examination of this viewing tendency is Maxim Gorky's famous 1895 review of the first Lumière program when it came to Russia. For Gorky, the views these films presented of domestic life and other everyday scenes were far from ordinary. They provided glimpses into a world that was strangely lacking in sound and color, a "kingdom of shadows."[65] Gorky knew that photography was a black-and-white medium and that what the Lumières were screening was moving photography; still, his senses were aroused in a manner that defied the simple and known facts of the presentation.

Contemporary discourses on early sound films suggest that viewers were again making the same sorts of projections, although probably to a lesser degree than viewers during the earlier period had. Hall articulated his dissatisfaction with the abrupt transitions of part-talking films in this way: "This sudden gift of voice to characters is frequently startling, for one may see a detective who has been silent suddenly boom forth in a terrifying fashion and thereafter figuratively have his tongue cut out."[66] Considering *The Jazz Singer*, *Harrison's Reports* noted that "Mr. Jolson sings with the Vitaphone several times. In one instance, after the song stops, one feels as if the characters were deaf and dumb." For another commentator, the need for actors to stay close to hidden microphones, keep still, and enunciate clearly "made the players resemble figures in a wax museum." A journalist covering a 1923 Phonofilm demonstration featuring a man and woman dancing to musical accompaniment found it "surprising that, while one could hear the instruments being played for the dancers, one could not hear the slightest sound of a footfall. Hence it seemed as if the dancers were performing in rubber shoes."[67]

These comments suggest that "absences" in the cinematic discourse could trigger perceptions of altered presences within the diegetic world. Among these presences, the most notably altered consistently was the human figure, for at least two reasons: the instant centrality of synchronized *speech* in the initial responses to sound film, and the long-standing centrality of human figures in classical Hollywood cinema. What then was projected onto these figures? The grayness of the medium, and the imperfect sound technology that many believed was never more imperfect than when it was reproducing the human voice. The result could be a viewing sensation whose power rivaled the uncanny realism of the first sound films.

The force of sound's novelty could impart to the image tremendous vibrancy, enough to make the singing Martinelli seem, to Hall, "so excellent, so real, that one felt as though Martinelli would eventually burst through the screen, as if it were made of paper."[68] But, as I have noted, Martinelli also seemed to Hall like a mere shadow on that screen. Figures now could seem anemic compared to the full-blooded characters and stars in silent films, and their voices could sound as attenuated as their countenances were wan. Something vital had been added along with the sound, but also something vital had been leached away.[69] Figures now seemed more vivid and animated, and yet, paradoxically, they did not necessarily seem more alive. In fact, with luminously pale skin and with voices that could be reedy and hollow sounding, these figures now could seem distinctly *less* alive than before.

This negative potential of sound film was intuited by Theodor Adorno and Hanns Eisler in their 1947 book, *Composing for the Films*. The authors wondered why musical accompaniment had so often been considered indispensable in silent film exhibition. They speculated that music helped to compensate for the lack of sound and color in the image, and masked its inherent ghostliness—then they added that "the sound pictures have changed this original function of music less than might be imagined. *For the talking picture, too, is mute.* The characters in it are not speaking people but speaking effigies, endowed with all the features of the pictorial, the photographic two-dimensionality, the lack of spatial depth. Their bodiless mouths utter words in a way that must seem disquieting to anyone uninformed."[70]

The authors point to two reasons why film speech during the early sound period could seem to issue from bodiless mouths, "speaking effigies." First, at that time every viewer was "uninformed." Second, nondiegetic music was not yet a norm of Hollywood sound cinema. There was disagreement as to how much, if any, nondiegetic music a film should contain. Some believed that music would annoy viewers who were trying to listen to dialogue; others worried that viewers would be wondering where the music was coming from.[71] Still others feared that viewers would find incidental diegetic noises distracting, as well.[72] As a result, dialogue scenes sometimes played out against inordinately quiet backgrounds. One who complained wrote in 1932, in the *Motion Picture Herald,* that "it seems strange that the power of music to make mobile and to vitalize has not been given more recognition in its application to the audible screen."[73] (The previous year Bakshy had written that most silent films, when screened without musical accompaniment, "appeared emaciated, bloodless, lacking in emotional appeal and dramatic accent.")[74] Unaccustomed viewers—and talking films with long stretches of virtually no sound *except* talk: Adorno and Eisler suggest that this combination could send disquieting sensations rippling through film audiences during the early sound period.

Comments from the period suggest that persons in sound films could indeed look to viewers like flat photographic entities. Luigi Pirandello wrote in 1929 that "the voice is of a living body which produces it, whereas on the film there are no bodies or actors as on the stage, but merely their images photographed in motion."[75] A critic commented the previous year that "the moment a character begins to speak from the screen his bodily unreality becomes marked—at least until one becomes accustomed to it."[76] Such feelings of unreality contributed to a general sense that more sensory information needed to be added to Hollywood films. A commentator in 1930 wrote that "the demand for color photography . . . increased to an almost unbelievable extent after the advent of sound and is steadily increasing. No doubt the incongruity of black and white images speaking lines and singing songs like living beings created a demand for a greater illusion of reality. This color photography helps to supply."[77] In 1929 Bakshy, after expressing his dissatisfaction with the illusion of reality on view in current films, wondered if "the introduction of stereoscopic projection coupled with color will solve this problem."[78] Cinema has long aspired to present an ever fuller sensory experience of the world. It is an impulse that André Bazin celebrated and one that Noël Burch, less delighted, has called "Frankensteinian."[79] Evidence suggests that this impulse grew more desperate when sound was added to the sensory mix.

Especially troubling was that this impulse could become even more desperate when faces were shown vocalizing in close-ups. Close-ups could seem to frame, as I have noted, huge physiognomies, marked men, and disgusting displays of lip gymnastics. Also, faces in close-ups could appear more *lifeless* than when viewed from other distances. Sound expert Joseph P. Maxfield found it "difficult and at times almost impossible to obtain a good illusion with extreme close-ups, that is, with pictures where the head and top of the shoulders only fill the whole screen. The reason for this partial failure is not wholly clear."[80] Another wrote that "in dialog sequences, quality and volume remain constant while the cutter jumps from across the room to a big close-up. At such times one becomes conscious that he is witnessing a talking picture."[81] Spiked increases in awareness of the artificiality of a film probably provoked more intense projections of cinematic discourse onto the faces on display. Close-ups, then, long valued by Hollywood for their capacity to strengthen character identification and glamorize stars, could distort and enervate human faces with a special power.

Regardless of the shot scale, sound film could seem to lack something, whether it was color (though it had always lacked this) or realism (though sound should have made films seem more real). Human presence in particular seemed afflicted. One option for figuratively describing this impression was to note a "shrinking of personality." Another was to invoke a critical reception trope of the period, one so ubiquitous in the contemporary discourses that we tend to pay it no mind, which is to call the films and the figures in them "talking shadows."[82] A third possibility was to call the figures ghostly.

Soundless feet could seem to wear rubber shoes or, as for a 1915 viewer of Edison's Kinetophone, could effect a more total, ground-up transformation: "A dog runs about noiselessly like a disembodied ghost, but his barking is far too loud." In 1929 a commentator described a film with "but two oral sequences in which the characters roared like monstrous ghosts." The same year, Pirandello attributed the inherent absurdity of sound film to the fact that "images do not talk, they can only be seen; if they talk their living voice is in striking contrast with their quality of ghosts."[83] Also in 1929, Bakshy wrote that "for reasons which it is difficult to discern, the total effect of the talking picture is generally thin, lacking in substance. Strange as it may appear, a silent picture seems to be freighted with sensory appeal. A picture like 'The Last Laugh' is a veritable 'eyefull.' In the talkies, much as you may be moved by the drama, you feel it is a drama in a world of ghosts."[84] And in 1990, a respondent to a Maine survey on cinemagoing recollected a 1928 film in which "the star was Conrad Nagel, and the 'talking' was of only partial duration—not for the whole picture. Spooky—hollow sounding voices—larger than life and ghostly. But fascinating."[85]

These comments suggest that the addition of synchronized sound triggered perceptions of ghostly figures in a shadowy world, just as the addition of movement had when, at the first Lumière screenings, the projected still photograph that opened the show was cranked suddenly to life.[86] Both times, the discursive element that was new raised awareness of the remaining silences and blank spots in the total sensory package, and the sensations that could result had the power to infiltrate and counteract impressions of the medium's advancement toward greater realism.

Tsivian and also Tom Gunning have described this dynamic of ambivalence running through the earliest responses to cinema.[87] They help us discern similarities between certain broad-scale patterns of film reception at two points in cinema history. While of course the two periods were really more different than alike, we can nevertheless say that at both times, conflicting perceptual cues clashed in the minds of viewers who were trying to make sense of a new representational technology; and at both times, a possible outcome of their efforts was to find the filmic world altered in a way that made it appear ghostly. At the dawn of the sound era, the both immediate and ingrained centrality of the human figure within the viewing experience guaranteed that the foremost manifestation in the freshly resurrected ghost world of the cinema would be an uncanny body.

SHADOWS IN THREE DIMENSIONS

One of the most pleasing numbers on the program followed. It was not a motion picture at all, but a shadow-graph dance, performed by real people behind a screen. When viewed through the teleview the shadows were not flat, as they would be ordinarily, but rounded, and separated as figures from each other. The effect was decidedly novel and pleasing.

"Vivid Pictures Startle," review of a demonstration of the Teleview, a stereoscopic film process, *New York Times*, 28 December 1922

The bloodless faces could appear ghostly. Ghostliness suggests a lack of physical substance, the semitransparent wispiness of an apparition. Impressions to this effect probably were helped along by the period's increased screen awareness, which would have made the figures seem as flat as shadows. Comments from the period, however, also suggest that synchronized speech could imbue figures with a physically emergent quality. Hall, for example, who wrote that it is "better to have words missed than to have them exploded from the screen in such a frightening fashion that it virtually killed the action of the story," also found, as I have noted, the singing Martinelli himself seeming ready to burst through the screen.[88] The two comments taken together suggest that in a reception environment in which discursive elements are tending to slip easily onto diegetic entities, perceptions of synchronized speech exploding from the screen possibly triggered perceptions of speaking bodies about to do the same—this at a time when the flatness of the screen *also* was asserting itself with a forcefulness to which viewers were not accustomed. I am describing a possible tension between the heightened awareness of the two-dimensionality of the screen image and the potentially frenetic visual intensity of the vocalizing human figure.

A theater chain executive wrote in 1930 that "no matter how effective your silent sequences might have been, they were still shadows, legends, phantoms. Once they become vocal, however, they become people; they come right off the screen into the laps of the audiences—whatever their effect was while mute, it trebles, and trebles again, in voice."[89] In 1932 Knox, describing recent improvements in motion picture sound technology, wrote that "many persons listening to Wide Range reproduction have expressed themselves as having the feeling that the actors are actually present in person. They seem to stand out in bolder relief, and one is not continually aware that it is only a picture."[90] It seems safe to assume that if improvements in synchronized sound technology could endow human figures with a quality of embodiment, the initial applications of the technology probably aroused similar sensations—with an added force deriving from the technology's newness. If so, the impressions of bloodlessness may have combined with ones of the vocalizing figures as more densely and protrudingly corporeal than the figures in silent films. This would help to explain why figures in silent films seemed to Bakshy "more phantom-like, but no less expansive and penetrating," than the ones in sound films. Possibly, then, viewers experienced a *composite* sensation of these figures. First, as Claudia Gorbman writes, "the recorded voice fleshed out the human body on the screen."[91] Also, however, the voice initially drained this body of its color and vitality. Such a body, at once lifeless and three-dimensional, might have born a resemblance to a living human corpse.[92]

A MODALITY

BELA LUGOSI: I just finished *Frankenstein Meets the Wolf Man* for Universal.
FRED ALLEN: Another musical, hey?

"Texaco Star Theater" radio program, 25 April 1943[93]

I began this chapter by making some contrasts between horror films, gangster films, and the lofty, experimental *Strange Interlude*. I conclude it by claiming that with respect to the coming of sound, the closest relative of the horror film is the musical. Describing their relationship now will help me refine my characterization of the uncanniness of the sound transition cinema while also previewing the means by which I will link that uncanniness to the origins of the horror genre.

Both genres seized on the abrupt tonal shifts that early sound film-makers sometimes effected in their films unintentionally. Consider movie musicals, in which musical numbers stand apart stylistically from the sequences that precede and follow them. A film shifts gears when a number starts, then shifts them back again after it is over.[94] The songs would threaten to break away from the rest of the film if their narrative motivation (the characters are putting on a show, the characters are falling in love) and the viewer's familiarity with the conventions of the genre were not holding the numbers firmly in place. This characteristic register switching has roots in the cinema of the sound transition.

During the transition, as Lastra and Altman note, two models competed for dominance as film practitioners experimented with different ways to integrate sounds and images.[95] One model, the scale-matching (or invisible auditor) approach, adjusted the sound scales of the individual shots to correspond to the shots' image scales. And so close-ups would be accompanied by "close-up sounds," while figures speaking in long shots would be harder to hear. The other model, the foregrounded-sound approach (which I have already found contributing to sensations of the unreality of close-up faces), placed dramatically significant speech atop a hierarchy that overrode the image scales of the individual shots and organized within itself all sounds according to their narrative relevance and presumed viewer interest.[96] Lastra writes that the scale-matching model, though it did not prevail, "found validation in an important early sound film form—the Vitaphone short—whose representational needs meshed seamlessly with the perceptual model of recording."[97] A model aimed to reproduce the experience of watching a live act from the vantage point of a theater seat proved ideal for the early Vitaphone shorts, which, Crafton observes, strongly resemble the numbers in many early musical feature films.[98] Through this pair of observations we can sketch a line of likely influence and development.

According to this sketch, the scale-matching model, which from the standpoint of narrative flow, represents the more disruptive of the two, gets funneled into the numbers in early musical feature films. The genre takes advantage of this model's assertion of an invisible auditor to position viewers in front of virtual live musical performances. Musicals latch onto—and codify—aspects of the more "disturbing" model, the one that tended to imbue single shots with too much weight and distinctness with respect to the other shots in a sequence. These codified aspects, with the weight and distinctness transferred from individual shots onto whole, segmented musical numbers, are in turn passed down through the history of the genre, which never stops encapsulating musical numbers to varying degrees.[99] Musicals thus carry forward into the sound era vestiges of the scale-matching model, and a short-lived idiosyncrasy of the transition furnishes raw material for a durable genre practice. We can compare this development to the inception of the horror genre as it relates to the sound transition. The precise nature of the parallel I want to draw is richly suggested by Katie Trumpener, who considers the first feature film that Douglas Sirk directed, when he was still in Germany and his name was still Detlef Sierck.

The film is *April, April!* (1935), which interests Trumpener because it manifests the "texture of transient moments" and because it poses what she refers to as "the problem of the overlap film."[100] Already the prospects for comparing the musical and horror genres seem tantalizing, even though the transient moment that is Trumpener's main interest concerns the overlap between the fall of the Weimar Republic and the rise of fascist Germany. Still, Trumpener also is interested in sound in Sierck's film, which, she finds, bears the markings of an early sound film. For her, the film's transitional status (in both senses) is most evident in its two brief musical sequences, especially where they begin and end:

> Sierck audibly and visibly shifts out of one modality (with its own particular use of space, sound, rhythm, and the bodies, gestures, and language of the actors) into a different modality, then back again. By now, nothing could be more familiar than such shifts. Since the early 1930s, indeed, they have formed part of the generic code of the musical, evolving from the practical need in early sound films to change the miking (and thus the mode of camera work as well) whenever there was a move from an action sequence into a singing sequence or vice versa. Ever since, when musical numbers appear or disappear in a musical, there is often a perceptible shift in the atmosphere, the emotional "weather" of a movie. The action of the film slows to a dream-like halt—or shifts into a different tempo; and then, suddenly, the onset of the music lifts the audience out of the inert everyday world into the more magical world of the song. When the music is rudely interrupted, or slowly fades away, the audience awakens, as if from a dream. If the movie itself works on its viewers as a kind of enchanted dream, a song sequence is a dream within a dream.[101]

Several points Trumpener makes here are worth underscoring: that aspects of musical films reach back to practical production realities of the sound transition; that the grouped, salient, formal characteristics of musical numbers can usefully be called a modality; that the modal shifts into and out of these numbers trigger changes in the "emotional 'weather'" of a film, with the numbers themselves constituting something like self-contained weather events traveling across the screen of the viewer's consciousness; and that this emotional weather is manifestly dreamlike, even against the dreamlike background of the film itself.[102] Each of these points correlates with an aspect of the uncanny body of early sound films.

The uncanny body was a modality. Its appearance marked a shift in a viewer's perception of the space, sounds, rhythms, bodies, acting gestures, and spoken language in a film. And like the numbers in a musical film, this body came and went. It might be called up by a voice suddenly sounding reedy or booming, a cut to a close view, an audible pop accompanying a film edit, or a combination of these events. Also, this shift, like the one into a musical number, reorganized a viewer's experience of a film. It provoked a change in the movie's "emotional 'weather,'" effecting a transition into a more deeply dreamlike state—although in the case of the uncanny body, this state was closer to a nightmare than to an enchanting reverie.

The patchy, inconsistent quality of early sound films thus becomes important for understanding the early developments of two genres. In the case of the musical, the numbers are not distinctive unless comparatively banal talking sequences precede and follow them. Put another way, there is no modal shift if the whole film is more or less uniformly dreamlike. Trumpener juxtaposes Sierck's film with ones directed by René Clair in which "the extremely subtle, balletic passage between spoken and sung sequences reinforces both the sense of waking dream *and* the sense of everyday life itself—street life, domestic routine—as a kind of unselfconscious but choreographed group dance, enchanting in its quotidian ordinariness. *April, April!* handles its transitions far more baldly, pasting its two musical sequences into the narrative with an audible montage, a visible shift in register and rhythm."[103] Gradual transitions of the sort Clair orchestrates, however beautiful, prefigure the formal distinctness of the musical film less strongly than do the abrupt starts and stops in Sierck's film.

Similarly, perceptions of the uncanny body were intensified by perceptions of the sometimes normal appearance of human figures in early sound films. That is, the relative instability of film style and reception during the period acted to set the uncanny body off against its surroundings more crisply. A dismayed fan wrote to *Picture Play* in 1928:

With the Vitaphone the smooth effect of varied action must be cut and always subordinated to the voice, to words, thus striking at the very heart of all that motion pictures have come to represent.

With the Vitaphone, one has a feeling of discord within, or a sensation like a tug-of-war. That part of one's receiving set which the cinema has developed is led to expect one thing, and before this is completed, the *mind* must be focused on the voice. It is a case of oil and water mixing.[104]

Impressions like this one—of churning internal disarray, fugitive parts within stormy wholes—enhanced the general "atmospheric conditions" for the integrations of both songs and living corpses into new Hollywood genre productions.[105]

We can think of the uncanny body as a form of reception interference or static. This shadow of life did not represent—from the standpoint of an institution dedicated to telling stories about flesh-and-blood living persons—a welcome side effect of adding synchronized sound to films. But neither were these incidental viewing energies counterproductive from the standpoint of every Hollywood interest. In the pressbook for *The Bride of Frankenstein* (1935), director James Whale made the following analogy as he reflected on the art of frightening audiences through the power of suggestion: "Lock yourself in a windowless room alone, turn out the light, and put your radio on in such a way that all you get is screams and moans and unearthly noises produced by static. Unless you are the rare exception, you will very hastily switch on the light, fully expecting to see some terrifying intruder in the empty room with you."[106] Whale, Tod Browning, and others made monsters out of the static of the sound transition. Browning's was not the first film to do this. The next chapter looks at some other early sound films as it examines the mechanism of this transformation.

CHAPTER 2

LUDICROUS OBJECTS,
TEXTUALIZED RESPONSES

There is chaos, as I have said, within the industry today. But
bad as it is, it is a good sign. It means progress. It is when the
show business gets orderly that you may look for danger signs.

William A. Johnston, "The Public and Sound Pictures," 1928

No tremendous talkie star has yet arisen, and there very
likely won't be such a star until things have stabilized a little.

Fitzhugh Green, *The Film Finds Its Tongue*, 1929

Bela Lugosi could make a stronger impression as an undead creature after George Arliss and Myrna Loy had stopped doing the same. Indeed,
virtually from the moment the sound transition began, the uncanniness
of sound film began to fade. This was in part because, virtually from the
beginning, the *novelty* of sound film began to fade. In 1932 Carl Laemmle
Jr. remarked that "the fact that the screen now has a voice is no longer
a novelty."[1] In 1930 the foreign correspondent who, as I note in chapter 1, implied that Parisians who did not understand English were going
to see Hollywood films, wrote that "the novelty of the first sound and
talking films has nearly worn off on this side, and while there will always be a receptive audience for singing and dancing pictures, straight
talkies must, of course, be in the language of the country where they are
being shown."[2] A history of film published in 1931 claimed that "before
1929 had ended, the novelty [of sound film], merely as a novelty, was
beginning to lose its power to draw patronage."[3] And, already by June
1927, the recorded score that had distinguished *Don Juan* (Crosland) at
its August 1926 premiere seemed like old hat; *Harrison's Reports* noted

that "the picture was accompanied by the Vitaphone, which at that time was a novelty; which now it is not."[4] To those who question the relevance of a professional reviewer's comment to understanding general film reception, I note that tracking the fading novelty of sound film through such comments actually permits us to be *conservative* when estimating what was happening with the viewership at large, since most reviewers—and especially ones in cities—saw more films than general viewers did, saw them earlier, saw newer prints, and saw them in theaters where there would be fewer technical problems and better sound and picture quality than elsewhere. Comments by critics and others writing during the period show that across the board, the novelty of sound film was always wearing off. The primal grip of wonder was always coming loose.

Simultaneously, Hollywood films were regaining their presound fluidity and polish. The practice of multiple-camera shooting, made necessary by difficulties associated with editing sound film, was phased out as soon as the superior multiple-*take* shooting system became viable again.[5] Also, release prints were standardized, which eliminated the need for projectionists to follow cue sheets and adjust volume levels during a screening, in turn reducing the chances for a sleeping or inept projectionist to jolt a film audience with wildly varying volume levels.[6] And Hollywood recovered editing options that sound temporarily had rendered difficult or impossible. As one theater manager recalled in 1932, "Years ago there were no 'dissolves'; nothing but a jump from one scene to another. Even one scene had jumps in it, for once the character got out of range of the camera, another had to 'pick him up' and continue the scene. As a result, the pictures were 'jerky,' and tiring to the eyes."[7] Lastly, sound films were including more nondiegetic music, and this helped considerably to smooth over the bumps in the viewing experience and "warm" the cinematic image.[8]

These technical changes combined with the waning of the novelty of sound film to effect a steady downturn in medium-sensitive viewing. A sign of this downturn can be read in a pair of comments that Bakshy made three and a half years apart. In February 1929 he wrote:

> Analogies between the stage and the screen assume that they deal with the same material. But they don't. The material of the screen is not actual objects but images fixed on the film. And the very fact that they have their being on the film endows these images with properties which are never found in actual objects.[9]

In August 1932, again reflecting on differences between theater and cinema, Bakshy explained why it was a mistake to import dialogue from a play into a film without first making some changes:

The stage is limited in its means and, moreover, cannot disguise its fundamental artifice and conventionality. But is it equally natural for this theatrically inflated speech to appear in the real world which is the province of the talking picture? After all, the material of the film is not an acted life, a life on the stage, but the real, honest-to-goodness life of people as it is lived in natural surroundings.[10]

Bakshy's dazzling turnaround suggests that the sense of sound film as a window on the world was fundamentally the one viewers were left with once the turbulence of the sound transition was fully behind them.

From the standpoint of the classic horror cycle, this return to viewing-as-usual was all for the good, for the unnatural goings-on in *Dracula* and *Frankenstein* would be made to seem more unnatural against the backdrop of a cinema that was itself, on the whole, seeming natural again. In 1930 sound engineer John L. Cass wrote that "if a medium of expression is to be powerful, the medium itself must be so utilized that it retires into oblivion as it does its work. This is true in the case of the printed word, the spoken drama, pantomime, the silent motion picture, and the talking picture."[11] For the purposes of the development we are tracing, *oblivion* might be too strong a word. Better to keep the medium— and all the weird and morbid effects that a heightened awareness of its artificiality can inflict on the inhabitants of a filmic world—in the background. Mordaunt Hall wrote in 1928 that "so far the shadow with a voice is a novelty, just as the silent picture was a novelty in the old days. It remains for the producers to consider seriously the new device and bend their efforts to making productions that will cause the audiences, in the interest in the story, to forget that they are gazing upon talking shadows."[12] Again, audiences *nearly* forgetting that they are gazing on talking shadows represented, for some filmmakers, the preferable outcome. These were filmmakers whose films concretely embodied qualities of the *unrealism* of early sound films and reflected them back at audiences who were in an excellent position to register and appreciate the results.

FILMS AS MIRRORS OF VIEWER RESPONSE

Modern Methods by Undertakers, With Actors
as Demonstrators

Headline in *Variety*, 21 January 1931

I have so far argued that early sound film viewers were medium sensitive and tended to project elements of the cinematic discourse onto the diegetic world. The third stage of the bridge I am building, from early sound film reception to early classic horror production, derives, like the first two, from Tsivian's reception study of early films in Russia. He finds some early films absorbing, or *textualizing*, general viewing responses to other early films. One example he considers concerns the often abrupt endings of films of the period, before editing became a standard practice and when the moment of a film's ending could catch a camera operator off guard. These endings, which tended to be less carefully planned than the beginnings and middles of the films were, could catch a viewer off guard as well. Tsivian describes the instant of the tail of the film flapping through the projector gate and the screen suddenly flooding with white light, startling some viewers and even making some of them feel disconcerted. He speculates that the high number of films of the period that end with a cataclysm of some kind—a car crash, a "fatal sneeze"—might be referring to viewers' encounters with these abrupt endings.[13]

An audience response, Tsivian explains, might also be echoed in a critical reception trope of the period. He notes that some commentators compared the first films to haunted portraits and magic mirrors, and he finds these tropes anticipating (and coinciding with) some filmmakers' approaches to transforming their own impressions of current and recent films into narrative premises, special effects, and other elements in their films. The haunted portrait and magic mirror tropes anticipate a subcategory of the trick film, a popular genre of the period, in which figures in portraits and mirrors come to life.[14] These trick films may reflect viewer impressions of films as retaining "copies" of persons that, in prints that circulate unbeknownst to those persons, take on lives of their own. During the sound transition, we find films again absorbing viewers' perceptions of the unrealism of the cinema of the period.

THE HOLLYWOOD REVUE OF 1929

> There are other such effects. For instance, Bessie Love
> is shown as a lilliputian inside the vest pocket of one of
> the characters. She exits from his vest pocket and walks
> on his arms. Soon she assumes her natural size.
>
> "The Hollywood Revue," Harrison's Reports, 24 August 1929

Some early sound films appear to textualize general impressions of the ambivalent status of vocalizing human figures on sound film, figures who could appear at once (and alternately) real and unreal, present and absent, flat and corporeal, and more animated and less alive than the figures in silent films. Also during the period, critical reception tropes point the way to some of the forms that these textualizations would take in individual films. One such trope is the figurative reference to sound films as "talking shadows." This trope—less common than "talking pictures," though not rare—anticipated a reviewer's response to a musical number in *The Hollywood Revue of 1929* (Reisner and [uncredited] Cabanne). During this number, a few times, the normal image suddenly becomes a negative one and then flips back again. Referring to this sequence, *Harrison's Reports* wrote that "by lights and shadows, the characters, during a dance, are made to appear at times as exotic beings, and at times as mere shadows."[15] The reviewer misremembers the technique behind this trick but signals his grasp of the underlying circuit of associations that the trick sets into play. Flashing before this viewer's eyes is a concrete manifestation of the potentially dual nature of speaking and singing figures on sound film—both lifelike and flatly photographic, both live persons and merely audible shadows.

Other moments in the film can be read along similar lines. One occurs when master of ceremonies Jack Benny introduces Bessie Love. Unable to find her at first, he eventually locates her tiny form inside one of his pockets. He sets her down and she grows to full size, whereupon her voice changes from a high-pitched squeak to a more full-bodied sound. Out of this brief sequence we can tease a few possible textualized responses.

Before Love appears, we hear her chirping inside Benny's pocket. This voice, if it seems to be issuing from Benny's body, does not seem to be issuing from his mouth. Also, the vocal quality of the sound is all wrong for Benny's body. I note in the previous chapter that similar complaints were leveled at many early talkies. (A reviewer in 1929, for example, wrote that "it is all very crude and unreal. The characters, as usual, seem to speak from their vest pockets.")[16] Then Love's head pops out of Benny's pocket, and a new set of potentially reflexive references is activated.

In a reception environment marked by heightened medium awareness, close and distant camera views could seem to yield, respectively, big- and small-sized persons. To viewers who had recently experienced such sensations, the manipulation of Love's size might have seemed vaguely familiar. Also, the moment possibly carried an extra charge at a time when some film sequences were still being assembled according to the scale-matching model, by which big bodies spoke with big voices and little bodies spoke with little voices. Here is another peculiarity of the transition cinema to which Love's introduction seems to make a winking reference.

Lastly, the transformation of Love's voice from an annoying squeak to the performer's "real voice" possibly struck a chord in viewers who were themselves growing accustomed to the sounds of their favorite stars and getting better at straining out of their speech all of the imperfections in the (steadily improving) sound technology. This brief sequence in *The Hollywood Revue of 1929* thus seems to dramatize a number of general viewer impressions of the unrealism of early sound films.

TWO VENTRILOQUISM FILMS

> There is more than a suggestion that the ventriloquist believes that he is so expert in the matter of throwing his voice that he has endowed the doll with a soul. Mad, yes.
>
> **Mordaunt Hall,** "The Ventriloquist," review of *The Great Gabbo, New York Times,* 13 September 1929

Another critical reception trope of the period compared watching a sound film to watching a bad ventriloquist's act. This comparison referred to the illusion-killing awareness of the distance between the loudspeaker behind the screen and the speaking mouth on the screen, an awareness that previously we might have called "the vest pocket effect" and that we may now call "the ventriloquism effect." A commentator referred to an early talking film as "a strange comedy, in which the actors are closely miming the lines with their mouths, while a mysterious ventriloquistic chorus leader, rigid and motionless in the center of the screen, at a certain depth, takes charge of the audible part of their silent speeches."[17] Pirandello compared sound films to "the vulgar muttering of ventriloquists accompanied by the buzzing, frizzling noises of phonographs."[18] Sound technician Lewis Physioc, trying to win adherents to the scale-matching model, described his sense of a problem that he associated with foregrounded speech:

> We see an object, and our experience reference estimates its nearness or remoteness. In both cases it is merely an estimate and considered individually, this estimate is satisfactory, but the moment we try to associate unrelated values of sight and sound it immediately violates this reference system and the results are unconvincing. To illustrate this further we cite the long practice by ventriloquists, in trying to furnish a voice that will fit their manikins. The success of their efforts lies in trying to furnish the combination that agrees with the experience of the auditors, and this experience refuses the possibility of a deep, gruff voice issuing from the diminutive figure of the manikin. We may also cite the shock to this experience of ours when

we hear, for the first time, a man of great stature speak in a delicate, high-pitched voice, or a Lilliputian address us in the deep basso of a giant.[19]

Physioc suggests that until audiences got used to foregrounded speech, watching a sound film could be like watching an incompetent ventriloquist butchering his art.

We can of course talk about the ventriloquistic nature of sound film without focusing on the early sound period. Altman, for example, writes that "the ventriloquist's art depends on the very fact which we have found at the heart of sound film: we are so disconcerted by a sourceless sound that we would rather attribute the sound to a dummy or a shadow than face the mystery of its sourcelessness or the scandal of its production by a non-vocal (technological or 'ventral') apparatus."[20] Without saying so, Altman is referring here to viewers who are used to sound films. Such viewers, rather than confront the disconcerting reality of the sound-image configuration before them, willingly attribute the speech to on-screen shadows. But this self-deception was not so easily perpetrated at the dawn of the sound era. The ventriloquistic nature of the *early* talking film has a special status. This was when, as we have seen, viewers were keenly aware of synchronization as a technological trick, just as most patrons who go to see a ventriloquist take pleasure in knowing that the act is an illusion.[21] And this was when the sense of human figures in sound films as "speaking effigies" (to recall Adorno and Eisler) was as strong as it ever would be.

Lips moved on the screen while a hidden machine talked, and viewers might be none too impressed by the results. It was clear from the whole sketchy setup that one voice could easily be substituted for another—as it was in *Blackmail* (1929), for which Alfred Hitchcock, reshooting parts of his originally silent film with sound, had actress Anny Ondra, whose Czech accent was wrong for her character, silently mouth her lines while a British actress with the "right" voice talked off-screen.[22] It was the right voice, but it wasn't Ondra's. Such sneaky substitutions were possible, and what was more, even an actor's *real* voice, warbling feebly out of the wrong spot on a flat screen, could strike a viewer as flagrantly inauthentic in nature.

All stars had a stake in representing themselves as the authentic source of whatever was interesting and exciting about their screen personas. Stars today who tell talk show hosts that they do their own stunts show this same investment. During the early sound period, the potential of voices to seem inauthentic posed special problems for some stars, among them Lon Chaney, who during the silent era had not merely played different roles but contorted his body and designed and wore makeup in ways that earned him the title "The Man of a Thousand Faces." The marvel of his makeup and performances was founded on the knowledge that it was really him up there. The less recognizable Chaney's makeup and physicality rendered him, the more amazed (and potentially skeptical) viewers could be at the transformations he underwent. When he made his first talking film, the skepticism that sound film could arouse needed to be addressed head-on.

The film was *The Unholy Three* (Conway, 1930), a remake of a 1925 film with the same title (and directed by Browning) in which Chaney also had starred. As part of the marketing campaign for the remake, MGM circulated a notarized deposition in which Chaney swore that all five voices that the film attributes to his character were in fact Chaney's own.[23] Chaney plays Echo, a ventriloquist who, disguised as an old lady, not only alters his voice to fit this character but also throws it into other people and even a few birds. (Echo is a criminal, and all these tricks figure in his scheme to rob houses.) Chaney was to be the Man of a Thousand *Voices,* too, and it was important that not one of those voices be rumored to belong to anyone but himself.

The ventriloquism trope of early sound film's critical reception suggests that awareness of the arbitrariness of the film voice-body combination could compel viewers to see through the body on the screen to the audiovisual chicanery that was the real source of the talking. But Chaney, heavily promoted as the designer of his own bizarre makeups, presented himself less as a star persona than, as Gaylyn Studlar notes, as a star *performer.*[24] He had to function as the end point of the viewer's fascination. Nothing propped *him* up, not any makeup artist and certainly not the bad ventriloquist that was the early sound film apparatus. Chaney addressed the "authenticity problem" of early sound films through the publicity stunt of the legal deposition and also by playing a ventriloquist. He asserted himself as the source not just of his own character's speech but of the speech of several other bodies on the screen as well. Echo was no mere echo. Chaney was the ventriloquist. It was really him up there, and it was really him talking.

The authenticity of a film star's voice and, by extension, his body could be cast in a dubious light during the period. One could issue signed statements attesting to the organic unity of the sound-image combination that constituted one's presence on the screen, or one could mine the perceived inauthenticity of this combination for dramatic purposes. Another ventriloquism film of the period is *The Great Gabbo* (Cruze, 1929). In it Erich von Stroheim plays Gabbo, a ventriloquist bound for greatness and ultimately ruin. From the outset we see that he is a tyrant to his lover, Mary (Betty Compson), and is incapable of relating to anyone but his dummy, Otto, whom he increasingly treats as though he were a real person. Early in the film, Gabbo loses his girlfriend, and in the end he loses his mind, although not before achieving great success as a ventriloquist. *The Great Gabbo* exploits, rather than resists, the transparently ventriloquistic nature of early sound film.

The film renders its ventriloquist character inauthentic in more ways than one. First, the character is grossly deficient as a person. Early in the film, Mary, preparing to leave him, tells Gabbo, "Little Otto there is the only human thing about you." She then says, directly to the dummy, "Goodbye, Otto. I'm sorry to leave you, because you're the only thing about him that seems to have a soul, even though you are only made of wood." Later, when Gabbo is sitting with Otto in a restaurant, an onlooker remarks, "Isn't he the funniest little thing you ever saw?" to which a man at her table quips, "Which one? The man or the dummy?" The joke, like the whole film, suggests that on some level Gabbo is interchangeable with his doll, the lifeless but artificially animated figure in whom Mary, the person who knows Gabbo best, finds greater reserves of humanity than she finds in him.

The same narrative that underscores Gabbo's washout status as a person asserts equally strongly his excellence as a ventriloquist. This second claim, however, is undermined by the total film. Von Stroheim and director James Cruze frequently seem indifferent to the dramatic requirement that Gabbo be made to appear to be originating Otto's speech. Gabbo can set Otto down and, by pumping a palm-sized bulb that connects via a cord to the dummy, remotely manipulate its jaw and somehow even move its head. At times it seems that von Stroheim has forgotten all about the bulb, as he frequently ceases working it while the dummy talks or sings on. Gabbo's virtuosic feats, moreover—which include smoking, eating, and drinking while Otto vocalizes—are a bit too virtuosic, for it is obvious at these times that the dummy's speech is issuing from a source other than Gabbo, one that is off-screen. This source can speak into a microphone planted right in front of him, and the resulting loud and clear speech is not quite like that of any human character heard in the film. The dummy's speech is nicely foregrounded and totally unreal, which is how the foregrounded speech of human characters in *any* film could sound until viewers got used to this convention. The illusion circumscribed by the narrative, that Otto is producing his own speech, fails to convince, and the illusion undergirding the narrative, that Gabbo is producing Otto's speech, fails as well. The manifestly ersatz nature of the talking human figure on sound film thus renders one character in this film doubly inauthentic.

One who found von Stroheim's performance less than persuasive was Mordaunt Hall at the *New York Times*, who wrote that

> Mr. von Stroheim is punctilious in the earnestness with which he attacks his role. He might perhaps have imbued it with a little more imagination, for when he is supposed, and only supposed, to make the dummy talk there is never a sign of movement in his throat. But so far as the effect of what happens is concerned this is not so important, for the audible screen is particularly well suited to ventriloquism. The dummy's mouth has only to move up and down, and it is taken for granted that the Great Gabbo is able to throw his voice in the direction of the ludicrous object, Otto.[25]

Hall suggests that to Gabbo's many false qualities, viewers in 1929 were free to add the patent phoniness of his professional bravura as well. He also suggests that to its first audiences, *The Great Gabbo* embodied shortcomings of the talking film that were at the time more than apparent.

SVENGALI

> And all that day, as she posed for Durien (to whom
> she did not mention her adventure), she was haunted
> by the memory of Svengali's big eyes and the touch of
> his soft, dirty finger-tips on her face; and her fear and
> her repulsion grew together.
>
> **George du Maurier,** *Trilby*

Whether any viewers ever found Gabbo or his dummy uncanny I do not know. It does seem to me more likely that such a feeling was elicited by another film of the period, *Svengali* (Mayo, 1931). In the most famous sequence in this film, the title character (John Barrymore) summons Trilby (Marian Marsh) across several Paris streets to his attic studio.

SHOT 1. Fade up on the interior of Svengali's studio. To the sounds of whistling wind are added, after a moment, those of chiming bells. We see a piano, a stool, and Svengali's rigid form. His back is to the camera. (Fig. 2, shot 1.1.)[26]

After a pause the camera begins moving toward Svengali. It starts veering to the right of the piano, then adjusts its trajectory so that it passes over it and to the left. Turning so that it keeps Svengali in the frame, and rising so that when it stops,

Shot 1.1   Shot 1.2

Shot 3.1   Shot 3.2

Figure 2. *Svengali.*

it will view him from a slightly high angle, the camera circles to a point where it takes in Svengali's still-unmoving form at a three-quarter frontal orientation. (Fig. 2, shot 1.2.)

SHOT 2. An open window with darkness beyond, Svengali's perceptual point of view. The chiming and wind noises continue.

SHOT 3. Extreme close-up of Svengali's closed eyes, bushy eyebrows, and nose. Timed to coincide with the start of the shot, Svengali's eyes open to reveal that they are white, glistening orbs. (Fig. 2, shot 3.1.)

After the eyes have opened, the camera remains close for a few seconds, then pulls straight back through a pane in the window seen in the previous shot. Svengali's motionless form, visible in the pane through which the camera has pulled, remains frame center. (Fig. 2, shot 3.2.) The chiming ceases; the wind noises continue. The pull-back continues until we are above the rooftop of another building.

SHOT 4. Rooftops. Following a very wide pan, perhaps 180 degrees, the camera begins moving forward over the rooftops. It

Shot 4

Shot 5

Shot 6

Shot 7

Figure 3

becomes increasingly clear that one window, roughly frame center and in the far distance, is the target of this movement. We continue to approach this window. (Fig. 3, shot 4.)

SHOT 5. Just before we reach the window, the camera pushes through a masked cut. Wind blows the sashes open, and we enter, never having stopped. The camera pans left and then closes in on Trilby's sleeping form, stopping on it. She stirs and tosses as though fighting off a headache or a bad dream. (Fig. 3, shot 5.)

SHOT 6. Close-up of Svengali, his eyes still white, only now they are glowing. (Fig. 3, shot 6.)

SHOT 7. Trilby sits up as though responding to a call. (Fig. 3, shot 7.)

As the sequence continues, we see Trilby struggling before fully rising from bed, her hand on her forehead as though in pain; Svengali, his eyes glowing white (as in shot 6); and Trilby, out of bed, moving in a trancelike state.

I find this sequence powerfully evoking the uncanniness of early sound films.[27] The setting is art director Anton Grot's miniature mock-up of nineteenth-century Paris. This Paris, although three-dimensional, looks totally unreal. Like the twisted exterior worlds seen in some German Expressionist films, this one conveys an intensely *interior* quality. This is a place untouched by fresh air and by any color not found on a gray scale. The sequence stands alone in the film in terms of style and tone. It is self-contained—like a musical number, and like a musical number, its beginning triggers a change in, to recall Trumpener, the film's "emotional 'weather.'" Certainly the film becomes more dreamlike when the sequence begins, a shift signaled by the camera's soaring flight and by Trilby's unwaking response to Svengali's summons. Her pained expression tells us that Svengali has come to Trilby in the form of a nightmare.

The sequence encourages viewers to project the monochrome color of the film onto the diegesis, in part, I believe, through sound cues. We have the whipping wind that never abates and the effects of which are not softened by a note of nondiegetic music. Instead we have bells tolling somewhere in this at-once vast and hermetically sealed-off world. The doleful chiming and the wind noises simultaneously invigorate and deaden the gaping emptiness through which the camera and Trilby move. This wind has always seemed to me to be whipping up the very grain of the film itself and casting it through the dusky air, across a space that seems at once empty and shot through with Svengali's godlike vision. Svengali unsettles the *grit* of the black-and-white film. This is the medium that sustains and transmits his power.

The sequence shows us what we simultaneously long and dread to see. There is nowhere else to look. In the opening shot, the camera seems to be caught in Svengali's orbit as it meanders toward him and as Svengali never relinquishes the frame. Nor does he give it up when the camera—at once anticipating and mirroring the spectator's fascination with and repulsion by the figure's blank, glistening eyes—backs away but for several seconds does not *look* away, not until we are far over the Paris streets.[28] The instant of Svengali's eyes opening is made more startling by its coincidence with the cut that brings us into the extreme close-up of this event. Viewers, suddenly closer to the character than ever before, have no time to adjust to the new proximity before they also must deal with those eyes. By fusing the instant of the eyes opening to the cut to the closer view, the film both imitates and elicits a viewing response that would construe a diegetic event in terms of a discursive action. (In a moment, Svengali will seem to take control of the discourse more boldly when, as one, his searching will and the camera take flight over the rooftops.)

Svengali's eyes initiate a series of reverse angles that stitch the space together and unify it through a supernatural causality. The sequence hyperextends the classical device of the point-of-view shot until it appears to represent not ordinary vision but the unnatural agency of a character's will.[29] These eyes, the source of the silent emanation that calls Trilby in her sleep, easily qualify as the most striking elements in the mise-en-scène. Their moist opacity foregrounds their status as eminently physical entities. More typically, eyes in Hollywood films tell viewers about the feelings of the characters to whom they belong. Synchronized speech supplied more such signals for viewers to interpret. Initially, though, as I have argued, the speech could have an arresting effect, as viewers stopped *on the speech* to marvel at its otherworldly materiality. Analogously, Svengali's eyes deny viewers access to a character's emotional interior while simultaneously drawing them into an intimate contact with their shockingly tangible surfaces.

These eyes are without question sentient, as the character they belong to controls everything we see happening. But if eyes are the windows of the soul, then these portals (if we can see *through* them at all) offer glimpses into a milky void. This figure—sentient but soulless, animated but inhuman—vigorously animates the world around him without breathing into it any shade of human coloring. In this sequence, Svengali has none to give. Sensations that recall earlier responses to talking figures on sound film are here being provoked by cues that have been hard-wired into one film. Significantly, at the center of the film's evocation of those earlier talking figures is one who is not saying anything at all.

In the piece in which Bakshy described his sense of the diminished human presence of Hollywood stars in recent films, he wrote that "the same shrinking of personality that was noticed in Mr. Arliss is also seen in John Barrymore. Excellent as he is in his flamboyant theatricalism in 'Svengali' (Hollywood), he never succeeds in coming off the screen."[30] I would disagree with Bakshy and say that, in this sequence at least, Svengali succeeds magnificently in coming off the screen; he just doesn't quite succeed in coming fully to life. This sequence contains the most vivid and concentrated textualization of the uncanny body modality of the sound transition to appear in a film outside the classic horror cycle.[31] With *Dracula*, the maestro's unwashed body would yield to the vampire's undead one, and morbid supernaturalism would emerge as the ideal repository of the uncanny body in the age of sound film.

CHAPTER 3

THE MYSTERY OF *DRACULA*

Precisely the same representation of a monster might be found frightening, repulsive, ludicrous, pitiful or laugh able by audiences in different social circumstances and at different times. Who now is terrified by Bela Lugosi?

Andrew Tudor, "Why Horror? The Peculiar Pleasures of a Popular Genre"

The first word out of the mouth of a horror film fan at the mention of the 1931 *Dracula* is likely to be "classic." All agree that the film casts a long shadow over the history of its genre and that its influence would be hard to overstate. The second word out of the same fan's mouth might be "creaky," "stagy," "funny," or possibly "bad." The film does not enjoy the same classic status as, say, *Casablanca,* in which the work's sterling quality and timeless appeal lift it high above the context of its first screenings. The capacity of *Dracula* to frighten and impress audiences remains resolutely fixed to the film's first screenings. Our next step in tracing the link between the coming of sound and the origins of the horror genre is to recover some of the lost original power, and strangeness, of Browning's film.

REAL EMOTIONAL HORROR KICK

The flaws inherent in *Dracula* are so self-evident that they are outlined in nearly every critique; only Lugosi freaks and the nostalgically inclined still go through the motions of praising and defending the film.

Michael Brunas, John Brunas, and Tom Weaver, *Universal Horrors*

"Dracula" is a story which has always had a powerful effect on the emotions of an audience, and I think that the picture will be no less effective than the stage play. In fact, the motion picture should even prove more remarkable in this direction, since many things which could only be talked about on the stage are shown on the screen in all their uncanny detail.

Bela Lugosi, 27 March 1931, read over radio station KFI Los Angeles[1]

For decades, *Dracula* has occupied a low place on the critical landscape of the horror film. The consensus has long been that the film represents a major disappointment and missed opportunity. Evidence of the size of the opportunity missed is typically found in the film's opening sequences, in which the real-estate agent Renfield (Dwight Frye) arrives at Castle Dracula and succumbs to his sinister host. After that, most agree, the film becomes a too-direct transcription of Hamilton Deane and John Balderston's 1927 theatrical adaptation of Bram Stoker's novel. The film becomes "stagy," an epithet endlessly invoked to say that the narrative unfolds in a talky and slow-paced fashion inside a boxy scenographic space that the camera ventures into only in the most perfunctory and bland ways. The unrestrained camera of the Transylvania sequences becomes a static recording device, Bela Lugosi overacts, and the promise of the opening goes largely unfulfilled.[2]

This estimation of the film is not quite as old as the film itself, for initially *Dracula* was a big box-office success, earning more money than any other Universal film released that year.[3] The film also impressed many critics. The *New York Telegraph* wrote that the film was "bound to raise the prestige of the screen." *Harrison's Reports* began its review by calling the film "Excellently produced!" Some found the film fast paced, and not just in its opening sequences. One wrote that *Dracula* was "packed with weird thrills, its lurid plot artfully introduced and suspense held for every foot of its unreeling." Another lauded the film's "spook-thrilling consistency."[4] Also singled out was the film's restraint, which, *Variety* claimed, kept the film from spilling neither humorously over the top nor disgustingly beyond the boundaries of good taste. This restraint, this reviewer felt, made the movie nothing like a canned version of the play: "Treatment differs from both the stage version and the original novel. On the stage it was a thriller carried to such an extreme that it had a comedy punch by its very outre aspect. On the screen it comes out as a sublimated ghost story related with all surface seriousness and above all with a remarkably effective background of creepy atmosphere. So that its kick is the real emotional horror kick."[5]

To be sure, the film also garnered criticism and even some pans.[6] The *Telegraph,* for example, wrote that "the weakness of its opening episodes, which lag, are more than counterbalanced by the compelling action of the last three-quarters of the picture."[7] Interestingly, this negative comment serves only to set the initial reviewers' praise of the film more sharply off against most of the later views, for this writer finds lagging episodes and compelling action in exactly the opposite places that most of the later critics do. One is tempted to wonder whether these first reviewers and the film's subsequent critics were watching the same film.

Opinions of Lugosi's performance as Count Dracula largely mirror this about-face in the critical assessments of the film as a whole. While today many find his performance indelible and often delightful, to most, Lugosi is a good actor only sporadically, and the pleasure that watching him affords is mainly of a campy nature.[8] In 1931 Lugosi's performance was something else entirely. Again, as with the film, not every critic was won over, but to many, Lugosi knew exactly what he was doing and he was very good at it.[9] One wrote that "Lugosi as the human vampire gives a convincing performance that will send chills down the spines of sensitive people." Another referred to his "brilliant portrayal." Another found him rendering the vampire "extremely convincing and horrible."[10]

The magnificent scariness of Lugosi's vampire and the "real emotional horror kick" of Browning's film are two mysteries of *Dracula's* first reception.[11] Although other films in the history of the medium have been praised on their first release, only to be remembered less kindly or not at all by posterity, the fall of *Dracula* was particularly precipitous, and the film's importance to its genre compels us to take a closer look. We must ask how this creaky and disappointing film could have once seemed so classy and frightening. We must ask how, for the critic writing in the *Film Spectator, Dracula* could have seemed so uncompromisingly singular in its intent and so sure in its execution that it verged on a kind of *purity:*

> A box-office success is being scored by Dracula because it is a production that is honest with itself. It makes no pretense at being anything but a horrible and impossible conception offered for the sole purpose of making its audiences gasp. It does not gather to itself any comedy relief on the theory that it is succeeding so well at doing what it started out to do that it should relieve the strain by doing something else, and thereby breaking the continuity of the effect that it is creating. It entertains an audience be-

cause it makes no concessions to the audience, and there is nothing in it to indicate that it cares two hoots whether the audience likes it or not.

Dracula is a successful picture because it has mixed its elements more intelligently than we find them generally in screen entertainment. The dominant note of the production is eeriness, a creepy horror that should give an audience goose-flesh and make it shudder. The picture never wavers in stressing this note. The sets, the lighting, the manner in which the lines are spoken, the costumes of the players, the tempo—everything bears down upon the theme without offering any abstractions that would divert our attention from what is happening before our eyes. . . .

The story of *Dracula* is about as forbidding as any story could be, and in itself contains not one element that makes a bid for popularity. But as a picture it is successful because it attends strictly to its business of being a picture with a single thought in it, a single straight line of story progression that does not stop anywhere to consider anything foreign to it. It is made honestly, and therefore, the public is paying to see it.[12]

For this critic, *Dracula* strikes its dominant note of eeriness so resoundingly that the film's comedy relief, supplied chiefly by the sanitarium attendant Martin (Charles K. Gerrard), does not even register as such. The "honesty" of the film has swept this critic up completely. How do we account for such a response? One way would be to reason that the film's first viewers, not having seen all the great horror movies that we have, were simply easier to scare. But this would represent a condescending and unproductive approach to our question. Better to ask what those viewers "knew" that we do not. They made sense of *Dracula,* as we do, by looking behind them; and of course, the texts that filled out their frame of reference differed quite a lot from our own. Stripping away *Dracula*'s retroactively applied generic labeling will help us see more clearly the impact of the sound transition on the shape both of the film and of its initial, auspicious reception.

THE MYSTERY OF *DRACULA*?

From where do genres come? Why, quite simply, from other genres.

Tzvetan Todorov, "The Origin of Genres"

But what is it that energizes the transformation of a borrowed semantics into a uniquely Hollywood syntax?

Rick Altman, "A Semantic/Syntactic Approach to Film Genre," in *Film/Genre*

The *Film Spectator* critic would seem to contradict Altman's claim that "nascent genres never appear to be pure."[13] But in fact *Dracula,* while perhaps uncommonly unified and distinct in its effect, did pose problems to marketers and critics who wanted to know how to categorize the film. Universal's publicity campaign was full of suggestions, many of them misleading. The campaign, for example, implied that the film was a mystery.[14] Many reviewers took the studio's lead and also classified the film in this way.[15] Further, Universal strongly suggested that the film offered viewers some form of a recognizable love story. We see this in posters depicting Dracula hovering over sleeping women and embracing swooning ones, in teaser display lines referring to "He of the fiery fingers, flaming lips and crimson kisses!" and in a studio-concocted newspaper contest asking readers to send in their answers to the question "What is a 'Dracula' kiss?"[16]

In a sense, the studio's strategy followed what was standard operating procedure for every Hollywood publicity department. This procedure was, as Altman writes, to "tell them *nothing* about the film, but make sure that everyone can imagine something that will bring them to the theatre."[17] Neither is it surprising that the *mystery* designation would figure prominently in the studio's promotion and the critics' reviews, since Deane and Balderston's play resembled the mystery plays that were popular during the 1920s. In Deane and Balderston's play, Renfield escapes Seward's Sanitarium by opening a secret panel and following a hidden passageway to Carfax Abbey.[18] Such devices would have been well known to patrons of mystery plays, among them *The Bat* (1920, adapted to film and directed by Roland West in 1926, remade with sound as *The Bat Whispers* and directed by West in 1930); *The Monster* (1922, adapted to film and directed by West in 1925); and *The Gorilla* (1925, adapted to film and directed by Alfred Santell in 1927, remade with sound and directed by Bryan Foy in 1930).[19] Each of these stories is set in an old dark house (or asylum or other old dark place) tricked out with secret panels and other surprises. Browning's film itself encourages the *mystery* classification by including, while no secret panels or passageways, other elements familiar from past stage and film mystery productions. Elements in *Dracula* with precursors in, specifically, *The Cat and the Canary* (Paul Leni)—Universal's 1927 adaptation of John Willard's 1922 play—include sinister lighting on faces, often from below (Fig. 4); clutching hands that emerge from unseen places (Fig. 5); and a heroine who tells of an encounter in her bed with a stalker whose breath she could feel as he drew near.[20]

Some critics noticed that there were problems with calling *Dracula* a

Figure 4. Top and middle: *Dracula*.
Bottom: *The Cat and the Canary.*

mystery. One found the film "ghastly and ghostly without benefit of trap-
doors and private detectives" and declared that "'Dracula' isn't mysterious. It is just plain spooky and blood-thirsty."[21] The problem with calling *Dracula* a mystery is that the film does not withhold the identity of
the "murderer" from its viewers. Viewers need only hear the warnings
of the frightened villagers and see Dracula rise from his coffin (both in
the opening minutes of the film)—indeed, they need only know the film's
title—to know who the murderer is. Likewise is *Dracula* a love story only

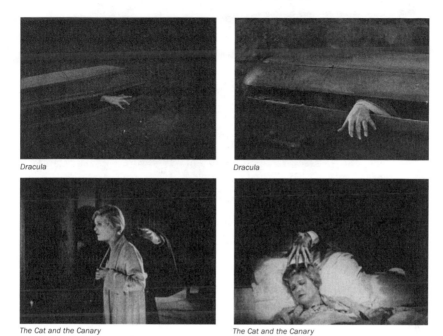

Dracula

Dracula

The Cat and the Canary

The Cat and the Canary

Figure 5

in the least-demanding sense of the term. Certainly the count looks suave in his tuxedo, and Lucy (Frances Dade) finds him attractive, and the physical contacts he makes with his victims happen in off-screen and other suggestively unseen places. But the film stops short of explicitly indicating or even strongly hinting that Dracula is interested in his victims for anything other than their blood.[22] The film skips over the moments in the play when Dracula kisses his female victims, and it includes no scene resembling one envisioned by novelist Louis Bromfield, in a treatment he wrote for Universal, in which, "with a look of obscene and loathsome gloating he seizes [Mina's] unconscious body, presses back her head, kisses her passionately."[23] In the film, advertised by the studio as "the story of the strangest passion the world has ever known," the passion was simply too strange to qualify as a love story in any conventional sense.[24] Even the relationship between Mina (Helen Chandler) and John Harker (David Manners)—a marginal character compared to his roles in the novel and play—was deemed too insubstantial to rate as a satisfying secondary romantic plot line. Critic Norbert Lusk called their relationship the mere "pseudo-love interest of the piece."[25]

Dracula was not much of a love story, and it was no mystery. And yet these labels performed a useful function. They supplied the film's makers, marketers, critics, and general audiences with a means to categorize, describe, and evaluate *Dracula* until such time as a more appropriate context for these discursive activities emerged. This was a context that these individuals were themselves in the process of creating. Until then, the misidentifying labels helped to promote a general sense that *Dracula* was a film of a sort that everyone had seen before. This impression was helped along by the studio's frequent reminders that the film was an adaptation of a hit play and a classic novel.[26] It was further encouraged by comparisons of *Dracula* to past film collaborations between Browning and Lon Chaney.[27]

To anyone wanting to associate *Dracula* with an existing body of films, the Browning-Chaney collaborations held out their morbidly strange plots and characters and, of course, Browning himself as a sturdy link. Referring to the Browning-Chaney films, a critic called *Dracula* "one of the best of the eerie procession."[28] But this association, like the *mystery* and *love story* designations, did not help everyone assimilate the film more easily. For one critic, the connection only made the film's singularity stand out more crisply. Lusk found *Dracula* "more macabre than any starring Chaney. And this circumstance, though emphasizing [Browning's] talent, militates against the picture, which lacks the very quality that was always present in the Chaney vehicles—humanness. However morbid the character, he was almost always possessed of human appeal. This cannot, of course, be said of Count Dracula, who is a monster, while his victims are obviously introduced to prolong his activities rather than stir any feeling for them as humans."[29] Lusk cannot help but admire (and also disdain) a powerful film that has been built around a character who elicits no viewer sympathy and who is not even, conventionally speaking, alive. The closest Chaney and Browning had come to anything so audacious was their *London After Midnight* (1927, lost), in which Chaney plays a vampire who is revealed in the end to be a Scotland Yard detective masquerading as a vampire to expose a criminal.

Lusk's criticism of *Dracula*'s lack of "humanness" points to the film's uneasy fit not just within the *mystery* and *love story* classifications but within the master classification of *Hollywood cinema*. What kind of Hollywood film offers viewers no characters with whom they may satisfyingly identify? Not a very successful kind, one might imagine. And yet *Dracula* was a hit with audiences and many critics (including Lusk).

The film was satisfying on its own terms, even to viewers who were not sure what those terms were. One critic warned readers expecting a mystery that "this is no subtle unraveling of a scientific puzzle. It is a bold, vivid presentation of unnatural horrors, leaving the audience fascinated, but shivering."[30] Another suggested that the secret of the film's success lay not in the vividness of its human characters but in a network of carefully wrought formal relationships that binds the whole film together: "Such a treatment called for the utmost delicacy of handling, because the thing is so completely ultra-sensational on its serious side that the faintest excess of telling would make it grotesque. Nice judgment here gets the maximum of shivers without ever destroying the screen illusion, the element that makes it possible is the pictorial plausibility of the scenes of horror in which impossible creatures move. That is, the mute perfection of the settings carry the conviction that the characters lack."[31]

No compelling human characters, no scientific puzzles or trap doors; and yet a mute perfection. Just as the film falls short when, today, we place it alongside other horror films, so *Dracula*, terrific as it was, frustrated reviewers who, in 1931, wanted to call the film a mystery. Of all the misclassifications, *Dracula*'s association with films of the old-dark-house mystery variety will be the most important for us, because looking at how the film fails to fit into this category can help us understand the *strangeness* of this creaky classic—in 1931—as a Hollywood film. Probing the inadequacies of the *mystery* label throws light on a genre-making process that, through *Dracula,* wove threads from old tapestries into something shocking and new.

The misidentifications of the marketers and reviewers, like the borrowed elements in the film, referred to film categories whose usefulness lay not in their inclusion of *Dracula,* but in their *proximity* to it. Todorov writes that "a genre is always defined in relation to the genres adjacent to it."[32] His claim can get us started thinking productively about *Dracula*'s false labels, spookily lit faces, and clutching hands.

One genre adjacent to the horror film was the filmed mystery play. Elements familiar from this genre appear in *Dracula*, where they are set new tasks. The ghoulish figure who comes to the heroine in her bedchamber is now not a man in disguise but an actual ghoul, and the sinister lighting and clutching hands now denote not events and persons that seem supernatural but ones that really are. This shift, which Todorov would describe as one from "the uncanny" (the supernatural explained) to "the marvelous" (the supernatural), points us past the superficial similarities between *Dracula* and the mystery plays toward the core of a new kind of film.[33] The atypicality of this core was acknowledged by Universal, if not to the general public, then to its exhibitors. A section of the pressbook titled "Here's How to Sell 'Dracula,'" and intended for the exhibitors' eyes only, began with this frank assessment of the film's appeal: "For its entertainment this picture depends upon thrills and 'horror' situations. Very little stress is placed on the love story . . the whole hinging on Dracula . . who, though dead for five hundred years . . comes back every night after sun-down . . seeking human blood."[34] The whole hinged on Dracula. The producers had a film with an unusually narrow focus and a singularly horrific appeal on their hands, and they knew it. Before their gamble paid off, the film's uniqueness appears to have made the producers nervous—signs of which can be read in the attempts to portray the film as more of a known quantity (a mystery, a love story, a Browning-Chaney-type film) than it really was. We also see it in this caution, in the pressbook, to exhibitors: "It would not be very good policy to use coffins in front of your house . . in other words . . don't go too far in gruesome exploitation . . keep it weird . . but don't suggest dead bodies."[35]

The studio's nervousness suggests that what is new can be frightening. Impressions the film made on its first audiences suggest the same. But no film, Todorov reminds us, can ever be completely new. *Dracula* took elements that viewers had seen before and arranged them into a new pattern. The elements came from filmed mystery plays, *Nosferatu* (Murnau, 1922) and other German Expressionist films, Stoker's novel, Deane and Balderston's play, Browning and Chaney's films, and other sources. The pattern derived in large measure from the uncanny body modality of the sound transition. To understand how, we need to return to Tsivian's concept of the textualized response.

THE VAMPIRE'S HISS AND THE MADMAN'S LAUGH

The thing is well nigh uncanny! Through the amazing
ability and ingenuity of the modern engineers, we have
made the shadow ghosts of men, women and children
to talk. . . . Before us we hear children shout and play,
where there are no children at all.

H. F. Richardson, "New Sound System," *Motion Picture
Herald,* 17 January 1931

DOCTOR: Did you hear that?
GRAY: Yes—the child.
DOCTOR: The child?
GRAY: Yes, yes, the child.
DOCTOR: There—is—no—child—here!

Vampyr (Carl Th. Dreyer, 1932)

A standard approach to considering the impact of the sound transition on *Dracula* might begin by examining how the film makes use of sound. We can begin there as well. Universal faced questions about how best to use sounds to evoke the supernatural worlds of the novel and play. One place to look for ideas was the studio's 1927 hit *The Cat and the Canary*, directed by German émigré Paul Leni.[36] This film had demonstrated that German Expressionist stylistic techniques could successfully cross the Atlantic and add box-office value to a Hollywood film.[37] Many characters look over their shoulders in this film. The vast and gloomy house where the guests spend the night is haunted definitely by a murderer and possibly by ghosts and an escaped lunatic. This film, had it been a sound film—and it was remade as one, now lost, *The Cat Creeps* (Julian, 1930)—would have been a feast of noises implemented, like the host of visual techniques Leni deployed, to make viewers jumpy. The *Motion Picture News* predicted that the film would "score best when presented mostly with mechanical sound effects rather than customary musical accompaniment."[38] We can easily imagine what some of those sound effects must have been: creaking hinges, banging doors, shrieking women, howling cats.

Also making use of sounds to rattle audiences were the Universal *Dracula*'s direct theatrical antecedents. Of Hamilton Deane's 1924 English play of *Dracula*, on which Deane and Balderston's 1927 Broadway version was based, a reviewer wrote that "noises are the sole contribution to alarm. If you shout loudly or strangely enough, and if only you can contrive to make the sound unexpected, somebody is sure to be terrified."[39] A reviewer of Deane and Balderston's play wrote similarly: "That it succeeded in freezing the very marrow of the majority of the local initial test cases is doubtful. . . . One jumps instinctively because of the noise and clamor of the procedure."[40] The aim to produce just such a response probably inspired this bit of stage direction in Deane and Balderston's play: when Dracula, cornered by his pursuers, vanishes with a "loud burst of mocking laughing."[41]

The *Dracula* plays encouraged Universal to conceive of a film liberally punctuated with loud and sudden noises. More inspiration for the same could be found in the studio's own recent forays into sound film productions of a macabre and scary sort. The studio's leading director of such films was Leni, who would have been a top contender for the job of directing *Dracula* had he not died suddenly in 1929. What is known about his only sound film, a part-talking old-dark-theater thriller titled *The Last Warning* (1929)—only silent versions of which survive—suggests that his approach to a sound *Dracula* would not have differed substantially from the effects accompaniment recommended for *The Cat and the Canary* by the *Motion Picture News,* nor from the *Dracula* plays' uses of sounds to startle audiences. The *New York Times* wrote that *The Last Warning* contained "too many outbursts of shrieking, merely to prove the effects of the audible screen, to cause any spine chilling."[42] *Variety* called the film's sound effects "multiple, continuous, and in detail," and predicted that the film included "enough screams to stimulate the average film mob into sticking through it."[43] Sound appears to have been used similarly in the sound *Cat and the Canary* remake, *The Cat Creeps.* The sound discs for this lost film turned up in the 1980s. William K. Everson listened to them and noted "much use made of howling winds, thunder, rain and creaking doors, to saying nothing of what sounds like wolves howling." He added that the film's female star "screams and sobs in the best Fay Wray tradition."[44] There was, then, no lack of precedent to lead Universal toward conceiving of a *Dracula* film brimming with noises.

Nor did the studio need to look far to find suggestions on how to unsettle audiences with, specifically, off-screen sounds. In his treatment, Bromfield described the moment of the count's first appearance as follows:

> Harker draws back from the window, dizzy by the great height. Behind him the howl of wolves is heard. He bangs the window shut and a moment later a voice is heard coming out of the shadows.
> VOICE
> It is a long drop, nearly two thousand feet.[45]

Only then would Harker and the viewers have seen Dracula. Elsewhere Bromfield indicates that when the protagonists make their way into Carfax Abbey, "weird sounds and what-nots can accompany this descent."[46] Surely a creepy sound blanket would overlay a visual frame already draped with cobwebs and shadows to enhancing effect, and the thicker the better.

When Universal began planning its film, then, sudden, off-screen, and ambient noises were among the near-at-hand options for using sounds to frighten a film audience. And these techniques do characterize some of what goes on in Browning's film. There is screaming; Renfield's presence is indicated a couple of times with a laugh that is heard before he is seen (a third time his shadow indicates it); and creaking, banging, and howling noises add to the atmosphere in a few spots. However, *Dracula* as a whole makes curiously light use of these techniques. Its major investment in the sound transition takes a different form.

We can begin to understand this form by considering the scene in which Dracula attacks Van Helsing (Edward Van Sloan). This scene comes in the long middle stretch of the film that critics today find draggy and inert. Dracula moves toward Van Helsing, who flashes a crucifix (Fig. 6, shot 1) and repels Dracula, who turns around and moves quickly toward the camera (Fig. 6, shot 2.1–2.2), disappearing past the right edge of the frame. In Browning and Garret Fort's shooting script, this moment is envisioned with the camera trained on Van Helsing and with Dracula's reaction signaled by an off-screen "snarl of rage."[47] In the film the noise comes from an *on-screen* Dracula and it sounds less like a snarl than like escaping steam. I imagine that many viewers today barely hear it. The noise accompanies Dracula's about-face and rapid movement into the foreground and out of the frame. It is not speech but hostile breath that has been made to seem part-and-parcel with the figure's turning action and forward propulsion. At this moment at the film's New York premiere, according to Hall, "there was no uncertain round of applause—handclapping such as is rarely heard during the showing of a motion picture."[48] Did Dracula's hiss play a role in this moment's provocation of an audible response?

I note in the first chapter that Tsivian has found objects coming into the foreground eliciting strong reactions in early cinema viewers. Now, at a time when viewers are in the process of overcoming a similar sensitivity for similar reasons, Browning hurls a vampire noisily in their direction. Dracula's forward movement is of the same sort that we might find in a 3-D horror film made in the 1950s. Looking back instead of ahead, we see the figure moving, more modestly but with sound accompaniment and a narrative thrust, along an axis similar to the one traced by the Lumières' train pulling into La Ciotat Station—in an 1895 film that, legend has it, sent viewers fleeing from their seats.[49] In each instance, an event that under other circumstances would draw little notice imbues a moment in a film with visceral power. Possibly, Van Helsing's repulsion of Dracula thrilled audiences in 1931, in part because it rekindled and recontextualized their own recent responses to sound films.

Shot 1

Shot 2.1

Shot 2.2

Figure 6. *Dracula.*

A contrast to both Dracula's hiss in the film and his snarl in the shooting script is the same moment as described in the "cutting continuity," a listing of shots compiled by editors as an aid to assembling the finished film. These lists appear to have been drawn up by editors who were screening the footage without sound.[50] The cutting continuity describes the vampire's repulsion as follows: "Dracula turns—runs to f.g. [foreground] with his cloak held over his face—exits past the camera—Professor in b.g. [background]—puts the cross in his pocket."[51] The document makes no indication of the hissing sound because none besides the sound

Figure 7

itself is made in the film. The cutting continuity also makes clear that elsewhere in the film, what is happening on the sound track can easily be inferred from what is happening on the screen—for example, when the flower-girl victim is found: "A policeman disc. [discovered] blowing his whistle—people come on—gather about—they bend over girl on ground."[52] The editors, viewers of a silent film that only they saw, can help us experience with fresh eyes and ears moments of the sound film that everyone saw. One such moment is when Renfield is discovered laughing madly in the ship's hold.

This laugh is heard first as the camera tracks over torn sailcloth and other debris on the ship's deck, then, after a cut, over a shot of Renfield glaring out of the hold (Fig. 7). The shooting script indicates that the character is to be discovered "looking up at them as he starts to laugh in a low, crazy way."[53] The "dialogue," a companion document to the cutting continuity that lists all lines of recorded dialogue (and other vocalizations, such as screams and laughter) in the film, describes the moment as follows: "Renfield (laughs crazily)."[54] The cutting continuity, however, describes the moment in this way: "Renfield disc. clinging to the railing on each side—he glares off."[55]

The cutting continuity has Renfield glaring only and not also laughing. The misdescription points to the uncertain status of the relationship between the aural and visual components of this shot. What the editor didn't hear, but helps us to, is how Renfield's laughter appears to float over this shot, how it remains strangely "off-screen" even after Renfield has appeared on screen. This laugh seems to us *near* Renfield's mouth but not quite *in* it. It is easy to imagine this moment calling to mind, in 1931, the experience of watching a film in which the sound and image lose synchronization, instances of which viewers at the time would have had no trouble recalling. Suddenly, a character's lips and the sound of her voice come unglued. The separation derails the viewing experience and possibly sends it rattling into uncanny territory. Viewers who a second earlier were comfortably ensconced in an unfolding narrative are suddenly put into contact with a cold and lifeless thing. There is no person there. The spirit of the person is elsewhere and does not inhabit this gray facsimile, this ghostly screen. Surely such a sensation qualifies as uncanny according to Jentsch's and Freud's criterion (described in my introduction) of thinking something alive and then suddenly realizing otherwise. Memories of this unpleasant experience possibly came to bear in the initial responses to this moment in *Dracula,* when a man who is losing his soul produces a laugh that is not altogether his own.

The moment represents a different approach to unhinging an audience with a laugh than the one described in Deane and Balderston's play, where, we may recall, the shocking power of Dracula's outburst, just before he escapes, resides in the abruptness and loudness of the sound. The moment also marks a contrast to the laugh heard at the corresponding moment in the Spanish-language *Dracula* (George Melford, 1931)—a film shot over the same period as the Browning production but at night, on the same sets, and with a translation of the same script but with a different cast and crew.[56] In the cutting continuity for this film, when Renfield (Pablo Alvarez Rubio) is discovered in the hold, the document indicates: "Renfield disc.—a light comes on—he screams—insane—he clutches at his head."[57] Here it is no challenge for the editor to determine by sight alone what is happening on the sound track, just as viewers do not hesitate for a moment in their determination of the source of this shrieking noise. Scary maybe, but not for the same reasons as in Browning's film.

Did these moments register more strongly in 1931 than they do now in part because *Dracula*'s makers and first viewers all shared recent memories of watching sound films in which similar sensations had been aroused unintentionally? These are just two moments in a film in which the uncanny of the sound transition touches virtually every quality of the work. This is achieved through a wide-ranging textual operation that begins with the figure of Count Dracula and spreads to the edges of Browning's film.

CHAPTER 4

DRACULA AS UNCANNY THEATER

Termed the Fantasmagorie (derived from the Greek for "phantasm assembly"), [Etienne Gaspard Robertson's] show played for six years, and because it dealt with the mysterious and unknown it appealed to Parisians, who were themselves in an uncertain, transitional period, having experienced the upheavals of the French Revolution.

X. Theodore Barber, "Phantasmagorical Wonders: The Magic Lantern Ghost Show in Nineteenth-Century America"

Viewers today call *Dracula* theatrical, and ones in 1931 might not have disagreed. Then, the film's theatricality simultaneously announced itself and transformed the whole film into an uncanny cinematic spectacle. This spectacle was made incandescent by the moment's proximity to the coming of sound. Lighting up the center of Browning's "phantasm assembly" was the figure of Count Dracula.

FIGURE

Or he is entombed alive in a sepulchre, beside the mouldering dead. There is in most cases an intense reality in all that he sees, or hears, or feels. The aspects of the hideous phantoms which harass his imagination are bold and defined; the sounds which greet his ear appallingly distinct.

Robert Macnish, *The Philosophy of Sleep,* 1834[1]

Compared to prior imaginings of Stoker's vampire, the one in Browning's film stands out for certain basic features that he lacks. He exhibits none of the overt sexual interest in his victims that we find in Deane and Balderston's play and Bromfield's treatment. And in contrast to the novel, Bromfield's treatment, and *Nosferatu,* in the movie the vampire's physical features do not give him an animal-like appearance.[2] Also absent are any salient traces of the character's formerly human status.[3] Further, the film mutes Dracula's ability to take different forms, making him appear neither younger as a result of his feeding (as in the novel and Bromfield's treatment) nor more ravenous and vile as the narrative progresses (as in *Nosferatu*), and always locating his transformations into bat, wolf, and human form in off-screen space.[4] Also, he is never explicitly shown, through a superimposition effect, to posses the ability to become physically insubstantial, as Count Orlok in *Nosferatu* is—and in his persistent corporeality the character differs from several other preexisting conceptions of Stoker's figure, including even the one in Deane and Balderston's play.[5] Except for when he passes through the web that blocks his stairway ascent in the castle (a penetration that happens off-screen) and when, in Seward's drawing room, his image fails to register on the mirrored underside of the cigarette case lid (where arguably his full-bodied presence on the big screen mitigates his absence on this small one), this Count Dracula remains thickly materialized at all times.

For Nina Auerbach, the playing down of the figure's incorporeal and animal natures is epitomized in the film's use of music from *Swan Lake* over the opening titles: "This musical equation with Tchaikovsky's Swan-Queen refines Dracula's bestiality into a theatrical trope. Stoker's Dracula infiltrated English households only furtively, as animal or mist; Lugosi's makes stagy, self-delighted entrances into his adversaries' drawing-rooms."[6] As Auerbach suggests, the major inspiration for this Dracula clearly was the figure as he appears in Deane and Balderston's play, the Broadway run of which also supplied Browning's production with the actor who would play the part. The play guided the filmmakers toward realizing a comparatively genteel version of Stoker's character, a streamlined and simplified version of the figure as he is drawn in the novel and elsewhere. If critics today cite this influence as the source of the film's biggest problems, viewers in 1931 seem to have felt differently. To better understand their responses to the film, we need to focus on the attributes this figure does possess, beginning with his voice.

Dracula's Voice

> When orchestral accompaniments and the noises of
> such things as steam engines, horses' hoofs, gun-fire
> and the like were synchronized with pictures, nobody
> became alarmed. They were an addition, that's all.
> But when screen actors began to speak lines, the silent
> drama was attacked. Voices invaded its peculiar domain.
>
> **James O. Spearing,** "Now the Movies Go Back to Their
> School Days," *New York Times,* 19 August 1928

Writing about the 1930 comedy *Feet First* (Bruckman), a reviewer found Harold Lloyd's voice to be "in character with his well reputed pantomime. He has a high pitch that is quite the kind most people wish and expect of him."[7] Lloyd's voice satisfied this reviewer's expectations concerning what a "voice of comedy" should sound like. Four months later, Lugosi's voice would set the standard for what a "voice of horror" should sound like, and for a time it had no rival. Low-pitched and thickly accented, Lugosi's voice exuded a sensuous strangeness that commentators since 1931 have taken pleasure in describing. From the "mellifluously thick Hungarian accent," to the "liquid, if sepulchral, voice," to the "stately, slightly over-ripe readings," to the "succulently foreign intonations," writers have suggested that Lugosi's voice constitutes within the film an entity with a material weight and density, one that even has its own smell and taste.[8] Dracula's speech oozes and flows. One can't help noticing its bizarre textures and halting rhythms—when, for example, he commands the usherette in the concert hall: "And after you deliver the message, you will remember nothing . . . I now say . . . Obey!" The character draws out pronunciations to exorbitant lengths, never more strikingly than when he tells Renfield, "I have chartered a ship to take us to England. We will be leaving tomorrow eeeeee-ven-ing." Though audiences who saw Lugosi on stage heard the same voice, ones who saw him on film experienced new dimensions of its power. If today the character's voice sounds mainly like the prototype for a thousand imitations, somewhere deep behind those imitations lies the "original" voice of this Count Dracula. To retrieve this voice is to find it sounding familiar even in 1931, although then not in a comfortably kitschy way. Then, Dracula's voice sounded something like human speech when it was first heard on synchronized sound film.

Dracula's speech evokes this earlier film speech, in part, through its slowness. A reviewer in 1931, ticking down a list of the film's effective touches, wrote that "slow, painstaking voices, pronouncing each sylla-ble at a time like those of radio announcers filled the theatre."[9] Though this writer does not mention any characters by name, we can assume that she is referring here to Dracula's and Van Helsing's speech, between which Dracula's is by far the more slowly pronounced.[10] This writer is reminded of radio announcers; I note in the first chapter that early sound film speech also was often delivered noticeably slowly. Though Van Helsing harks back to those voices, too, Dracula does so more forcefully.

One reason why is that Dracula's speech, in addition to being slow, is sensuously strange. The film foregrounds this quality of his speech when, after the concert, Mina teases Lucy about her infatuation with the count:

MINA: (mocking the cadences of Dracula's words as he spoke them in the previous scene): "It reminds me of the broken battlements of my own castle in Transylvania." *(laughs)* Oh, Lucy, you're so romantic!

LUCY: Laugh all you like. I think he's fascinating.

MINA: Oh, I suppose he's all right, but give me someone a little more normal.

LUCY: Like John?

MINA: Yes, dear, like John.

This exchange suggests that some part of Lucy's attraction to Dracula is to his voice, a voice that (at first) holds no fascination for Mina. Give her someone a little more normal, like John, as blandly conventional a male romantic character type as one is likely to find in a Hollywood film. If this exchange hints at a reading of the count as embodying a "dan-ger" lurking in the initial appeal of synchronized speech—get too hung up on the unearthly materiality of the speech and you risk bumping into an uncanny body—then clearly the implication is that Lucy chose the wrong path. In the world of possibilities for enjoying the evocative po-tentials of sound film, she chose a dead end.

The film also implicitly invites viewers to compare Dracula's and Van Helsing's voices. This juxtaposition is encouraged by more than just the slowness of the two characters' speech, for each character also wields a type of *authority* through, in large measure, his voice. There is Dracula, whose halting rhythms and odd pronunciations are dreadful but com-pelling. He is vanquished at the climax, expunged from the world of the film as he, an abomination, must be. And there is Van Helsing, whose first line, "Gentlemen, we are dealing with the undead," is sounded with an enunciative richness and a commanding tone that rivals the doomy

Figure 8. *Dracula.*

gravity of Dracula's words. With this pronouncement, which Van Helsing makes just after examining Renfield's blood, the character sets into
motion a development of discovery and pursuit that will eventually lead
to the vampire's destruction. That Van Helsing is an agent of rational
thinking, vision, and action is underscored by his goggle-like eyeglasses
and white lab coat, and by the beakers and test tubes that we see in the
shot in which he says this line, which is the first time we see him (Fig.
8).[11] These props clue viewers in to Van Helsing's rational and scientific
nature, as does his voice. Although foreign sounding, his voice is not in-
scrutably and oddly foreign sounding in the way Count Dracula's is. This
Van Helsing does not speak in the pigeon English of the character in the
novel, and no one would believe that actor Edward Van Sloan lacked familiarity with the English language—which is something press stories at
the time implied about Lugosi. Van Helsing's speech is crisp and correct;
his is a voice of reason. His voice, like Harker's, foregrounds qualities
of synchronized speech that sharply contrast ones we can hear embodied in Dracula's voice. Whereas Harker benefits from sound's ability to
make routine Hollywood character types seem more dramatically present,
Van Helsing benefits from a type of authority that sound also made more
emphatic. Van Helsing's voice—the one to trust and believe—is a cousin
of the voice-of-god narration that started booming on newsreel sound
tracks immediately following sound's arrival.

Van Helsing's alignment with this authoritative power of synchronized
speech was more apparent in 1931 than it is today, in part because the
film, until its rerelease in 1936, contained a concluding curtain speech
delivered by Van Sloan.[12] In it the actor stood on a stage in front of a
blank movie screen and spoke directly to the camera. This speech, through
its direct audience address and its assertion, through mise-en-scène, of a

live, on-stage human presence, recalled the 1926 short film in which Will Hays proclaimed to the world the wonders of the Vitaphone.[13] In Van Sloan's speech (taken from Deane and Balderston's play), the figure steps outside the world of the film—dramatically, as he interrupts the "End" title screen—although not quite out of character, to deliver one last thrill to audiences. Here is the speech as it appears in the "dialogue" production document: "Wait! We hope the memories of Dracula won't give you bad dreams—So just a word of reassurance. If when you get home tonight and the lights have been turned out and you're afraid to look behind the curtains—or you dread to see a face appear at the window—why just— just pull yourselves together and remember—that, after all, *there are such things.*"[14] Here Van Helsing/Van Sloan playfully validates the viewer's belief in a bogeyman who, like himself, draws authority from the power of the voice on sound film.

Exquisite Mincing Grace

> The casting of Bela Lugosi, as the criminal investigator, was a stroke of luck. He at times paints his acting with a phosphorescent glow and the touch of horror he thus adds to the proceedings helps in the widespread coagulation of veins.
>
> Review of *The Thirteenth Chair* (Browning, 1929), *Los Angeles Times,* 1 November 1929[15]

The weird textures of Dracula's speech enfold his visual form in a way that calls to mind figures in earlier sound films whose slow and unreal-sounding speech could trigger perceptions of their bodies as ghostly or corpselike. The film sets the vampire visually apart in more straightforward ways, as well: through lighting effects (see Fig. 4, in chapter 3); makeup that lightens his face relative to the other characters'; and the figure's glossy hair and impeccable formal attire.

Also distinguishing the figure is his bodily stillness. Dracula's form frequently constitutes within the film a strikingly unmoving presence. And when the character does move, it is with a slowness and a precision that does not break the spell that Lugosi consistently weaves around himself when he is at rest. A scene featuring some quick movements on Lugosi's part serves to illustrate how distinctive his physical actions are throughout the film. In it, Dracula smashes a cigarette case after Van Helsing has tricked him into looking into the mirrored underside of its lid.

Following the briefest of glances into the mirror, Dracula acts quickly but in too controlled a fashion to suggest a ferocious, animal-like movement. The action proceeds with almost balletic precision and fluidity, from the downward slice of the arm (Fig. 9, shot 1.1–1.2), to Dracula's withdrawal to a position from which, stock-still, he stands glaring at Van Helsing (Fig. 9, shot 1.3) and where, before and after a shot of Van Helsing (Fig. 10, shot 2), he regains his composure so slowly that the transition is almost imperceptible (Fig. 10, shot 3). No one else in the film moves like this. Of Browning's film, Frank McConnell writes that "the clash of time-senses comes across brilliantly in the movie, due primarily to the exquisite mincing grace of Lugosi's movements. Where everyone else walks and gestures with 'normal' theatricality, he choreographs himself in slow-motion."[16] This apparently was precisely the right choreography to follow for a figure hailing from the misty elsewhen of Transylvania. Comparing the historically unspecific quality of the film's opening sequences with the scenes set in contemporary England, Arthur Lennig writes that "the film actually has a double time sense; it is both modern and historical."[17] Lennig and McConnell together suggest that along with his boxes of earth, Dracula brings to England his own distinctive *time-sense*.[18] Putting it another way, and recalling Trumpener again, the "emotional 'weather'" of the movie changes whenever he makes an appearance.

This idea of clashing time-senses will become increasingly important for tracing a development that links up some of the most important early films in the classic horror cycle. In *Dracula* more than in any other film in the entire cycle, the time-sense associated with the monster calls to mind the altered perception of human figures in earlier sound films. This was when the medium appeared to thicken and turn gray, when it seemed to slow down the speech and movements of figures whose speech and movements were being constrained by demands placed on them by reigning opinions about "proper" film speech and by the new sound technology's myriad problems and limitations. *Dracula* mobilizes this perception to make one figure seem to be moving within this viscous medium still. Count Dracula stalks the normativized world of a Hollywood cinema directly on the cusp of a posttransition sound era.

The film evokes earlier moments in the transition through not only speech but also bodily stillness and movements and through costuming, makeup, and lighting. Perceptions previously triggered (mostly) by sounds are now being triggered by sounds as well as other formal elements in this film. In this way, *Dracula* initiates a process of transfer and transformation, from sound-induced perceptions of visual distinctness

Shot 1.1

Shot 1.2

Shot 1.3

Figure 9

to a visual distinctness that has been concretely realized. This process played a crucial role in the early development of the horror genre.

Dracula dramatizes this process by giving the count less and less to say over the course of the film. Most of the character's best-remembered lines come early, after which, increasingly, his eyes do much of his talking.[19] Renfield talks on board the ship to England while Dracula, staring at him with pin-spots lighting his eyes, says nothing. He commands Mina's nurse wordlessly.[20] Upon hearing a wolf's howl, Renfield goes to his cell window and alternately listens to and pleads with Dracula (who

Shot 2

Shot 3

Figure 10

has not said anything) not to make him do *that*. Later Dracula, in the form of a bat, flutters above Mina, who waits for him to emit a tiny squeal before saying, "Yes . . . Yes . . . I will."

The dramatization of this process, by which ephemeral effects of sound are being etched permanently into the visual field, becomes most explicit in a scene that has been criticized for telling when it should be showing.[21] In it Renfield relates a recent encounter with his master:

> RENFIELD: He came and stood below my window in the moonlight, and he promised me things, not in words, but by doing them.
>
> VAN HELSING: Doing them?
>
> RENFIELD: By making them happen. A red mist spread over the lawn, coming on like a flame of fire. And then he parted it, and I could see that there were thousands of rats with their eyes blazing red—like his, only smaller. And then he held up his hand and they all stopped. And I thought he seemed to be saying, "Rats . . . *Rats* . . . RATS! Thousands, millions of them, all red blood. All these will I give you, if you will obey me."

Maybe a shot of the rats would have been exciting, but it is worth noting that this scene, while it has been telling, has been showing as well, for during Renfield's speech (Fig. 11, shot 1) the scene cuts to Dracula standing unobserved on the veranda, enshrouded in mist (Fig. 11, shot 2). This shot presents viewers with an image of Dracula *twice* removed from speech. First, Renfield says that Dracula made him promises not by saying things but by doing them and by only seeming to say things. Second, we never see Dracula producing his inaudible speech but only hear about it from Renfield, in the course of whose narration the vampire appears, silent and motionless, a fixed icon charged with supernatural presence.[22]

Shot 1

Shot 2

Figure 11

If Dracula's speech appears to "call up" his image in this scene, it does so in a highly mediated fashion. The scene encapsulates something we see going on in the larger film—the increasing distancing of Dracula's image from his speech. The film, at the same time that it is leaning heavily on its strategy of *re-estranging* synchronized speech in order to call back the corpselike quality of human figures on sound film, is working to sever this umbilical link to the earlier cinema. The film is dismantling a modality built out of the novelty of sound film and the coarseness of the transition cinema and reconstituting it out of visual emblems, sounds, bits of narrative filament, and other reusable materials. These are genre conventions. The uncanny body of the sound transition is migrating from the sphere of reception into the discursive field of a new genre practice.

The Floating Soul

> Next came the "Floating Soul." With eerie music and lighting, the curtains opened to reveal a robed figure standing in the middle of the darkened stage. Through voodooism the person's soul began to glow, left its body, and floated around the stage. After the show many patrons swore that the glowing object floated well beyond the proscenium arch.
>
> **Mark Walker,** *Ghostmasters: A Look Back at America's Midnight Spook Shows*

Reinforcing the unnaturalness and visual distinctness of the vampire in *Dracula* are edits and camera movements. One technique involves rolling the camera toward Dracula's unmoving form. This happens after Renfield

Shot 1

Shot 2.1

Shot 2.2

Figure 12

cuts himself (Fig. 12). A more striking instance of this movement is when viewers see Dracula for the first time. If Dracula says less and less over the course of the film, he does not do so in a steady or continuous fashion, for he says nothing in a number of shots in the opening Transylvania sequences as well, including the shot in which viewers first see him.

Here is the shot as the shooting script describes it:

CAMERA MOVES BACK TO FULL SHOT, picking up Dracula, as we discover him with his back to Camera, bending over and closing the box from which he has just emerged. Beside the box from which he has come, are two oth-

Shot 1.1

Shot 1.2

Figure 13

ers, lids off, piled high with earth. Dracula straightens up and Xes to the two boxes—surveys them carefully, his back still to camera. Then he turns facing camera for the first time, and, moving into fore, towards stairs, starts to ascend. This movement brings his face into camera until the entire screen is filled with the menace of his inhuman eyes.[23]

This description differs from the sequence as filmed in a few ways. In the film, Dracula does not lower the lid, turn around, or come forward but, when the shot begins, is already upright and facing front, and Karl Freund's camera is already approaching his unmoving form (Fig. 13). The opossum seen in the previous shot is heard squealing over this one, and like Dracula's hiss when he rushes away from the crucifix, this sound quietly emphasizes the camera's movement, making it seem strangely audible. Dracula's introduction differs not only from the shooting script— and Bromfield's treatment, where, we may recall, the count is first presented as and through a sound—but also from the corresponding shot in the Spanish-language version, where, in a static long shot, a crate opens and smoke and light pour out, and Dracula (Carlos Villarias) is seen straightening up from behind the raised lid.

The vampire's introduction also can be contrasted with Van Helsing's. When we first see the doctor, his voice, glasses, lab coat, and lab equipment all mark him unambiguously as a man of science. These elements constitute "signs" that viewers "decode" unproblematically. The first shot of Dracula is laden with signifiers of a different kind. The dim, soft-focus pillars and arches in the background, and the figure's tightly wrapped cape, provide minimal distraction from the bright center of the frame, which is Dracula's face. Compared to the first shot of Van Helsing, this introduction provokes a more purely emotional response. Playing a role in eliciting this response is the forward-tracking camera. It differs from the track away from Van Helsing in his introductory shot, a movement that serves an unexceptional function—merely showing us the most important person at the table and then backing up to reveal who else is seated there. This is a standard variation on a Hollywood establishing shot.[24] The track in to Dracula, on the other hand, pushes through a space containing comparatively fewer depth markers toward a luminous face. Even though it is clear what is moving—the camera and not the subject— this shot engenders in viewers a (mild) sensation of a disembodied face floating into the foreground.

This effect is comparable to that of the same camera movement when construed by a medium-sensitive viewer. Surveying responses to forward-tracking cameras during the early cinema period, Tsivian writes that "in an age when a face approached by the camera was described as 'bearing down upon the viewer,' the track-in played the role of a transformer of energy: the energy of the moving camera was converted into the energy of the face, figure, or detail that was coming towards the viewer."[25] Did recent, shared, "emotional memories" of forward-tracking cameras similarly empower Freund's camera to act, in 1931, as an uncanny "transformer of energy"?[26] Was this one of the moments in the film that inspired a reviewer to write that "there are times when the force of the evil vampire seems to sweep from him beyond the confines of the screen and into the minds of the audience"?[27] Again 3-D, that other cinema technology that was a boon to the genre, comes readily to mind.

Dracula Is Already *There*

Dracula is in the house!

Van Helsing in the Browning *Dracula*

Camera-to-figure (and vice versa) movements act, like the sinister facial lighting, to accentuate the supernatural presence of the vampire at particular moments in the film. Another camera movement combines with a tendency of editing to do the same. These are movements and edits that discover Dracula within the frame rather than pick him up, say, walking into view through a doorway or coming around a corner.[28] We've seen this technique at work in Dracula's first appearance, where he is already upright and facing front when the shot begins. And we saw it when, during Renfield's speech, the scene cuts to Dracula not walking out of the mist but planted in the doorway.[29]

The game the film is playing with Dracula's figure is clearest in the scene

Shot 1   Shot 2

Figure 14

in which Van Helsing finds the bite marks on Mina's neck. In a medium shot of Harker and Van Helsing, Harker asks, "What could have caused them, Professor?" The two look off as they hear a voice say, "Count Dracula!" (Fig. 14, shot 1). The next shot reveals that the maid was not answering Harker's question but announcing a visitor (Fig. 14, shot 2). In this pair of shots, figure blocking, line delivery, and editing are all carefully coordinated so that, in addition to answering a question that viewers already know the answer to, the shots imbue the ostensibly mundane event of a caller's arrival with a preternatural suddenness. The moment is managed differently in the corresponding pair of shots in the Spanish-language version, in which Dracula *steps into view* through the doorway.

Something similar goes on the two times we see Dracula rise in Carfax Abbey. Both times, the camera drifts left past the opening crate (Fig. 15, shot 1.1), stops on a window as we hear the lid bang shut (Fig. 15, shot 1.2), then returns to pick up his straightening form (Fig. 15, shot 1.3). The averted gaze of the camera spares viewers the undignified sight of a man climbing out of a box, and it sidestepped the risk of offending local censors who might have found such a sight too graphic.[30] Also, the movement functions to discover Dracula within the frame. As we saw in the sequence from *Svengali,* cinematic discourse in this film consistently bends to one figure. It keeps "coming to" Dracula rather than the other way around.

Also relying on cuts and camera movements are Dracula's physical transformations and other supernatural feats. In one instance, the scene cuts from a bat to a sleeping Mina and then cuts back to Dracula in human form. Another time it cuts from a bat to a sleeping Lucy and then *pans* back to Dracula in human form. Earlier, when Dracula passes through the spider's web that blocks his way, three shots cover the ac-

Shot 1.1

Shot 1.2

Shot 1.3

Figure 15

tion: one of Dracula approaching and nearly bumping into the web (Fig. 16, shot 1); one of an astonished Renfield looking on (Fig. 16, shot 2); and one of Dracula on the other side (Fig. 16, shot 3). As with the transformations, this handling of the figure's penetration of the web might strike a jaded horror film viewer as a cheap trick.[31] But there were no such viewers in 1931, and no review I have found expresses dissatisfaction with the vampire's stairway ascent or with his transformations. The initial positive response to *Dracula* suggests that what can seem ordinary to us, or like a cheat, could seem extraordinary then.[32] This was when

Shot 1

Shot 2

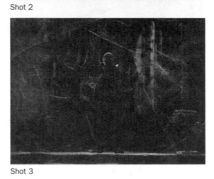

Shot 3

Figure 16

such "ordinary" discursive elements as cuts and camera movements ex-
hibited greater potency than they had in years (and soon would again)
to invest the entrances, awakenings, and physical transformations of a
vampire figure with visceral power. Still, if this power has waned, not
every subsequent viewer has missed the subtle eeriness of this formal pattern in Browning's film. Joyce Carol Oates, considering the same tendency in the representations of Dracula's risings and transformations
that I have just described, writes that "the subliminal message is: Blink
just once, and the vampire is already *there*."[33]

GROUND

For Depression-era audiences, the picture may have
carried all sorts of half-conscious metaphors about
people paralyzed and enervated by mysterious draining
forces they could not control.

David J. Skal and Elias Savada, referring to *Dracula,* in
*Dark Carnival: The Secret World of Tod Browning—Hollywood's
Master of the Macabre*

Dracula is the figure around and through which all the spooky goings
on occur. The whole hinges on Dracula, and I have suggested that the
film gives us the Harker and Van Helsing characters in part to act as foils
that make the vampire's weirdness stand out in bolder relief. But the film
was praised on first release not just for one character but also for its atmosphere. As in *Nosferatu* and other versions of the Dracula story, this
vampire is a figure of contagion, and he carries with himself a corruption that confines itself not only to his form and to those of his victims.
This corruption expands to the limits of the diegetic world and the filmic
frame. Dracula is the figure of menace, but we must also consider the
ground against which he moves. We can picture this ground consisting
of three layers: the soundscape surrounding the vampire's speech; the
arrangement and density of the narrative across the whole film; and the
film's construction of scenographic space.

Mute Perfection

I can easily see that this revelation is going to give the
magazine illustrators a great chance to kid the speakies.
Heretofore they have pictured "the silent drama" being
filmed amid a perfect bedlam of noises, but now the
joke is reversed, for the noises are being made in the
quietude of the grave!

Rob Wagner, "Silence Isn't Golden Any More," *Collier's,*
25 August 1928

We sense a feeling of silence and emptiness between
the few spoken sequences, which begin to sound like
a foreign body within the film.

Michel Chion, "Wasted Words"

The peculiarity of Dracula's speech gets a tremendous boost from the voluminously empty soundscape out of which it soars. The film contains no nondiegetic music and is spare in its use of ambient sounds. This quiet, which has long prompted complaints from critics who find the film static and slow, helped to make the film frightening on its first release.[34] Simultaneously, the quiet clearly marks *Dracula* as a product of the sound transition period, when, as I note in the first chapter, films could be unusually quiet compared both to late silent films, screened in most venues with live musical accompaniment, and to sound films that, starting around 1932, contained increasing quantities of nondiegetic music. Further, the quiet of *Dracula* helps us locate the film as, specifically, a product of the *late* transition. Crafton explains: "Generally by late 1930, Hollywood films showed that producers were responding to the critics' clamor for less foregrounding of sound effects, more narrative integration of dialogue, and less aural overstimulation. But characteristically, they responded late—in the 1930–1931 season—and they overreacted, interpreting the critics' call for less noise as a call for silence."[35] The industry's overreaction amounted to good luck for *Dracula*'s makers. This is because a "silent" sound film can be more disturbing than a noisy one, even when the noises are of the creepy sort that Universal could have thickly layered onto its film.

In chapter 1, I note commentators complaining about the unpleasant effects of watching a film, silent or sound, against a background of silence. These complaints echo ones that Tsivian finds running all the way back to the first years of cinema history. He quotes viewers who, faced with films unaccompanied by music, describe horses that "seem to gallop in that yawning void," "the weird and spectral feeling overtaking us when this pianist left his post for a few minutes," and viewers feeling "immediately gripped by a terrible, frightening emptiness, a kind of naked, cold, alien, limitless void, which has no connection with the external world—with us. An unbridgeable abyss yawns between us and the film."[36] It was this abyss, which reopened at the dawn of the sound era, that opened a little wider in the season of *Dracula*'s release.

In a season of quiet films, *Dracula* still managed to set itself apart. A reviewer wrote that "Browning is to be commended for allowing several episodes to be enacted in comparative silence."[37] This silence, thicker than in the Spanish-language version, which includes nondiegetic music and many loud sound effects—and which anticipates the genre's characteristic uses of sound better than Browning's film does—registers today as yet another of the film's disappointments.[38] A different way to approach the quiet is to regard it in the context not of post-1931 horror films, as we might, but of earlier sound films, as *Dracula*'s first audiences did.

In 1929 Bakshy looked forward to a time when sound film will "develop the specifically cinematic method of 'close up.' It will be able to focus an individual utterance, and at the same time put out of focus all the other voices—a procedure unquestionably in advance of the method of the 'realistic' stage which, in order that certain characters may be heard, enforces a most unrealistic silence among all the other characters."[39] Bakshy objects to the unrealistic silences that must be enforced when a character in a film (or play) is speaking. He is calling for the better modulation of the film sound track.[40] For Bakshy these background silences can make a film seem stiflingly static, like canned theater. Certainly the quiet of *Dracula* has gone a long way since 1931 in earning the film its reputation as a piece of stage-bound cinema. *Dracula*'s quiet seemed stagy in 1931 as well, although then, I contend, it was with results that are unique in the film's reception history. Then, the quiet reactivated the medium-sensitive viewing response. A black-and-white sound film, especially one without music, can, as Adorno and Eisler noted, elicit sensations of human figures as "speaking effigies." If the film in question is a vampire film, the flaring into prominence of the cold and lifeless properties of the medium can be made to work considerably to that film's advantage.

The world of *Dracula* is suffused with a quiet that does not affect all the diegetic inhabitants equally. The vampire, with his strange speech, pale face, and slow-motion movements, draws the effects of this quiet to himself. And so what sounds to viewers today simply like dialogue delivered theatrically to the accompaniment of nothing at all functioned originally to imbue a larger-than-life figure with an appalling lack of humanity. The film's supernatural narrative premise breathed life (of a sort) into the "talking shadows" of the "silent" sound film screen. *Dracula* pulsated with the colorless luminescence of the medium, and Philip Glass's 1999 score for the film can be understood to plug gaps that originally constituted crucially operative elements within the film's formal workings.

In 1981, comparing watching *Dracula* on video to watching it in a movie theater, Everson observed that "since most of the action is done in a stagelike fashion, little is lost in terms of composition, and the slowness of pace, emphasized by the total lack of a musical score, is rather less apparent than in a theatre, where the long periods of silence seem somehow magnified."[41] Contrary to what he himself believes, Everson here suggests that more than a little is lost in the transfer to video, for anything that diminishes the vaulting quiet of Browning's film correspondingly diminishes the otherworldly menace of its title figure.

Dead Time

> Contemporary audiences, other than those making a deliberate historic leap, would find, say, the 1931 *Dracula* impossibly slow.
>
> **Andrew Tudor,** *Monsters and Mad Scientists: A Cultural History of the Horror Movie*

Dracula gained effectiveness also from its skeletal narrative structure, which is something else about the film that critics since 1931 have disdained. The plot is not one of twists and turns. The film does not disorient or spook viewers by making its story line hard to follow. No developments are ambiguous, and there are not very many of them.[42] Another treatment Universal considered, one by Frederick Stephani, describes Seward and Harker renting a motor launch and pursuing Dracula back to his native land, gathering information on his progress from passing boats as they go.[43] In the film there is no chase back to Transylvania, just the short run over to Carfax Abbey. From novel to play to film, the narrative becomes increasingly streamlined, a sign of which we can see in what happens to the number of coffins that Dracula takes with himself to England: in the novel it is fifty; in Deane and Balderston's play, six; in the film, three.[44] Compared to the novel and play—and to another early sound horror film, Carl Dreyer's *Vampyr* (1932), the narrative of which is famously hard to follow—the narrative of Browning's film is exceedingly thin, slow paced, and straightforward.[45] This seems not to have been a problem in 1931. At that time, I believe, *Dracula*'s narrative thinness constituted one of the film's major strengths.

Critics like to say that Browning's film is too much like the play and not enough like the novel. In fact, some differences between the film and both the novel and the play can help us see how the thin narrative may have fueled the film's initial effectiveness. Consider the Harker and Renfield characters. In the novel, Harker travels to Castle Dracula in the beginning, makes it back alive, then joins forces with the other protagonists to vanquish Dracula. Meanwhile the lunatic Renfield is on hand to baffle his doctors and refer mysteriously to his master. In the play, no one travels to Castle Dracula, and in the sanitarium and abbey scenes, Harker and Renfield play roles similar to those they play in the novel.

Only in the film does *Renfield* travel to Castle Dracula and then return to become the lunatic we know from the novel and play. In the film one character, in effect, slides into another character. Something similar goes on with the settings. In the novel the action begins in Transylvania, moves to England, then returns to Transylvania. In the play the action stays centered on the sanitarium and abbey throughout. Only in the film does the action begin in Transylvania and then move to England and stay there. While noting the likely influence of *Nosferatu* on *Dracula,* we may observe that, as with the transplantation of the Harker and Renfield characters, there is something halfway about the film's handling of the original settings.[46] This is a symptom of the functional interchangeability of these elements within the film's formal machinery.

The visual and atmospheric similarities between the castle and abbey are underscored when, at the concert, Dracula says of Carfax, "I shall do very little repairing. It reminds me of the broken battlements of my own castle in Transylvania." This line combines two different lines from the play, neither of which asserts a similarity between the two locations.[47] The parallel also is stressed in the pressbook, in a newspaper story noting that "many scenes are laid in an ancient Abbey leased by Dracula— a location which in its ruined construction is greatly reminiscent of the castle in Transylvania."[48] It is as if the studio, anticipating the disappointment of viewers who will never get a second look at the majestically gothic vistas that open up the film, wanted to reassure them that the abbey made an equally fine setting for the vampire's demise.

The producers made a money-saving decision regarding the location of the climaxing action, one that pushed the film's narrative closer to that of the play and, apparently, cost nothing in terms of profits and prestige earned. The substitution worked as well as it did because, initially, the abbey performed essentially the same function that a return to Castle Dracula would have—and not only in a narrative sense. The *Motion Picture Herald* noted that "there is one beautiful scene in a haunted castle with a winding staircase, from which Renfield plunges to his death."[49] But Renfield plunges to his death in an abbey, not a castle. The mistake is understandable given that reviewers write on deadlines and that the film upgrades Carfax from a house (what it is in the novel and play) to a ruined abbey, then goes out of its way to make its interior look like a dungeon. Still, for one viewer, the resemblance was strong enough to turn the abbey into a castle in recollection. The mistake also is understandable given that this sort of detail was incidental to the experience of watching this film. It mattered less *where* Renfield plunged to his death than that it happened inside some vast, gothic interior space. Likewise, *who* went to Castle Dracula was less important than the fact simply that someone did.

The narrative thinness—thinner than in the Spanish-language version, which contains a half hour of material not seen in Browning's film— acted, like the quiet of the film, to make the film's creepy atmosphere more palpably intense. There had to be *some* story to get viewers into the world of the film. A seventy-five-minute shot of Lugosi saying moody things on a grand staircase probably would not have made for a very scary or memorable filmgoing experience. But *too much* story, such as the novel supplies with its busy epistolary format and its account of the endlessly prolonged efforts to save Mina and hunt down Dracula's scattered coffins, would have diminished precisely the quality of the film that its first viewers found so compelling. The only partial substitutions of Renfield for Harker, and Carfax Abbey for Castle Dracula, suggest that it didn't really matter who went to Transylvania and where the action climaxed. *Vampyr* engulfs viewers in a labyrinthine narrative space signposted with few reliable indicators of what is happening and where the action is going. *Dracula* confronts viewers with a shallow and uncluttered narrative space whose signal virtue is that it permits the raw uncanny of the medium to shine through unimpeded. The glacially slow pacing of the plot contains gaps that are large enough to house the film's primary workings, which are only superficially narrative in their nature.

We can take as a counterexample old-dark-house mystery films, the genre with which *Dracula* was often initially associated. These films tend to emphasize the importance of the action's setting. In the prototypical setup for such a film, the gathering of guests for the reading of a will, the location of the reading can be loaded with significance. In *The Cat and the Canary,* the place is the house wherein Cyrus West died and is believed to have taken up residence as a ghost. The importance of location also may be underscored by a film's promotion. The *1931 Film Daily Yearbook* offered this suggestion to exhibitors of "mystery house" films: "Secure window in empty store near the theater. Display a miniature house similar to the house of mystery in the attraction. Have ribbons running from the different windows with cards pasted at the ends explaining the various mysterious elements leading up to the murder."[50] Not surprisingly, we find films about "mystery houses" amenable to promotional displays that graphically map out their spatio-narrative topographies.

The films also may highlight the importance of the *time* of the action. In *The Cat and the Canary* the will is to be read at midnight twenty years to the night after West died, in a room containing a clock that stopped the instant he died and that (of course) starts up inexplicably at midnight on the night of the reading. Such pains taken to establish the significance of the time and place, like the bodies pitching out from behind sliding panels and like the other secret spaces in the house, all serve to emphasize the importance of the time and place to the deepening mystery. Likewise do the *identities* of the characters matter within the frameworks of these narratives. Just as a reviewer is unlikely to get the location of a major character's death wrong—as the *Motion Picture Herald* reviewer did when he described Renfield's fall—so is one unlikely to misremember the murderer's identity, since mystery films are designed to keep viewers guessing about just that. In such films the "true" identities of the characters play featured roles in the prescribed viewing experience.

In *Dracula* all of that intrigue is swept away when the film names the killer in its title. The action begins in a historically vague Eastern European setting and then moves to a nondescript modern interior location that houses, conveniently if implausibly, both Renfield's cell and Mina's bedchamber. Such details did not trouble many first viewings of the film because they were not essential to those experiences of the film's unfolding. Likewise, the precise *who* of each character, with the exception of Dracula (upon whom the whole hinged), mattered less than in the watching of other sorts of films. Hence John Harker barely has a thing to do and fades into the narrative wallpaper, where he belongs, and Lucy becomes a vampire and then is barely glimpsed again by viewers, who apparently do not notice or care. The strength of the Browning *Dracula*'s narrative was that there was *just* enough of it. The narrative thinness may mainly reflect the production's curtailed budget and the studio's desire to incorporate as few potentially objectionable original story elements as possible. If so, then the result was more lucky than inspired—for the result, after all that narrative furniture had been cleared away, was an enormous scaffold of a film hung with blanketing silences. This vast, empty structure supplied a perfect backdrop for the film's action.

In her reflection on Browning's film, Oates writes that "images that may endure in the memory for decades can be discovered, upon a re-examination, to have been strung out like beads on an invisible yet always palpable 'plot'—the tyranny, not just of genre, but perhaps of film generally. Its great, raw, even numinous power resides in *images;* its weakness is virtually always narrative, *plot.*"[51] McConnell, writing about the film, refers to "the plot of the movie itself, insofar as there is a plot at all." For him *Dracula*—and also *Frankenstein*—"are marked by a monumental technical simplemindedness, and by a capriciousness of plot construction which, in its very banality, achieves a unified effect of overwhelmingly weary poetry."[52] In the case of *Dracula*—and, for reasons explored in the following chapter, much less in the case of *Frankenstein*—this poetry has grown more prosaic over time, as the film's complex dialogue with the cinema of the sound transition has become a one-way conversation. It is a testament to Browning's film that sensitive critics like McConnell and Oates can still hear it at all.

The *Stimmung* of Staircases

> The actor's body "builds space"; flights of steps allow this dynamism to assert itself.
>
> **Lotte Eisner,** *The Haunted Screen: Expressionism in the German Cinema and the Influence of Max Reinhardt*

> The sound film betrayed with words the mystery of gestures. . . . The veil of *Stimmung* would seem to be rent without hope of repair.
>
> *The Haunted Screen*

Finally, the film gains atmosphere through its approach to constructing scenographic space. McConnell observes, in addition to their uncomplicated stories, the "monumental technical simplemindedness" of the first two films in the classic cycle. He suggests that we should look for ways in which stylistic qualities of the films mirror the simplicity of their narratives. I have highlighted places in *Dracula* where camera movements, editing, and lighting accentuate the supernatural presence of the vampire. Taking a step back from these moments, we begin to discern aspects of the film's style that support McConnell's claim.

Dracula does not deploy stylistic devices to confuse viewers about what is happening in the story. Camera movements and editing patterns do not mislead viewers about the contents and dimensions of the spaces depicted—and here again the film differs pointedly from *Vampyr*, where stylistic techniques pervasively confound viewers' efforts to get to the bottom of the film's mysteries and even, at times, to know exactly where they are in diegetic space.[53] Significantly, *Dracula* does not lead viewers very *deeply* into its diegetic spaces, either. McConnell writes that

> the classic horror film . . . has no "depth." One manifestation of this negative quality is in the arrangement of camera angles. With surprisingly few

exceptions, these films maintain the point of view of a neutral third observer: one seldom sees the monster from the point of view of the victim or the victim from the point of view of the monster. . . . The effect of the third-person point of view is literally to flatten the horror, to convert the potential depth-perception of panic into a two-dimensional tableau which, again, underscores the factitiousness of the monster.[54]

Though McConnell is not specifically considering Browning's film in this part of his essay, his comments provide us with a good starting point for asking how *Dracula* builds space through stylistic techniques.

The events of *Dracula* take place within a spatially flattened world. We see this not so much in the editing, which is on the whole, if somewhat bland and sluggish, classically analytical. Rather, this flat quality asserts itself mainly in camera movements, the use made of the settings, and the compositions of individual shots. At few moments does the camera move into or out of depth, and these mostly are confined to movements toward Dracula's unmoving figure.[55] Also, no locations are presented as architecturally complex or confusing. Even the massive castle interior, whose depths we are shown, stays mostly behind the action. Dracula leads Renfield to a guest room that could be located, based on what we see, right at the top of the main entryway staircase. Harker and Van Helsing need only to run a few steps into the abbey and open two doors to find Dracula's crate. We are shown only bits of Seward's Sanitarium and are not given a sense of where these are in relation to one another. Moreover, the viewer's eye is rarely drawn into the depth by mise-en-scène. As David J. Skal notes in his comparison of the English- and Spanish-language versions: "The American compositions are remarkably flat, like a play performed on a narrow stage apron. [Spanish-version cinematographer George] Robinson's camera work is distinguished by its use of multiple planes of focus and action. Foreground objects create tension and depth, while middle-ground devices (cobwebs, windows, branches, bars, etc.) further split and define the visual field."[56] Turner, also indicating his preference for the Spanish version, describes the scene where Dracula shows Renfield his room and where "the camera and players move more freely and the flaming fireplace becomes more than a backdrop."[57] Undynamic compositions, restrictions on the camera's movement through depth, and inattention to the number and complexity of the chambers, vaults, and corridors of its interior spaces all combine to flatten the world of *Dracula*.

An emblem of this visual flatness is the massive staircase seen in Carfax Abbey near the close of the film (Fig. 17.1). The manifestly planar

Figure 17.1   **17.2**

quality of the action in this sequence is established through more than set design, as two subsequent disappointed critics have noted: "Even the return to architectonic vastness in the concluding sequence at Carfax Abbey is flattened by full-light and lenses of greater focal-length." Another pair of critics refer to the "flat, stagebound mise-en-scène of the climax."[58] And Turner helps us see how—again, on the same sets and with the same story—the Spanish *Dracula* concretely illustrates a road not taken when he celebrates that version's "stunning camera moves, especially when [Melford and Robinson] utilize the unique 'Broadway Crane' to carry the action onto the high stairs."[59] In Browning's film, then, we have architectonic vastness that runs in two dimensions but not a third. This is a flatness that we can see "spreading out" from the abbey staircase in shots, intercut with the first ones we get of the staircase, in which Harker and Van Helsing make their way across the abbey grounds, traversing the frame on roughly the same diagonal traced by the winding steps (Fig. 17.2).

Why didn't Universal follow the available guidelines and precedents for fleshing out the spaces in its film along more exciting lines? There was Bromfield's treatment, which described "an immense flight of stairs leading down, down, down into the depths of the castle. Dracula . . . descends the stairs. The camera follows him."[60] And there was Stephani's treatment, which has Harker wandering "through many queer-looking rooms which are lighted by torches, always guided by this mysterious opening and closing of door. (sic) He does not encounter a human soul, but in every room stands a coffin."[61] And there was *Nosferatu*, with the multiple archways strung through its depths and with the roomy castle grounds on which Hutter (that film's Harker) wanders during the day.[62]

At least some reasons for the restraint were pragmatic. The studio was concerned that some camera movements originally planned for the film would prove too difficult to execute. Next to one such movement, described in a version of the script, Laemmle Jr. wrote, "This might be a cumbersome shot if you are going to use the columns and catacombs from the Phantom."[63] No doubt such concerns escalated with the scaling back, shortly before production on *Dracula* began, of "A" picture budgets at Universal.[64] Also, the studio apparently feared that a film with strong "German influences" might be too darkly lit to follow and too fantastically conceived to win broad appeal. In the same script version, next to a description of a "fantastic cabriolet at top speed," Laemmle Jr. wrote, "Why is this fantastic?? Should be realistic!"[65] The final shooting script is careful to stipulate that "the castle is grim and eerie, but there is nothing about it to suggest any sort of fantastic, unreal architecture—nothing of the impressionistic Caligari school."[66] Such worries no doubt pushed the studio toward construing the film's spaces in ways that more or less adhered to the road-tested expedient of Deane and Balderston's play. Still, if not all (or any) of the thinking behind the film's planimetric quality was exactly visionary, the results nevertheless were impressive. We can understand this flatness to have contributed to the film's resonance with the uncanniness of earlier sound films. The affinity becomes easier to see when we examine the film, once again, alongside old-dark-house mystery films, with *The Cat and the Canary* serving once more as our prototypical example.

> You are made to feel as though you were walking
> through the West slaughter house.
>
> **John S. Cohen Jr.**, review of *The Cat and the Canary*,
> *New York Sun*, 1927, quoted in the *Universal Weekly*,
> 24 September 1927

The *Cat and the Canary*'s reviewers suggest that a house whose function is to serve as a setting for murders and other mysterious happenings is, prototypically, a house with trick springs and sliding panels to spare. Likewise, the films' *narratives* tend to be spring-loaded with booby traps and other surprises at their every turn. Shocking plot twists and other jolts are favored over organic unity and in-depth character development. The loose formal organization of the films, and their tendency to build in intensity through a serial accumulation of sensational effects, are reflected in the tendency of the *Cat and the Canary* reviewers to string together, more or less indiscriminately, elements of the film's narrative and style as they catalogued the film's appeals. One wrote that "ghosts, greed, a house with secret doors, a maniac, a murder, jewels and a slight love story winding thru the whole are the ingredients of the plot."[67] Another noted that the film's weird atmosphere is "accomplished by using unusual types for the people of the story; by shadows that flicker menacingly on walls; by flapping white draperies whose quivering folds give ghostlike effect to long halls; by unexpected entrances of the characters, and most of all, by the use of lights whereby the feeling of the supernatural permeates the story."[68]

Entering into this simple entertainment formula is the film's aggressive spatial aesthetics. In the film, a bustling visual style joins with a narrative of twists and bumps to screw the viewing experience ever more tightly into an experience of the house. One critic wrote that "the all-important spooky atmosphere is created by swinging the camera this way and that; and making furniture, hallways, sliding doors and the like, actual characters in the plot."[69] Another wrote that Leni "actually makes furniture talk; a long deserted hallway tells a story; he calls attention to a door by making it oversize and gets attention without taking it from the action in the foreground."[70] The number of critics who find Leni actually making the furniture talk or turning it into characters strongly suggests that these critics were all writing with the same set of Universal publicity materials at their elbows. Still, whether their comments give voice mainly to their own opinions or merely to the studio's best hopes for them, such laundry lists of the film's attractions clearly reflect just the sorts of responses that the film itself was designed to elicit. In this light, Hall's variation on the "talking furniture" claim, whether he came up with it himself or only borrowed it, is instructive: "There are scenes in this piece of work that are amazing, especially those in which Mr. Leni photographs his characters through the backs of chairs and first gives one an impression that the books on a shelf are long, narrow, deep-sunken windows of a fortress, while the lines of the furniture bring to mind the interior of a cathedral."[71] Here Hall suggests that Leni so insists on rendering the spatiality of the house that he manages to turn solid objects (books and chairs) into portals and cavities (windows and cathedral interiors).[72]

Viewers are rooted so firmly in the setting of such a film in order to encourage their identification with characters who themselves are experiencing the house as a space of mystery and surprises. This guiding objective of Leni's film is perhaps never clearer than in its opening moments, when we glimpse the long hallway set that plays a role in the film's em-

Figure 18. *The Cat and the Canary.*

phasis on visualizing the mysterious recesses of the deserted West mansion (Fig. 18). We see this emphasis in the floorboards that run this hallway's length and pull the spectator's eye into the depth. We also see it in the camera's movements on this set, most strikingly in a shot at the film's beginning in which the camera dollies down the hallway, turning to the left and right as though it is a person looking from side to side. Let this hallway serve as our emblem of the space in *The Cat and the Canary,* for this hallway, with its lengthwise planking marking out a path for the camera's wandering eye, serves as the viewer's on-ramp into Leni's film.[73]

Here we come to a way that old-dark-house films can be understood to embody, if in a simplistic and hyperbolic fashion, a basic principle underlying the whole of mainstream narrative cinema—and this is important for our further understanding of the atypicality of *Dracula* as a Hollywood film. In *The Classical Hollywood Cinema,* under the subheading "The Winding Corridor," Bordwell writes that "the spectator passes through the classical film as if moving through an architectural volume, remembering what she or he has already encountered, hazarding guesses about upcoming events, assembling images and sounds into a total shape."[74] Viewers of old-dark-house films project this sort of narrative space onto the scenography with a special intensity. So suggested James Price, in an article titled "The Dark House" that appeared in the *London Magazine* in 1963:

> There is another important way in which the image of the dark house helps to expose the nature of the cinema; and that is the clarity with which it demonstrates the cinema's use of the experience of space. The camera moves along corridors and under arches, reproducing for the audience the sensations an individual would experience in the camera's position. In *L'Année Dernière à Marienbad,* for example, the endless prowling through

the passages of the hotel has a simple, literal meaning: it is to make us experience the building *as a building,* as a relationship of spaces and levels, in which the characters are imprisoned.

This is not just one of the tricks the cinema can play if it wants to: it is part of its basic language.[75]

The Cat and the Canary, the paradigmatic old-dark-house mystery film (and a long way from *Marienbad*), supports with a manic energy both Price's and Bordwell's claims. Viewers poke and inch their way through the architectural volumes of these fun-house films, encountering one surprise after another for the length of a long, dark, and winding corridor. For their money, viewers of *The Cat and the Canary* gain a ticket *into* the world of Leni's film.

> It is undeniably a mere shadow on a plane surface.
>
> "The Moving World: A Review of New and Important Motion Pictures," *Independent,* 27 April 1914

If the hallway in *The Cat and the Canary* serves as the viewers' on-ramp into Leni's film, the staircase in *Dracula* seals viewers off from the world outside the movie theater and locks them into an encounter with a very different kind of film—different, I have suggested, not just from old-dark-house films but from most any Hollywood film. Old-dark-house mystery techniques pass through the "wall of sound" and come out behaving differently.[76] How does *Dracula*'s peculiar spatiality lead us back to the sound transition? The visual flatness played a role in drawing viewers into the film's engagement with the uncanny body by reinforcing the film's evocation of a certain kind of presence.

Critics after 1931 agree that if *Dracula* evokes any kind of presence, it is a highly theatrical kind. That is, the film recreates the experience of watching a live play. But if *Dracula* reproduces this experience, it does so incompletely. The players and sets are gray; the spectator's viewpoint shifts about instantaneously as it never does in the watching of a play; characters loom into the foreground and then vanish past the frame's edges in ways that do not resemble exits stage left and right; and so on. The imperfectness of the theatrical illusion takes on special significance in the case of this horror film, for through its cracks, *Dracula* asserts a different sort of presence. This is the presence of the film itself within the theater auditorium. The success with which *Dracula* stages this (non)illusion, far from spoiling the fun, intensified the sensational horror appeal of the film for its first audiences. To understand how, we need to return briefly to the beginning of the sound transition.

The first sound films asserted the liveness and presence of the figures they presented by placing them in settings that were meant to blend visually with the spaces in which the films were screened. Performers on stages, gesturing and bowing to imagined audiences, were meant to help "suture" the virtual space of the performance into the physical space of the theater.[77] This assertion of human presence simultaneously was one of theatrical presence. Such films were meant to evoke a different sort of presence than the sort that most Hollywood films are meant to evoke—what Gilberto Perez calls "dramatic presence," an effect, he notes, that the coming of sound enhanced.[78] Dramatic presence pulls viewers into narrative space. This is where Leni strived so energetically to pull his viewers. It is where the makers of all Hollywood films strive to pull theirs. *Dracula* is no exception in this regard. What makes *Dracula* different is its assertion of the theatrical presence of the vampire as a means to supersaturate the narrative space of the film with an atmosphere of the uncanny.

Count Dracula is made to appear present within the space of exhibition, and in this investment of the film's energies, Lugosi's flamboyant theatricality pays dividends. His performance harks back to the touted liveness and presence of the speaking and singing figures in the first sound films. At the same time, his character embodies the disappointments and strange fascinations that could be engendered by screen figures for whom the addition of synchronized sound meant an accompanying surge in the conspicuousness of their artificial natures. Count Dracula textualizes—and resolves—the contradictory sensations that could be aroused by figures who seemed both more and less present, and more animated and less alive, and more ghostly and more solid. The semi-theatricalization of the vampire figure is achieved through acting, costuming, makeup, stagy silences, a thinly stretched narrative that provides minimal distraction from—and just enough stimulation of—the raw uncanny of the medium, and a compressed spatiality that keeps the action, whether it is on the abbey steps or in a sanitarium drawing room, strung along a narrow stage apron. In the end, precisely where in the diegetic world Browning placed his vampire was not important. It was any stage. It was the stage in front of you. Hence the effortlessness of the substitution of the abbey cellar for the castle crypt and the boxy feel of the space in the long middle part of the film. These spaces merged with the interior of the theater auditorium to create an ideal showcase for the film's main attraction, which was a talking corpse.

Count Dracula is alive but dead, ghostly but solid, and in these ways he embodies the category violation and hybrid impurity that, theorists of horror and the gothic note, constitute basic ingredients of monstrosity in films and in works of fiction produced in other media.[79] Dracula upsets borders separating states that are supposed to be mutually exclusive. For many critics writing after 1931, the most intolerable of these category violations concerns the line separating what is "theatrical" from what is "cinematic." To critics for whom the mutual exclusivity of these qualities is a given, the initial success of *Dracula* poses an unsolvable mystery. Such critics hold too tightly to opinions about what makes a good film cinematic and a good horror film scary.[80] What made *Dracula* both was its insistence on the theatrical presence of the vampire, for the harder the film pushed this claim, the more *absent* this figure became. Dracula, who is always already there, is always *never* there. He is flesh without color, animation without life. The more adamantly the film asserted the contrary, the more vividly it thrust an undead figure before the eyes of its viewers.[81] This same push-pull dynamic momentarily haunted screenings of the first sound films. *Dracula* forged a link, through its first audiences, to those screenings. This was a link that winding corridors, complicated and vague plotting, and copious sound effects and music would have only weakened. Instead, the film hung a huge gray backdrop and re-presented the uncanny body modality of the sound transition. No other film in the history of the genre would ever do it so directly.

CHAPTER 5

FRANKENSTEIN AND THE VATS
OF HOLLYWOOD

A few picture makers in their enthusiasm for sound with
shadows have hastily proclaimed their belief that the talking
film will deal a death blow to the stage. This, in my humble
opinion, is no more likely than a man falling in love with
the articulate shadow of a lady. True artists of the stage with
color and flesh and blood will always be with us, for man
can't make a man.

Mordaunt Hall, "The Reaction of the Public to Motion
Pictures with Sound," September 1928

During the Middle Ages, magic claimed to evoke the Devil
and other wonders, and produced legends, such as that of the
Golem, that persisted in literature and finally arrived from
the vats of Hollywood as Frankenstein—the synthetic man.

Parker Tyler, "Supernaturalism in the Movies," June 1945

STRONG MEAT AND MONSTER FOOD

Frankenstein surpassed *Dracula* at the box office and with the critics.[1]
Many reviewers hailed James Whale's film as superior to Browning's,
finding the film not only artistically more impressive but also scarier and
more shocking.[2] How scary the film was on its first release is suggested
by the fact that at the time, and unlike any time since then, the view of
Boris Karloff's monster as a sympathetic figure was not unanimously
taken for granted. The monster's accidental drowning of the little girl,
for example, a scene that critics have long singled out as especially mov-

ing, prompted one initial reviewer to write only that "what pity the thing is capable of showing, it shows here."[3] Another noted the character's "blandly innocent but sinister bearing towards the child he drowns."[4] In late 1931, the monster was simply too disturbing to win every viewer's sympathy.

Also suggesting the initial magnitude of the monster's menace are anecdotal reports of the stir the film caused in theaters where it was first shown. Hall claimed that the film "aroused so much excitement at the Mayfair yesterday that many in the audience laughed to cover their true feelings." Another reporter wrote that the film, "if gasping males and screaming females count for anything, succeeds." The pressbook boasted: "The trick is to see how much an audience will stand. According to several previews, they will stand a lot of the strong meat and monster food of which 'Frankenstein' was made."[5] One eyewitness account suggests that some in those first audiences could stand, if a lot, not all of the strong meat and monster food of which the film was made. Whale's longtime companion, David Lewis, told Whale biographer James Curtis: "Up came the first shot in the graveyard . . . and you could hear the whole audience gasp." Lewis continued: "The film has been imitated so much that today those scenes don't bother people. . . . But in 1931, this was awfully strong stuff. As it progressed, people got up, walked out, came back in, walked out again. It was an alarming thing."[6] Some of those first impressions turned out to be long-lasting. In 1989, lifelong fan and promoter of the genre Forrest J. Ackerman recalled: "The Monster backed thru the door and slowly turned toward the audience. I was 15 years old and I was marked for life."[7]

Critics since 1931 have continued to find *Frankenstein* outstripping *Dracula* in every important way. Many have called the film "timeless." Also, Karloff's monster has overtaken Lugosi's vampire as an indelible icon in U.S. and world popular culture.[8] In 1997 James Heffernan wrote that the monster's image "has been reproduced and disseminated as widely and as often as the *Mona Lisa*."[9] In 1991 a 60th anniversary appreciation noted that "with the possible exception of Chaplin's Little Tramp, he remains the most recognizable black-and-white character in cinema history." In 1971 a fortieth anniversary appreciation began by remarking that "the face is unforgettable." One can travel much further back in time and continue to find similar claims. In 1935 a reviewer of *The Bride of Frankenstein* wrote that "so vividly are etched the memories of the Monster's first screen appearance that it seems scarcely possible that the original 'Frankenstein' was shown on Broadway in December, 1931."[10] We keep peeling back the pages and finding that the monster's image has bled through every one. How far back can we go and still find this to be the case?

Lewis, Ackerman, and others suggest that we can go all the way back to the film's premiere. In fact, and not surprisingly, the monster thoroughly dominated popular perceptions of the film on its first release. The monster was repeatedly singled out in the reviews as the film's outstanding achievement.[11] In its promotion of the film the studio, too, fixed on the monster's image, and especially his head. The pressbook exhorted theater managers to "let the monster look from every billboard—His face is your good fortune!!"[12] Practical applications of this guiding principle of promotion frequently involved cutting out the head of the monster from posters and displaying it on every available surface of a theater lobby and facade. One exhibitor's inventive approach was written up in the *Motion Picture Herald:* "For ten seconds before the trailer was thrown on the screen the house was darkened. During this period groans and moans, produced on a special disc, came from behind the screen. Then, while the house was still dark and the screen still blank, a deathly green head and the hands of the 'monster' were projected on the blackness of the ceiling, played across the screen and up to the ceiling on the other side. This effect was made possible by means of a special slide projected with the aid of mirrors."[13] Heads on ceilings, heads in lobbies and on sidewalks, and even door hangers shaped like the monster's head and printed on the front with this caution: "BEWARE—WHEN YOU MEET HIM FACE TO FACE."[14] The producers had a tremendous visual icon at the center of their film, and they knew it.

Here is an important continuity for us to consider. We have a face whose iconic power today rivals that of the *Mona Lisa* and whose "unforgettable" status registered instantly at the moment of its first appearance. More true now than when it ran is a November 1931 *Saturday Evening Post* ad for the film that declared the monster "Thundering Down the Corridor of Time" (Fig. 19).[15] While, to be sure, the film has experienced ups and downs over the course of its long post-life, we can nevertheless say that *Frankenstein,* like *Dracula,* was an immediate sensation and that, unlike *Dracula,* it continues to endure.

The horror genre also was an immediate sensation, and it continues to endure. One reason why *Frankenstein* resembles the genre in this regard, and *Dracula* does not, is that each film engendered fear in its first audiences by implementing different strategies for exploiting its medium. *Frankenstein* is a film "for the ages" because it does not presuppose a

Figure 19

viewer who has just spent three and a half years watching early sound films. To such a viewer, *Dracula* was a scary movie. So was *Frankenstein,* but not only to such viewers. Still, while in one sense *Frankenstein* represents a break from *Dracula*—and a necessary one if Universal's efforts of one year were to launch a new genre—shared textual operations also bind the two films together. In both films we find unpredictable, context-contingent responses being converted into responses that are being provoked not by technological novelty and other temporary, reception-based dynamics but by text-embedded triggers that are, comparatively speaking, context independent. *Dracula* sets this development into motion. *Frankenstein* carries it much further, so far in fact that a viewer's having just weathered the sound transition ceases to be a prerequisite for appreciating the film's horrific appeals. The result is a "timeless" horror movie, one that in 1931 put to rest doubts, as *Variety* expressed them, "whether nightmare pictures have a box office pull, or whether 'Dracula' is just a freak."[16]

Frankenstein propelled the horror genre into the mature sound era. The film reconstitutes what I have been calling the uncanny body modality of the sound transition, although not in such a way that it relies, as a kind of crutch, on viewers' recent encounters with this phenomenon to jolt those viewers with fear. The historicity of the viewer becomes less of a factor with *Frankenstein*. However, the film does speak to a sense of the cinematic uncanny that was stronger in 1931 than it is today. This was a sense of human figures in *silent* films as distant and unreal beings. We must, then, view Whale's film alongside two figures of the cinematic uncanny.[17]

FRANKENSTEIN AND THE UNCANNY OF EARLY SOUND FILM

Looking forward, the future holds great possibilities. Makeup is only beginning to reach its artistic stride. We have far to go, just as cinematography has. Color, third-dimension, and all the other developments that lie in the future offer us great possibilities and as great problems as they offer the cinematographer.

Jack Pierce, "Character Make-Up," *American Cinematographer,* May 1932

Whereas *Dracula* depends for its horror effects on viewers' recent experiences watching sound films, *Frankenstein* arouses fear less by presupposing the earlier reception phenomenon than by reproducing the basic engine of its effectiveness. The connection to the uncanny body is more one that we can pick out in retrospect than one that, through the film's first audiences, actively shaped the film's first receptions.

To consider *Frankenstein*'s formal affinity with the uncanny body is to consider, most basically, the film's narrative premise. The monster is unquestionably animated; this indeed is what the whole film is about. However, he is not alive in the same way that the other characters in the film are. The story of his origin, like his physical appearance, underscores the deeply compromised nature of the monster's living state. This creature has been made alive by electricity, and—like the human figures who, earlier, had been touched by the electric "spark" of synchronization—he is not less striking for having been brought only *partially* to life.

In Whale's film the scene in which the monster comes to life—influenced by the scene in *Metropolis* (Lang, 1927) in which the robot is transformed into a likeness of Maria (Brigitte Helm)—retains and in fact intensifies the earlier film's copiously visible presence of electricity. One way *Frankenstein*'s laboratory equipment intensifies this presence is by making the electricity copiously *audible* as well. The snapping and sizzling bolts and arcs, to say nothing of the life-giving lightning crashing down outside the tower, accommodate a reading of the creation scene in *Frankenstein* as an evocation of the wild and potentially dangerous creative energies that adding synchronized sound to motion pictures unleashed. Crafton notes that electricity figured heavily in the initial promotion of sound film. In a chapter titled "Electric Affinities," he writes that

> few commentators, if any, saw sound as a natural outgrowth of silent cinema production practice. On the contrary, the talkies were something new, part of the electrifying spirit of the twenties. Sound film's alleged origins in thermionics made it essentially *different* from the classical Hollywood cinema. As a result, no one knew which form the new medium would take. It might resemble Broadway theater or vaudeville, a phonograph or radio with pictures, or it could substitute for a live orchestra. The one thing that hardly anyone anticipated was a quick, smooth continuity between silent and sound movie production.[18]

Sound film, then, briefly appeared in the popular imagination as an outgrowth of electricity, and for a time no one was sure what form this outgrowth would eventually take. Feelings of uncertainty prevailed as a once "classical" cinema came somewhat undone and as the great electrical intervention of synchronized sound coursed through newly startling Hollywood films. Perhaps Whale's vision of a new-made corpse brought to life during an electrical storm dramatizes a dark side of the narrative of progress that the industry related as it brought sound film to public notice. *Frankenstein* hints at the recognition that each step toward a more perfect cinema harbors the potential to unearth long-forgotten and dreadful things in the cinema's past.

Once animated, the monster—like the opera singer who seemed to Hall "so excellent, so real, that one felt as though Martinelli would eventually burst through the screen, as if it were made of paper"—comes at viewers in startling ways.[19] We get a sense of the monster as a physically emergent figure from posters in which he is shown bursting through a wall (Figs. 20.1–20.2).[20] The monster, even though he never actually does this in the film, appears to have been the perfect sort of figure to depict in just this way. So suggested the makers of the "Cutawl"— a tool for excising shapes from posters for use in three-dimensional theater displays—when, in a 1932 ad, they depicted a cutout figure clearly intended to call the Universal monster to mind (Fig. 20.3).[21] Horror films have been hurling monsters at us ever since. Sound, like 3-D cinema, energized this assaultive impulse of the genre. Whale's monster is physically emergent, unrestrainably so as the other characters in the film learn, and he blends aspects of liveness and deadness into an unwholesome composite—just like his counterparts in earlier sound films.

Beyond these general outlines, other aspects of *Frankenstein*'s resonance with the uncanny body can be found on the film's sound track. Legend has it that for the opening graveyard scene, James Whale placed a microphone inside the casket to record the sounds of the dirt hitting the lid.[22] This moment impressed the *Variety* reviewer, who called it the film's "Shudder no. 1."[23] The moment also apparently created enough of a general sensation for the studio to get wind of it, for in the prologue to the sequel, Lord Byron (Gavin Gordon) recaps, to the accompaniment of footage from the first film, some highlights in the monster's story up to now, saying: "I take great relish in savoring each separate horror. I roll them over on my tongue. . . . The first clod of earth on the coffin. That was a pretty chill." That the sound as well as the sight of the clod hitting constituted a chill is suggested by the fact that in Byron's recap, in which almost no diegetic sounds from the original scenes can be heard, we do hear this gravelly thud. The sound in the sequel can be read as a "textualized response" to the sound as heard in the original film.

Other sounds in the 1931 film include those of the monster's footsteps as he approaches Henry Frankenstein (Colin Clive) and Dr. Waldman

Figure 20.1

20.2

Figure 20. Images of the Frankenstein monster or his look-alike.

20.3

(Edward Van Sloan) from the other side of a closed door.[24] These quiet sounds alert viewers to the approach of a figure they have seen only under a sheet and bandages until now. The film, along with the original promotional campaign—which, while the film was in production, teasingly touted the secrecy of the monster's appearance—have predisposed viewers to take careful note of these scuffling noises. Mise-en-scène (in the case of the dirt hitting the lid), narrative (up to the point when we hear the monster's footsteps), and marketing (on the occasion of the film's first release) all compel viewers to listen closely to these sounds—and to listen with a combination of fascination and dread. In these ways *Frankenstein* elicits responses that can be compared to some initial responses to ordinary sounds in films released during the transition, when, as I note in the first chapter, "footsteps—scrunch, scrunch—on the path" could transfix a film viewer. Also, recall that this was when ordinary noises could sound to viewers quite unreal. (A commentator in 1932 referred to recent improvements in "the reproduction of common sounds, such as hand clapping, footsteps, and rustling paper, which have in the past sounded far from natural.")[25] Whale makes these noises fascinating and unnatural sounding again by recontextualizing them, first to set the right mood at the start of his film (Shudder no. 1), and later to portend the imminent arrival of an unnatural being.

Viewers also listen closely to the monster's vocal utterances. The monster does not speak eloquently as in the novel, nor haltingly and with a tiny vocabulary as in the 1935 sequel.[26] Instead he grunts and snarls, making sounds that the film's first critics noticed and tried to describe. (One mentioned the figure's "mooing"; another referred to his "barking.")[27] We can understand this subspeech to be performing a function similar to Dracula's moody pronouncements in the earlier film, though with an important difference. In early 1931 Lugosi's Hungarian accent and off-kilter line deliveries were foreign sounding enough to cast viewers back onto the initial strangeness and materiality of synchronized speech. Now, just a few months later, the memories of those sensations had grown more distant. Now the experience of being so astonished by the weird textures of synchronized speech that one might forget to pay attention to its semantic content was further out of reach. Whale compensates for the added distance by presenting a figure whose "speech" possesses no semantic content whatsoever. Viewers so confronted have no choice but to register the sensuous qualities of the creature's guttural noises and strangely plaintive coos—and to project the unearthliness of these sounds onto the speaker's body. This is one way Whale uses sound to make the monster exude an uncanny materiality that altogether suits his status as a figure built out of fresh corpse pieces.

Monstrous speech in *Frankenstein,* if more extreme, also figures much less centrally than it does in *Dracula* within the larger strategy of setting the monster visually apart. The film shifts this responsibility decisively away from speech. This was an inspired move because synchronized speech, now less strange, had less power to estrange than it did earlier in the year. In late 1931 it was necessary to take more radical steps to concretely alter the visual appearance of the monster. Glossy hair and a tuxedo would no longer do the job. It is within this framework that I wish to consider the contribution, to the film and to the early development of the horror genre, of makeup artist Jack Pierce.

Pierce coated Karloff's skin with blue-green greasepaint because this color photographs on black-and-white film especially gray.[28] Pierce thus managed to make the monster's face look *grayer than gray.*[29] This also is the way human faces in earlier sound films could look. Now, late in 1931, those faces were not so gray. And so, while the other characters in Whale's film look merely like characters in a black-and-white film, the monster wears the pallid complexion (and bodies forth the unearthly speech) of the figures in earlier sound films.

Pierce also blackened Karloff's lips and gave him sagging eyelids meant to suggest, as the shooting script indicated, "a dead thing."[30] If these makeup touches reflect the studio's desire to be faithful to a figure Mary Shelley describes sparingly—but of whom she does mention "watery eyes, that seemed almost of the same colour as the dun white sockets in which they were set, his shriveled complexion, the straight black lips"—they also mimic a possible result of leveling a medium-sensitive gaze at a human face on black-and-white film.[31] Tsivian quotes this comment made during the early cinema period: "Look at that grimacing, greyish face; those lips, black as earth with their soundless mouthings; that eye with its glassy sheen . . . When the muscles contract into a cadaverous smile, then, however much the trombones may ring out, a human being can not help but give a shiver."[32] So, in contrast to *Dracula,* which reverts to a theatrical mode of presentation to reawaken sensations of the lifeless faces in earlier sound films, *Frankenstein* takes a much straighter route and projects an emphatically gray and dead-eyed face directly onto the screen.

Pierce made the monster's head more monstrous by laying a bony flat ridge across the top of Karloff's forehead. This, the signal attribute of the creature's *otherness,* completely transforms Karloff's appearance while simultaneously leaving most of the actor's face free to express the character's emotions.[33] The impulse to strike just this balance—between recognizably human features and disturbingly distorted ones—preceded Whale's and Karloff's, but not Pierce's, involvement in the project. Originally, Robert Florey was supposed to direct the film and Lugosi was offered the role of the monster. The script for a test sequence that Florey shot (and which has not survived) stipulated that the monster's face was to be "moulded so as to be just a trifle out of proportion, something just this side of human—but that narrow margin is sufficient to make it insidiously horrible."[34] *Variety* suggested that Whale's film achieved the balance Florey was hoping for when it wrote that "the figure of the monster is a triumph of effect. It has a face and head of exactly the right distortions to convey a sense of the diabolical, but not enough to destroy the essential touch of monstrous human evil."[35] I want to compare the distorted quality of the monster's head with the sometimes troubling appearances of heads in earlier sound films, especially when they were shown vocalizing in close-ups.

In chapter 1, I note commentators during the sound transition finding faces in close-ups appearing grotesque, and others finding synchronization especially unconvincing in shots so framed. I argue that for these reasons, perceptions of the uncanny body probably intensified with cuts to a close-up view. Close-ups spurred viewers to transfer, without regard for a filmmaker's intentions or a film's narrative, the discursive attributes of a shot onto its diegetic contents. With *Frankenstein,* Whale accomplishes something similar on the viewer's behalf, only he makes the transfer stick, and he jettisons the requirement that the head be framed in any particular way. In his film, the distorting and enervating effects of the early sound film close-up become the concrete attributes of one diegetic subject, regardless both of the distance between it and the camera and of the level of a viewer's medium awareness. To be clear, I am not claiming that early sound film close-ups "produced" the head of the monster in Whale's film. Rather, Whale's film is calculatedly achieving ends similar to ones accidentally achieved by some early sound films. Simultaneously, *Frankenstein* is aggressively co-opting effects that its predecessor *Dracula* also managed, and doing so in ways that would be of greater use to horror filmmakers for a longer period of time.

The monster circulates within a total film that, like *Dracula,* sustains and amplifies the figure's horrific otherness. Whereas Browning resurrected, with temporarily sensational success, the theatrical uncanny of earlier sound cinema, Whale fashioned a blunter instrument to achieve longer-lasting results. His film is technically unpolished and, in spots, noticeably awkward and crude. Some critics who commented on this raw quality did not find it offsetting the film's merits. One wrote that "Mr. Whale has directed 'Frankenstein' with more regard for individual scenes than for the story as a whole, and thus the continuity is not always smooth. But the individual scenes are so admirably managed and the camera work is so good that the picture turns out to be a first-rate horror offering." Some even found this quality *enhancing* the film's gruesome appeal. A critic wrote that "'Frankenstein' the film is anything but a classic in filmcraft. As a rather crudely constructed blood-curdler it will certainly thrill those who find their pleasures in things morbid and horrible." Another found *Frankenstein* "just the film for those who are tired of aggressive prettiness in the cinema."[36] Qualities of the film that contributed to impressions such as these include elements of its sound design as well as some of its editing patterns and camera movements.[37]

The film contains no nondiegetic music.[38] This absence functions, as in *Dracula*, to foreground the photographic qualities of the image, which viewers then project onto the monster figure. In *Frankenstein* this absence also functions in other ways to force viewers into a more direct contact with the film's overtly synthetic nature. Music, however scary, would have cushioned these frequently harsh encounters. *Frankenstein* gains effectiveness from viewers' awareness of Whale's film as a "crudely" manufactured entity.

Alerting viewers to the film's artificial nature are some of its sets (Fig. 21). Again some reviewers took note. One, who liked *Frankenstein*, found the film's realism "offset by many palpably obvious studio sets. Mountains and rocks look utterly unreal and one wonders at Universal passing shots in which creased backcloth is unmistakable." To another critic, however, everything in the production was "absolutely real, never once smacking of papier mache." A third view, offered by Everson, finds that the film's "relative crudities, including the total lack of a musical score and the obvious use of studio 'exteriors,' give it a kind of rough hewn realism."[39] Everson hints at a productive approach to understanding what is going on in Whale's film.

Some of the film's "rough hewn realism" owes to unsteady camera movements and jarring film edits. Brian Taves describes Whale's takeover of the project from Florey: "Nearly all the shots planned for the moving camera, particularly to give dimension or develop a distinctive long take, were eliminated by Whale, and he added few such flourishes of his own. Yet he kept most of the expressionistic set design derived from the sketches Florey and [Charles D.] Hall collaborated on, even though

Figure 21. Studio "exteriors" in *Frankenstein*.

Whale's uncertain use of camera effects sometimes prevented this element from integrating purposefully in the film."[40] "Uncertain camera effects" in the film include, in the opening graveyard sequence, a lengthy lateral movement that overshoots all the interesting visual elements in the shot and stops on an uninteresting tangle of branches (Fig. 22); a track-in to Henry and Elizabeth (Mae Clarke) on their wedding day that wobbles noticeably on its approach; and a movement past some town revelers that shakes as the dolly rolls over uneven ground. Potentially distracting edits include match-on-action cuts that don't match (Fig. 23); a violation of the 180-degree rule of continuity editing (Fig. 24); and a scene that begins, somewhat incongruously, with four shots in a row featuring close-up views of faces (Fig. 25), including two consecutive shots that each depict a different head occupying virtually the same space (shots 2 and 3).[41]

Whale fans wishing to explain away these "gaffes" might point out that this was only the third film that Whale had directed up to this point. Indeed, critics noticed an improvement with his next film, *The Old Dark House* (1932), about which the *New Yorker* wrote that "there is a smoothness here that the Frankenstein picture didn't have. . . . Altogether, the movie people have bothered with this film, given it polish." About the same film the *Los Angeles Times* wrote that "Whale, improving as a director, reveals a sense of pictorial pace for the first time."[42] However, if Whale was on a learning curve when he directed *Frankenstein*, it is interesting to note that his *previous* film, *Waterloo Bridge* (1931), also is considerably more technically polished than *Frankenstein* is. Of *Waterloo Bridge* a reviewer wrote that "the picture escapes the dread label of a photographed play. It moves smoothly, cumulatively."[43] This film, which lists the same cinematographer, supervising editor, and editor as

Shot 1.1   Shot 1.2

Figure 22

Frankenstein, displays none of the awkward camera movements and clumsy edits that we see in *Frankenstein.*[44] Curtis describes

> Whale's own style of composition and cutting, which had advanced with such assurance on *Waterloo Bridge* and which, for *Frankenstein,* regressed to some degree. . . . Whale liked to move the camera liberally, but did not show the same concern for matching shots that he had on the previous picture. Possibly inspired by F. W. Murnau's *Nosferatu,* in which the German director purposely jump-cut his action to convey a heightened sense of unearthliness, Whale coarsened his style to the point where *Frankenstein,* in places, became more a series of related images than the seamless piece of theater he had made of *Waterloo Bridge.*[45]

If *Nosferatu* inspired *Frankenstein*'s jump cuts (the most striking instances of which I will consider shortly), this inspiration yielded fruit of a different sort than we find in Murnau's film—for nowhere does *Nosferatu* convey an impression of stylistic coarseness. In that film's most famous jump cut, the edit that brings Orlok closer to the camera is a dissolve, not actually a cut, and the fluidity of the transition adds to the unearthly quality of the vampire's advance. Jump cuts in *Frankenstein,* on the other hand, look like just that, and their power derives from their jagged abrasiveness, not from any effect of seamlessness.

Jump cuts and other manifestly artificial qualities of *Frankenstein* combine to produce a provocation-and-response circuit of a sort that we have seen before. A cut crudely pastes analytical space together in a way that reminds viewers that pieces of film that have been pasted together are constituting the world on view. Whale's film, in other words, is coaxing viewers into a state of medium awareness. Viewers so stimulated are inclined to project discursive aspects of this patched-together film onto the

Shot 1

Shot 2

Shot 3

Figure 23

diegesis, and here is one reason why Whale's film depicts a world that resonates so powerfully with the creature at its center. This resonance galvanizes the viewing experience and accounts for much of the film's rough-hewn realism and richly morbid atmosphere.

Others to view Whale's film along reflexive lines include William Nestrick, who writes that "editing reassembles separate shots into an illusion of continuity. It is a mechanical stitchwork, a piecing together

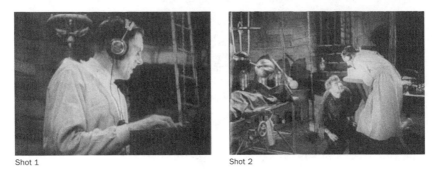

Shot 1   Shot 2

Figure 24

Shot 1   Shot 2

Shot 3   Shot 4

Figure 25

that becomes another cinematic equivalent of the Frankenstein Monster." Similarly, Heffernan writes that "film versions of *Frankenstein* implicitly remind us that filmmaking itself is a Frankensteinian exercise in artificial reproduction."[46] We may note that if editing produces a cinematic equivalent of Frankenstein's monster, then some films are more "Frankensteinian" than others—and Whale's film is that exceedingly.

Also, we should be clear on which Frankenstein's monster is supplying the basis for our metaphor. It is Whale's monster, for as Heffernan points out, his film originates the conception of the creature as a stitched assembly of corpse pieces.[47] Whale's monster consists of dead things that have been fused together to make a (somewhat) living entity. If this is what a film is, too, then Whale's film more than most lets its viewers in on this secret. Frank McConnell writes that "the creation of the monster in the movie *Frankenstein* is not effected by the near-alchemy of the English novel, but by an absurdly reductive production line of anatomical bits and pieces: the process which made possible Ford, paperbacks, and napalm."[48] To this list McConnell could have added Hollywood movies, most of which conceal their provisional and manufactured nature much better than *Frankenstein* does. Whale flaunts the manifestly *built* natures of his film and monster to extraordinary degrees, and the result in each case is not a shambling semblance of a whole but a whole, synthetic, uncanny film body.

The film's stylistic bluntness produces its most striking results in the sequence in which the monster is revealed to viewers for the first time. Frankenstein and Waldman are seated at a table discussing the monster, who has come to life a few days ago. Under their dialogue comes the quiet footstep sounds of the approaching figure. There is a cut to a low-angle view of a closed door, which opens as the monster backs through the doorway (Fig. 26, shot 1). Next is a cut to another low-angle view of the monster, still rear-facing and now in a medium shot (Fig. 26, shot 2.1). The figure turns around to face forward (Fig. 26, shot 2.2), after which is a cut first to a medium close-up (Fig. 27, shot 3), then to a close-up of his face (Fig. 27, shot 4).[49] This sequence more than any other crystallizes the film's formal affinity with the uncanniness of early sound films.

First, the footstep sounds fill viewers with anticipation and compel them to pay close attention. Then the door opens. In his *London Magazine* article on "dark house films," James Price wrote:

> The images of the cinema are presented in several ways, but the technique represented here of the door opening to reveal something horrifying is one of the most basic. The image is presented simply, suddenly, and with maximum emphasis. That is one half of the relationship; the other half is the act of seeing on the part of the audience. The opening door discloses something which has been hidden; and the audience's reaction is one of mingled disgust and pleasure. This response is fundamental. The cinema lives by exposing things we long, yet dread, to see.[50]

Shot 1

Shot 2.1

Shot 2.2

Figure 26

Price frames our moment in Freudian terms. If Whale's film stages a return of the cinema's "repressed," then this sequence presents this return the most forcefully. The door that opens marks the moment of the monster's arrival. Before now we have only heard about him, seen him under wraps, and, just before, listened to his scuffling advance. Now, at last, the thing we long and dread to see is here—although not quite. Whale has not fully revealed him to us yet.

Whale delays the full revelation in a few ways. One is to bring the

Shot 3

Shot 4

Figure 27

figure through the door with his back to us. Another is to lower the camera, which hides the flat top of the monster's head for as long as he remains turned around.[51] Then the monster turns around—and here the sequence begins in earnest to entwine its unveiling strategy with its excitation of the medium-sensitive response. The figure looks directly into the camera lens. Such a look was, in 1931, long forbidden in classical cinema because it was thought to disturb a viewer's comfortably voyeuristic status by seeming to acknowledge her and the camera's existence.[52] The monster's glassy-eyed stare represents a moment of self-conscious filmmaking. This self-consciousness intensifies with the cuts that push viewers into the close-up of the monster's face.

The camera leaps more or less along a straight line. Like the direct look at the camera, such axial cutting violated a tenet of Hollywood filmmaking. This was the thirty-degree rule of continuity editing, according to which, when cutting closer to or further away from a person or other subject, the camera should be moved out of the original camera-to-subject axis by at least thirty degrees. Otherwise the edit will convey a sense of discontinuity and constitute a jump cut.[53] Editing in this sequence accomplishes something similar to what we see in the promotional images of the monster smashing through a wall, for as Bordwell notes of this kind of cutting, "in the sound era most directors avoided it because it makes the scene jump out a bit spasmodically at the viewer."[54] Sacrificing smoothness and an unobtrusive style, Whale uses axial cutting to punch his monster out of the screen and into the space of the theater.

Whale liked to use this technique to spring his monsters on viewers. He used it to introduce, in 1933, a bandaged Invisible Man and, in 1935, the Bride of Frankenstein. Ted Kent, who edited both films, said of *The Invisible Man:* "Whale had a full shot, then a medium, then a chest shot—

boom, boom, boom. I didn't like that. There is no such thing as a *right* way to cut a scene, but to me an introduction of a character in that manner is making the audience conscious of the film element; it reminds them that they are watching a film."[55] Reminding viewers that they are watching a film is an unproductive thing for a Hollywood director to do in most contexts. Whale found a context in which doing just this would, rather than awaken them from the dream of the film, plunge them deeper into it. All at once, Whale reveals Pierce's makeup and, working from the opposite direction as well—from the viewers to the screen—he projects with a brilliant intensity something very much like the uncanny body of the sound transition onto the monster's head. Whale, who does not need a close-up to imbue this head with horrific otherness, saves the potentially dreadful power of the close-up for this special moment in his film. People got up, walked out, came back in, walked out again. It was an alarming thing.

FRANKENSTEIN AND THE UNCANNY OF SILENT FILM

> Reception works like a diffusing lens: whatever comes into its field "goes out of focus" and comes to look like something else rather than itself.
>
> **Yuri Tsivian,** *Early Cinema in Russia and Its Cultural Reception*

The monster, for all his barking and mooing, is mute. He does not talk in this talking film. The monster's status as a "silent" figure alerts us to a second formal affinity in Whale's film. This affinity is with the silent cinema, a body of films that in 1931 appeared to be speeding into the past at an accelerating rate. Silent films, with their intertitles and overtly gestural acting styles, once the norm of Hollywood and other cinemas, were looking increasingly remote. Already by early 1931, Jesse Lasky could speak of "what film folk are now so apt to refer to as 'the golden days of the silent films.'"[56] Already by late 1931, the monster could seem like a figure who had wandered into Whale's film from that dead epoch.[57] Considering mute characters in talking films, Michel Chion writes that "the silent ones of the sound film should bear no particular relation to the silent cinema, and yet . . . In the modern cinema they can represent, by a sort of proxy, the memory of a great Lost Secret the silent movies kept."[58] Chion's reflection calls to mind Price's comment about doors that open in films to reveal hidden things. He suggests that we should look beyond *Frankenstein*'s similarities to the uncanny of the sound transition to more fully understand the film's deeply reflexive nature. Chion and Price mark our starting point for understanding how Whale's film dramatizes a development that began unfolding in the general reception sphere at the beginning of the sound transition and that continued well past its end. This was a change in perceptions of human figures in silent films, from perfectly adequate human agencies acting out conventional stories to silent beings inhabiting spectral, faraway worlds. In *Frankenstein* we find the classic horror cycle's incorporation of the uncanny body shifting in order to take advantage of this change in the general viewing environment. Signs of this shift are clearest in the appearance and behavior of Whale's monster. The monster supports Tsivian's claim about the "diffusing lens" nature of film reception.

One way the film evokes silent cinema is through its uses of sound and the lack of it. The monster can be dramatically soundless. Chion writes that "the mute character occupies an undefined position in space, so that he might emerge from offscreen at any moment. It is as if not being tied down to a voice gives him a sort of angelic—or diabolical—ubiquity. One might find him anywhere without knowing how he got there . . . as if his mutism or muteness extends even to footsteps and other sounds he makes when he moves."[59] The monster exhibits this sort of ubiquity when he shows up on Henry and Elizabeth's wedding day. This is when we learn that the creature's vocal sounds not only are inarticulate but can also be hard to locate, as they send Henry first upstairs and then down to the wine cellars in search of their source. This gives the monster time to appear outside the large window of the room Elizabeth waits in, alone, and to open the window and enter. The sounds of the monster's off-screen footsteps when he was on the other side of the door separating him from Frankenstein and Waldman were scary; now what's scary is the absolute soundlessness of his on-screen booted feet as he closes in on Elizabeth, who is oblivious to the monster's presence. Only after she sees the monster, who from her perspective (as from ours a moment earlier) has materialized out of nowhere, does he loudly snarl. This abomination, called up by Frankenstein from the beyond, possesses attributes that suggest that the "beyond" from which he was called is the world of films when the footsteps of *no* figures made sounds. In silent films this attribute was universal and so constituted a nonattribute. In this sound film it endows one figure with a diabolical ubiquity.

The monster's vocal muteness and general capacity to be soundless invite us to read him as a figure of silent cinema stalking the world of Whale's film. Something that does the same is the film's self-conscious indebtedness to *The Cabinet of Dr. Caligari* (Wiene, 1920).[60] Aspects of *Frankenstein* that show this influence include the artificial-looking sets and the narrative, which revolves around a mute figure who is the unnatural creation of a master figure and who steals into women's bedchambers and is seen carrying his victims away over unreal landscapes.[61]

If some sets and plot elements in *Frankenstein* nod to *Caligari,* the monster points enthusiastically at that film's mute character, Cesare (Conrad Veidt).[62] The monster calls to mind the German Expressionist acting style, which to many Veidt in *Caligari* epitomizes, when in the creation scene he shows a sign of life by moving one arm, and when on the dissection table he feigns unconsciousness while surreptitiously moving one arm into a position to strangle Waldman. These isolated limb movements recall actors in German films moving a part of their bodies—an arm, a hand, a leg—while keeping the rest of their bodies still.[63] *Frankenstein* naturalizes this sort of unnatural movement by, in the creation scene, having all but the arms of the monster strapped down and by, in the scene with Waldman, making such a movement reflect the creature's desire to grab Waldman before he moves out of reach.

Karloff also evokes the Expressionist style when he conveys the monster's childlike newness. Even sitting down is not something that at first comes naturally to this figure. After the monster backs through the doorway, Frankenstein orders him to sit down and he does so, stiffly, then leans forward and extends both hands to their fingertips while holding his body rigid (Fig. 28.1). Then, in a close-up, he turns his head very slowly toward the sunlight that Frankenstein has let into the room (Fig. 28.2). A moment later he stands and reaches toward the light, again slowly and again in a manner that serves the dramatic requirements of the scene while simultaneously calling to mind the highly stylized German Expressionist performance aesthetic (Fig. 28.3). The figure's link to the earlier movement is reinforced by Pierce's makeup. The flat-topped head was new but viewers who had seen *Caligari* had seen that pale complexion and those blackened features before (Fig. 28.4).

Viewers who had *not* seen *Caligari* also had seen that pale complexion and those blackened features before. Whale's film, by borrowing heavily from one silent film, forged a connection to the whole of silent cinema. This was to a cinema not as it once existed—for *Caligari* would hardly qualify as a fair representative of that—but as it was coming to appear in viewers' memories. Silent films were looking increasingly the-

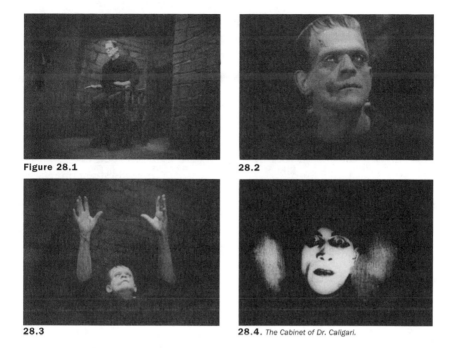

Figure 28.1

28.2

28.3

28.4. The Cabinet of Dr. Caligari.

atrical, artificial, and stylized. They could seem to depict places so far removed from the here-and-now world of the sound film that these places seemed ancient and otherworldly. I noted in the first chapter that *The Jazz Singer* altered perceptions of figures not just in its talking sequences but also in its silent ones, making those figures appear, to one viewer, to have been struck deaf and dumb. The tumult of the sound transition produced not only talking ghosts but also silent ones—in silent sequences in part-talking films and in the all-silent films that continued to be screened throughout the transition period.[64] Sound film instantly changed perceptions of silent film, and viewers seeking safe refuge in the same old thing had, for a time, nowhere to turn. *Frankenstein* evoked the uncanny of early sound cinema at the same time that it evoked a silent cinema newly estranged by the same.

By considering how German Expressionist film acting has been described during the sound era, one begins to get a sense of the hazy references that *Frankenstein* was channeling through its narrowly focused references to *Caligari*. Lotte Eisner notes that "the brusque, exaggerated gestures of actors in an Expressionist film frequently make modern audiences laugh. This is not merely due to its being shown at the speed of sound projection (24 frames per second); at the original speed (often 16 frames per second) the effect can be just as astonishing."[65] John Barlow writes of the German film *Raskolnikow* (Wiene, 1923) that "sometimes there is indeed too much intensity, as in so much expressionist silent film acting, and the rolling eyes and twisted mouths begin to be slightly comic."[66] Karloff, never guilty of creating unintentionally comical moments through his performance, does import into Whale's film elements of an acting style that can look "funny" to viewers whose regular diet of films consists mostly or entirely of sound films. Add to Karloff's performance Pierce's makeup, and we have in the monster a potent emblem of the rolling eyes and twisted mouths of the earlier movement.

The above comments about German Expressionist film acting resemble ones that have been made, also in the sound era, about silent-film acting considered as a whole. Of silent-film acting, Mary Ann Doane writes that "the absent voice reemerges in gestures and the contortions of the face—it is spread over the body of the actor. The uncanny effect of the silent film in the era of sound is in part linked to the separation, by means of intertitles, of an actor's speech from the images of his/her body."[67] But Doane is writing in the 1980s, one might object, and so of course the facial contortions of the actors look strange. What has this to do with the power of Whale's monster to evoke silent films *in 1931?* I suggest, quite a bit. In 1930 Hall wrote of the sound film *White Cargo* (Williams and Barnes) that "Maurice Evans, who plays Langford, looks as if he were acting for an old-time silent film." Alexander Walker, considering critical responses to the silent and sound versions of the 1929 film *Interference* (Mendes and Pomeroy), writes that "critics who saw both found the mime of the silent film overdone and intrusive: a sign of how quickly the habitual response to the silent film was waning." Early in 1928, *Harrison's Reports* wrote of the 1927 silent film *The Chinese Parrot*—released seventeen days after *The Jazz Singer*—that director Paul Leni "permits the old style of acting, with the twisting of the muscles of the face and the like. This makes the picture-goer of today laugh; he knows that such acting is out of date."[68] Clearly, the sound era was still very new when it had already become the case that one of the worst things a critic could say about the acting in a film, sound or silent, was that it resembled the acting in a silent film. Like the acting in German Expressionist films, acting so judged could look bizarre and old to audiences accustomed to the performance styles on view in newer films. The silent style, moreover, although much older to viewers today, probably was more *strikingly* old when *Frankenstein* first appeared, because then it was, while just as strange, much more vividly remembered.

In their 1994 film history textbook, David Bordwell and Kristin Thompson write that "to modern viewers, performances in Expressionist films may look simply like extreme versions of 'silent-film acting.'"[69] It may be necessary to interpret "modern" much more broadly than these authors intended. In 1930 Paul Rotha, considering *Caligari,* wrote that "of the acting there is not a great deal to be said, for the parts did not call for any great emotional skill beyond melodrama."[70] Had the German Expressionist acting style, mannered and self-conscious in the extreme, come to look, already in 1930—and to a viewer who should have known better—simply like "melodrama"? This label has of course long been applied to refer to what people find overdone and unintentionally comical about silent films, including their acting. And so it seems that the very qualities that once had set the German acting style apart from other contemporaneous styles functioned, virtually from the moment the sound transition began, to make the German style resemble—and even come to *represent*—silent-film acting conceived in the vaguest possible terms.

The monster's makeup meshed with general perceptions of the oldness of silent films in another way as well. I argue throughout this book that the coming of sound temporarily changed the visual appearance of mainstream Hollywood films, especially of human figures in the films. A concrete change in the way the films and figures looked happened at around this time as well, when, more or less coinciding with the start of the transition, the industry switched from orthochromatic to panchromatic film.[71] Thompson notes that because orthochromatic film was insensitive to certain colors, namely reds and yellows, makeup needed to be applied carefully; otherwise an actor's lips might appear black. She also notes that this problem can seem exacerbated in poorly preserved prints, which tend to be more contrasty.[72] The sight of blackened lips in scratchy, contrasty copies of films originally shot on the abandoned, orthochromatic stock no doubt contributed to impressions of silent films as remote and antique artifacts. Such impressions helped turn Cesare into an emblem of an outmoded film practice; and they helped Whale import into his film a vivid evocation of an irretrievably bygone cinematic era.

Unlike the monster in Browning's film, then, that in Whale's film embodies two time-senses: the uncanny of early sound films; and, retroactively projected virtually from the moment the sound transition began, the uncanny of silent films. *Frankenstein* marks the moment at which the uncanny body splits into two strands as it continues to penetrate forward into the unfolding classic horror cycle.

FROM MODALITY TO MONAD

> Just as individual texts establish new meanings for
> familiar terms only by subjecting well-known semantic
> units to a syntactic redetermination, so generic meaning
> comes into being only through the repeated deployment
> of substantially the same syntactic strategies.
>
> **Rick Altman,** "A Semantic/Syntactic Approach to Film Genre"

In roughly a year, Universal moved the uncanny body out of the theater auditorium first into a film that was briefly scary, then into one that to this day retains impressive measures of its dignity and its power to shock and disturb.[73] From reception phenomenon, to *Dracula,* to *Frankenstein*— this third stage made a solid foundation on which to build a genre. Whale's film was for the ages; Browning's was for about one year. This difference is reflected in formal qualities of the two films and in their first and subsequent critical receptions, as I have tried to show. We also can see it reflected in differences between Universal's marketing of the two films' stars.

In its promotion of *Dracula,* the studio fixed on Lugosi's foreign birth and accent to spin a story around the actor that was designed to make him seem darkly mysterious. While the reviewers highlighted Lugosi's skills as an actor, the marketers seemed intent on playing up the man's similarity to the vampire in Stoker's novel. A newspaper story in the pressbook claimed: "They always gasp when they meet Bela Lugosi!"[74] A *Motion Picture Classic* interviewer described Lugosi's appearance: "The tall, too-pallid man with the enormous predatory hands, the narrow, red-lit pale blue eyes, the soft, caressing voice, the atmosphere of charnel house and carnival surrounding him, a rank miasma." This interviewer reported that in answer to a question, Lugosi's "voice came, remote and far away, dying down, rising to a penetrating cry."[75] The look, voice, and demeanor of the actor thus strongly resembled those of the character he played.

The studio went to similar lengths to show that aspects of Lugosi's personal history further strengthened his link to the role. A story in the pressbook noted that "Lugosi was born in almost the exact spot in Hungary where the earlier scenes of the story are laid, and thus his slight Hungarian accent in Universal's screen production of this strange book is exactly 'in character.'"[76] Another pressbook story quoted Lugosi: "I have played the role on the screen, and I often sit in the dark theatres, watching, and wondering if the sinister character in the picture is Bela Lugosi— or Dracula." The actor's uncertainty stemmed from his experiences with an "actual human vampire," recounting which, Lugosi said that "it was her sharply pointed teeth which made these wounds in my throat."[77] Such publicity emphases on Lugosi's foreignness, personality, and personal history all referred viewers *outside* the text of Browning's film to major sources of the film's authentic horror.

The marketing of *Frankenstein,* by contrast, stressed differences between Karloff and the part he played. Karloff was no slab of meat. A story in the pressbook marveled at how little the actor's face resembled the monster's: "This was a staggering job, but when the make-up men had Karloff's classic and highly intellectual face made over to suit them, the production department was so concerned about it that they bottled Karloff up in a room in a closed stage." Another pressbook story noted that the actor's voice, too, differed considerably from that of the monster: "One of the softest and best bred voices I ever listened to bade this interviewer enter."[78] And *Modern Screen* reported that likewise was Karloff's demeanor not remotely monsterlike: "Off stage Karloff is the typical, charming, well-mannered upper-class Englishman."[79] Unlike the promotion of *Dracula,* then, which variously ascribed the authenticity of the film's horror to extratextual sources, the *Frankenstein* campaign emphasized that this film's horror was all craft; it was all *in* the film.

Universal further promoted Whale's film as a work of singular artistry by claiming that Karloff not only wore his makeup but also designed and applied it.[80] This was part of the studio's plan to bill Karloff as the successor to the departed Lon Chaney.[81] To this end, and in contrast to the claims that Lugosi was born in almost the exact spot where events in *Dracula* take place, the studio announced, in its campaign to promote *The Mummy* (Karl Freund, 1932), that Karloff's dressing room was the same one that Chaney had once occupied.[82] And in contrast to the stories about Lugosi's encounter with a real vampire were ones about the Christmas when the boy Karloff received a box of paints that he immediately took upstairs and applied to his face to gruesome effect.[83]

I highlight these differences in the marketing of the two stars because I find them mirroring a deeper sense in which the initial appeals and effectiveness of the two films also differed. *Dracula* scored at the box office and won over many critics; but much of that film's power was rooted in sources that lay outside the film itself. *Dracula* exploited possibilities that were at the time lingering heavily in the air of general viewing. The film packed itself loosely around a center of attraction that consisted largely of one figure—which drew to itself the moment's uncanny reception energies, intensified them, and directed them back at viewers who were perfectly situated to appreciate the at once cinematic and theatrical tour de force that was Browning's film. The film's power was founded on a network of contingencies. Everything had to be just right for the film to be effective—and early in 1931, everything was. But those energies were fading fast, and with them would fade the magnificent scariness both of Browning's film and of Lugosi's vampire figure.

Frankenstein also was a financial and critical success, and it has persisted through the years in a way that *Dracula* has not. One reason why is that fewer ephemeral viewing conditions underpinned this film's initial successes. Viewers at the end of 1931 were perhaps especially well primed to receive a marking-for-life when they saw Whale's film; but all viewers from that moment on would take in the monster's deformed head, blackened lips, and glassy, hooded eyes when the door banged open and he turned around to face Whale's camera. The authentic horror of *Frankenstein* raised the film above the moment of its first screenings. The film turned heads at the other studios and laid to rest all doubts as to whether *Dracula* was "just a freak." Here was a film to imitate. Elements in *Frankenstein* and, now that the producers were reassured, *Dracula* began in earnest to be elaborated into new patterns, new films. The uncanny body could melt away, leaving scarcely a trace of itself, and it wouldn't matter. The future of the genre it helped give rise to was all but assured.

CONCLUSION

What allows the repressed fantasy to come again into view?
Metaphorically speaking, we notice, the Freudian uncanny
is a function of *enlightenment:* it is that which confronts
us, paradoxically, after a certain *light* has been cast.

Terry Castle, *The Female Thermometer: Eighteenth-Century
Culture and the Invention of the Uncanny*

A ghost? No, somethin' of flesh and blood, yet of neither,
a horrible monstrous creature with a head as big as two
men put together, and skin with the shine of a new shillin',
and eyes that are no better than a dead codfish!

Villager in *The Man from Planet X* (Edgar G. Ulmer, 1951)[1]

In this book I have argued that the coming of sound stirred up sensations of the strangeness and ghostliness of cinema, sensations that also
characterized some perceptions of the medium during its first years. The
introduction of sound resensitized viewers to the artificial nature of cinema, and the resulting resurrection of the forgotten phantoms of the earlier time haunted the sound film screen long enough to shape the beginnings of a Hollywood genre. In *Dracula* the debt to the sound transition
is clearest because there it is the least mediated. With *Frankenstein* the
uncanny body embeds itself more deeply in a film text that relies less on
temporary and external factors for its expressive power. Some films released during the cycle's second year continue the first-year developments
that I have traced, while others reflect different impulses and initiate new
trends. Well beyond the cycle's second year, we find horror films con-

"Remember how big and clunky the first ones were?"

tinuing to elicit responses in ways that call to mind films not only from the cycle's first year but from the sound transition as well.

Horror film production stepped up after *Frankenstein* proved that the success of *Dracula* was not a fluke. Studios and independent producers launched efforts to cash in on the new public demand. Two films from 1932, the independent *White Zombie,* directed by Victor Halperin, and Universal's *The Mummy,* directed by Karl Freund, are notable for the ways they extend and develop classic horror's engagement with the uncanny of silent cinema.

Director Victor and producer Edward Halperin could not afford the rights to adapt a stage or literary property whose name audiences would instantly recognize. Nor could they secure the brand recognition that would be theirs by making a sequel, since they had originated neither horror hit of the previous year. But they did have Bela Lugosi, and perhaps in an effort to compensate for the production values that they could not lavish on their film, or perhaps purely in a spirit of capitalist show-manship, they loaded *White Zombie* not with one monster but with a modest legion of them. Lugosi plays Murder Legendre, a mortal man who with his voodoo powers creates and commands the cinema's first zombies. These pale mute figures, raised from the dead (so the film suggests while leaving room for doubt), supply the labor for Legendre's sugar mill and act as their master's slow-moving but lethal thugs. When the young woman Madeline (Madge Bellamy) comes to Haiti, Legendre covets her and, through his black magic, turns her into the film's eponymous "white zombie."

Although not an adaptation, *White Zombie* did draw on other texts. Two were William Seabrook's 1929 fanciful nonfiction book about Haitian voodoo practices, *The Magic Island*, and Kenneth Webb's 1932 play *Zombie*.[2] In these texts the Halperin brothers found elements to appropriate and set to new tasks. Some changes they made to these elements strengthened their film's resonance with the uncanny of silent films. For example, both Webb's play and the Halperins' film feature a "white zombie." In the play a male character meets this fate, while in the film it is a woman. Both productions also featured leading ladies who had enjoyed greater success acting in silent films than they were so far enjoying in the sound era. The screen actress in the play's brief Broadway run was Pauline Starke. A reviewer of the play, echoing comments made in many reviews of early sound films, wrote that "Starke, late of the movies, is present in the flesh and speaking-voice, and the speaking-voice is not quite so good."[3] In the film production the actress whose career was in trouble was Madge Bellamy, and, in contrast to the play, it is her character that becomes a "white zombie."

The Halperins' film was billed as Bellamy's comeback. A story in the publicity section of the pressbook began: "'I pulled a Zombie,' declared Madge Bellamy." The story went on to explain the actress's meaning: "Miss Bellamy has been dead for two years as far as the screen is concerned."[4] Her comeback attempt was not successful, and in 1943 Bellamy would generate some Norma Desmond–style publicity by firing a pistol at her lover.[5]

The film thus transfers the white zombie fictional character onto that production's fading screen actress figure. When Madeline succumbs, she becomes mute, and more intriguingly, Bellamy adopts what looks like a silent-film acting style for the duration of the time her character is a zombie (a state from which she awakens at the end of the film). Long stretches of the film are accompanied by virtually no diegetic sounds and by often frenetic nondiegetic music. Madeline and the other soundless, whitened zombies evoke the ghostly figures in silent films. The whole film is densely laden with figurations of silent cinema and, I believe, does not easily support an interpretation that satisfyingly pulls them all together. The film is a rich and slightly demented condensation, a dreamwork, a film overflowing with meanings and sensations and one to be admired for the measure of *incoherence* that ultimately makes the work cohere rather beautifully and accounts for much of its enduring poetic and haunting quality.

Both the ambitiousness of the filmmakers and the practical limitations circumscribing their production efforts are evident in *White Zombie*'s many jittery optical wipes. Other technical problems further mar the production; and, strangely, these do not detract from the film's mesmerizing power. The film's wipes, wooden performances, and other overtly artificial qualities continually remind viewers that they are watching a film, and *White Zombie* does not suffer for this. Similar to what we see with *Frankenstein,* the film's ostensible flaws refract onto the diegesis and narrative, suffusing both with an almost humidly rich atmosphere of the uncanny.

The simultaneously awkward and atmospheric *White Zombie* suggests that a special affinity may exist between horror films and the low-budget production practices that have characterized much of the genre's output throughout its history. The technically challenged sound transition cinema was the birthplace of the horror film. What do we make of the fact that so much of the genre's future would proceed through similarly choppy waters? While, of course, most of the factors determining this historical confluence of production mode and genre practice have been nonaesthetic, I hope that this book has supplied a new basis for asking whether some ramifications of this confluence have indeed been aesthetic. To consider this question is to ask how films like *Strangler of the Swamp* (Wisbar, 1946), *Carnival of Souls* (Harvey, 1962), and *Night of the Living Dead* (Romero, 1968) draw power from their makers' exploitation of the highly limited means at their disposal. These films remind us of *White Zombie,* and not just because pale, undead figures populate all four. They inspire us to ask whether the history of low-budget production has traced a natural path forward for the ongoing egress of the uncanny body into the still unfolding sound era.

In *The Mummy* the elements that evoke silent films do all come together, and they do so somewhat strikingly. The film stages the most lavish and spectacular pageant of death and reanimation yet seen in a classic horror film. It is also the first film in the cycle to feature altogether fluid and sure camera movements and cutting and to incorporate nondiegetic music in ways that foreshadow its conventional application throughout the sound era. The film is polished and smooth, and correspondingly, its engagement with the uncanny of silent films spreads across the work in the form of a network of elegantly interlaced themes.[6] One could call the film an *allegory* of the uncanniness of silent film in the age of sound. Close observers are cued to the possibilities for such a reflexive reading at the beginning of the film, in a shot in which a tripod and camera are shown positioned next to, and pointed at, the swathed and 3,700-year-old figure of Karloff's Im-Ho-Tep.[7] Similarly suggestive elements include the celebrated flashback sequence, which viewers enter through the graphically explicit framing device of the mummy's pool. After the smoke blows away, the waters of the pool continue briefly to ripple over the first flashback image. This effect, like the graphic frame, underscores our sense that everything to be seen in the flashback will be a flat (if momentarily undulating) image. The absence of diegetic sound, the continuous non-diegetic music, the sometimes stiff gesturing of the actors, the costumes reminiscent of a biblical epic of the DeMille variety, and the undercranked camerawork all clearly mark the flashback sequence as a miniature silent film set off within the larger work.

The film distributes its narrative events across three time periods: the ancient *then* of Im-Ho-Tep's lifetime, the brief *now* of the mummy's discovery in 1921, and the sturdy and emphatic *now* of the film's main action (and first release) in 1932. This is when Im-Ho-Tep as Ardath Bey, wrinkled and paper-dry dealer in Egyptian antiquities, emerges and tries to form a union with the living reincarnation of his past love, Princess Anck-es-en-Amon (Zita Johann). But this union, the film makes clear, is not possible as Im-Ho-Tep, thwarted at the climax, turns to dust and a few bones. We can trace across this story a metanarrative development in which the fledgling star Karloff engages in a struggle to break free of the conventions of the genre to which his stardom was owed. While according to the logic of the burgeoning cycle, a monster must be an undead thing and must perish, a bona fide movie star must be able to play characters who seek and sometimes find romantic love. He must be able to play characters who persevere and prevail. Karloff appears as a conventional, if doomed and belated, romantic leading-man figure in the "silent" flashback segment of the film. His character is briefly, normally alive then. But just as time was fast-acting on the once vital world of the silent film, making it seem increasingly remote and strange, the logic of the cycle was mandating the enclosures both of the flashback segment and of Karloff's body in the trappings of grim makeup, desiccated cloth strips, and a story about an unholy revenant. The march of the explicit narrative action dashes the "hopes" of Karloff the star while fulfilling the destiny of Im-Ho-Tep the monster. *The Mummy* displays a moment of productive tension between a new star's emerging persona and a new genre's coalescing conventions.

White Zombie and *The Mummy* are linked by what was only one developmental thread of the cycle's second year. With the genre's rapid diversification, the uncanny body modality quickly became diluted as producers freely appropriated the *horror* label to sell a wide variety of films. As early as *Dr. Jekyll and Mr. Hyde* (Mamoulian), released on the last day of 1931, filmmakers daringly departed from the arguably narrow course set for the genre by its first two entries. Mamoulian injects into the cycle elements that are barely glimpsed in the earlier films. In place of the vaguely amorous Count Dracula is a fiend who arises directly from the sexual frustrations of Henry Jekyll (Fredric March), a flawed man with good intentions who offers viewers a stronger character to identify with than the milquetoast Harker, the stiff Van Helsing, or the histrionic Henry Frankenstein. Contrasting these slight characters is one whose motivations and plight are etched in deeply psychologized terms. The film variously conspires to implicate viewers in Jekyll's fomenting sexual longing. When the barmaid Ivy (Miriam Hopkins) undresses, we share Jekyll's perceptual point of view as she looks straight at him, giggling and tossing her garters our way. This direct look at the camera, like the one in *Frankenstein*, elicits a response—although not the same kind. The film continues the theme of mad science developed in Whale's film, but jettisons all business pertaining to body parts (with the exception of Ivy's, which are displayed at length) and undeath, and presents instead a figure who is perversely Neanderthal in nature. Hyde's quick-witted turns of phrase contrast the unearthly and corporealizing speech of the vampire and monster in the earlier films. If this figure's body is uncanny, too, then clearly the template is shifting, and new ideas are flowing into the simultaneously expanding and solidifying incipient generic patterns set out during the cycle's first year.

More variations soon followed. First National–Warner Bros. wrapped the face of a living man in synthetic flesh and spooked audiences with Technicolor close-ups of his distorted visage (*Doctor X*, Curtiz, 1932). MGM permitted Browning to display actually deformed persons in a fiction film (*Freaks*, 1932). Paramount unleashed a crazy vivisectionist who transforms animals into feral, suffering, humanlike creatures (*Island of Lost Souls*, Kenton, 1932). In none of these films do the monstrous incarnations at their centers evoke the dead-alive figures in early sound films the way the monsters in *Dracula* and *Frankenstein* do; and in none is the uncanny of silent films evoked as strongly as we find in *Frankenstein, White Zombie,* and *The Mummy.* The swift "genrification" of the horror film meant that, as quickly, good horror films could come along that were altogether "unfaithful" to one of the major impulses that gave rise to the genre in the first place. By the time we get to *Dracula's Daughter* in 1936, vampirism is suggestive more of lesbianism conceived as a form of deviant sexuality than it is of the clammy weirdness of early sound films. And with *The Bride of Frankenstein,* the undead status of the monster comes more to resemble a pathetic disability, something the creature must and can't overcome in order to find love and a place in the world, than it does the corpses and ghosts of the earlier cinemas. In the sequel the monster learns to speak, and viewers are urged by the story and by Karloff's performance to care deeply about the semantic content of his rudimentary phrases. This speech is a far cry from the moos and barks of the character in the earlier film. The uncanny body exerts less explanatory power the further out into the cycle we travel.

Viewed together, the cinema of the transition and the first year of the classic cycle suggest that the coming of sound was, in one important respect, not unlike other moments in the history of the medium. The horror film is an opportunist genre. On the heels of the cinema's emergence, trick films by Méliès and Pathé turned some living bodies into skeletons and chopped the heads off other ones. With color at its disposal, Hammer horror exploited the eye-catching sight of red blood and packed its mise-en-scène with lurid art-direction flourishes. 3-D delivered a burst of fresh possibilities and a jolt of animating energy to the genre. The coming of sound marked another such moment in the history of uncanny cinema. This was a moment of emergence, technological change, and instability that meant money and sometimes art for a few enterprising dabblers in the macabre.

Notes

INTRODUCTION

1. I periodize the transition following Donald Crafton, who notes that the Hollywood release seasons ran from Labor Day to Memorial Day and that the end of the transition coincided with the end of the 1931 season (Donald Crafton, *The Talkies: American Cinema's Transition to Sound, 1926–1931,* ed. Charles Harpole, vol. 4, *History of the American Cinema* [New York: Charles Scribner's Sons, 1997], 267–68, 380).

2. Two who single out horror-film screams are Les Daniels, *Living in Fear: A History of Horror in the Mass Media* (New York: Charles Scribner's Sons, 1975), 130; and Rhona J. Berenstein, *Attack of the Leading Ladies: Gender, Sexuality, and Spectatorship in Classic Horror Cinema* (New York: Columbia University Press, 1996), 16. For an overview of sound in horror films that considers screams and off-screen sounds, see Peter Hutchings, *The Horror Film* (Harlow, UK: Longman, 2004), 127–47. The critical emphasis on off-screen sound in classic horror relates to the long-standing view that suggestion rather than graphic display represents the special strength of the premodern horror film. See, for example, Berenstein, 82–83; Dennis Giles, "Conditions of Pleasure in Horror Cinema," in *Planks of Reason: Essays on the Horror Film,* ed. Barry Keith Grant (Lanham, MD: Scarecrow, 1984), 49; and Curtis Harrington, "Ghoulies and Ghosties," *Sight and Sound* (April–June 1952): 158–59. On the potential of sounds originating in unseen places to seem mysterious and frightening, see Rick Altman, "Moving Lips: Cinema as Ventriloquism," *Yale French Studies,* no. 60 (1980): 74; Bela Balazs, "Theory of the Film: Sound" (1945), in *Film Sound: Theory and Practice,* ed. Elisabeth Weis and John Belton (New York: Columbia University Press, 1985), 120; Michel Chion, *The Voice in Cinema,* trans. Claudia Gorbman (originally published in French in 1982; repr., New York: Columbia University Press, 1999),

36–37, 46–47; and Mary Ann Doane, "The Voice in the Cinema: The Articulation of Body and Space" (1980), in Weis and Belton, 167.

3. I am excluding from my consideration of the cycle's first year Rouben Mamoulian's *Dr. Jekyll and Mr. Hyde,* even though it was released on 31 Dec. 1931.

4. For an argument that reception should be viewed as an important influence on production, see Rick Altman, "General Introduction: Cinema as Event," in *Sound Theory/Sound Practice,* ed. Altman (New York: Routledge, 1992), 2–4.

5. David Bordwell, Janet Staiger, and Kristin Thompson, *The Classical Hollywood Cinema: Film Style and Mode of Production to 1960* (New York: Columbia University Press, 1985), xiv.

6. For an example of a connection drawn between *Dracula* and the Depression, see George Turner, "The Two Faces of Dracula," *American Cinematographer* (May 1988): 34. On connections between *Frankenstein* and the Depression, see David J. Skal, *The Monster Show: A Cultural History of Horror* (New York: W. W. Norton, 1993), 132–33; and S. S. Prawer, *Caligari's Children: The Film as Tale of Terror* (New York: Da Capo Press, 1980), 22–23. For a summary and critique of such approaches to *Frankenstein,* see Paul O'Flinn, "Production and Reproduction: The Case of *Frankenstein*" (1986), in *The Horror Reader,* ed. Ken Gelder (London: Routledge, 2000), 123. Mark Jancovich both entertains and questions the notion that the Frankenstein monster can be read as a Depression-era proletarian figure, in *Horror* (London: B. T. Batsford, 1992), 58. Finally, James Twitchell compares the zombies in *White Zombie* (Halperin, 1932) to figures in bread lines (James B. Twitchell, *Dreadful Pleasures: An Anatomy of Modern Horror* [New York: Oxford University Press, 1985], 265).

7. Ernest Jones, *On the Nightmare* (1931; repr., London: Hogarth Press, 1949), 98.

8. Approaches to the genre that emphasize its narrative characteristics include Noël Carroll, *The Philosophy of Horror or Paradoxes of the Heart* (New York: Routledge, 1990); Andrew Tudor, *Monsters and Mad Scientists: A Cultural History of the Horror Movie* (Oxford: Basil Blackwell, 1989); Twitchell; and Skal, 1993.

9. Tom Gunning, "'Those Drawn with a Very Fine Camel's Hair Brush': The Origins of Film Genres," *Iris* 20 (Autumn 1995): 60.

10. Ibid., 59.

11. Yuri Tsivian, *Early Cinema in Russia and Its Cultural Reception,* trans. Alan Bodger (London: Routledge, 1994), 11.

12. Rudolf Arnheim, "A New Laocoön: Artistic Composites and the Talking Film" (1938), in Weis and Belton, 113.

13. Sigmund Freud, "The 'Uncanny'" (1919), in *The Standard Edition of the Complete Psychological Works of Sigmund Freud,* vol. 17 (London: Hogarth Press and the Institute of Psycho-Analysis, 1955), 226. Also see Ernst Jentsch, "On the Psychology of the Uncanny" (1906), trans. Roy Sellars, *Angelaki* 2, no. 1 (1995): 11.

14. Freud, 224 (ellipsis original).

15. Altman makes a similar claim when he writes that *"the coming of sound represents the return of the silent cinema's repressed,"* by which he means a "re-

turn to the theatrical model" (Rick Altman, "The Evolution of Sound Technology" [1980], in Weis and Belton, 51).

16. Nicholas Royle, *The Uncanny* (New York: Routledge, 2003), 75.

17. See, for example, the first chapter of Carroll, 1990.

18. Richard Watts Jr., "On the Screen," rev. of *Dracula, New York Herald-Tribune,* 13 Feb. 1931, 20.

19. Mordaunt Hall, "The Mystery of the Wax Museum," *New York Times,* 18 Feb. 1933, 13.

CHAPTER 1. THE UNCANNY BODY
OF EARLY SOUND FILM

1. "George Bernard Shaw—Fox Movietone," *Photoplay,* Sept. 1928, 57. Mordaunt Hall found the film conveying "Mr. Shaw's true personality by an unimportant little chat" (Mordaunt Hall, "The Reaction of the Public to Motion Pictures with Sound," *Journal of the Society of Motion Picture Engineers* 12, no. 35 [Sept. 1928]: 608). On the slipperiness of the concept of realism in relation to the early sound period, see Claudia Gorbman, *Unheard Melodies: Narrative Film Music* (Bloomington: Indiana University Press, 1987), 45–49.

2. Hal Hall, "Some Talkie Observations" (interview of William A. Seiter), *American Cinematographer* 11, no. 2 (June 1930): 19.

3. Alexander Bakshy, "The Movie Scene: Notes on Sound and Silence," *Theatre Arts Monthly* (Feb. 1929): 102. Bakshy voiced a similar opinion in "The 'Talkies,'" *The Nation,* 20 Feb. 1929, 236.

4. "Facts about Talking Pictures and Instruments—No. 4," *Harrison's Reports,* 8 Sept. 1928, 144.

5. "When Movies Talk," *New York Times,* 17 May 1928, 24.

6. Alexander Bakshy, "Hollywood Tries 'Ideas,'" *The Nation,* 22 June 1932, 708.

7. Delight Evans, "Strange Interlude," *Screenland,* Sept. 1932, 60.

8. Abel Green, "Strange Interlude," *Variety,* 6 Sept. 1932, 15 (This reviewer signed his name "Abel.").

9. "Strange Interlude," *Film Daily,* 8 July 1932, 22.

10. Crafton, 100.

11. "I Am a Fugitive from a Chain Gang," *Motion Picture Herald,* 22 Oct. 1932, 31.

12. J. C. M., "The Current Cinema: Silk-Shirt World—The Lockstep with Music—Robinson Becomes a Type," *The New Yorker,* 28 May 1932, 51. Jason Joy of the Studio Relations Committee worried that *Scarface*'s Tony Camonte resembled Al Capone too closely in name and deeds (Joy to E. B. Derr of Caddo, 4 June 1931, quoted in Richard Maltby, "'Grief in the Limelight': Al Capone, Howard Hughes, the Hays Code and the Politics of the Unstable Text," in *Movies and Politics: The Dynamic Relationship,* ed. James Combs [New York: Garland, 1993], 150). On similarities between the backgrounds of the films' stars and those of the characters they played, see Jonathan Munby, *Public Enemies, Public He-*

roes: Screening the Gangster Film from Little Caesar *to* Touch of Evil (Chicago: University of Chicago Press, 1999), 39–40, 41, 63.

13. Respectively: Sid Silverman, "The Public Enemy," *Variety,* 29 April 1931, 12 (This reviewer signed his name "Sid."); Norbert Lusk, "The Public Enemy," *Picture Play,* Aug. 1931, 56; and "The Public Enemy," *Screenland,* June 1931, 84. *I Am a Fugitive from a Chain Gang* was a "starkly realistic expose"; *Kameradschaft* (Pabst, 1931) moved "like an epic news reel, and you feel the reality of every incident"; also, this film was "a human document, intense, direct, forceful in its concentrated action"; *All Quiet on the Western Front* (Milestone, 1930) was a "powerful document against war." (Respectively: "I Am a Fugitive," 31; "Kameradschaft," *Film Daily,* 10 Nov. 1932, 6; "Kameradschaft," *Motion Picture Herald,* 10 Dec. 1932, 50; "All Quiet on the Western Front," *Film Daily,* 27 April 1930, 12.)

14. Silverman, "The Public Enemy," 12.

15. Todd Graves, "Fed Up on Gangsters," *Picture Play,* Dec. 1931, 73. Munby notes that this also was a cinema well equipped to address head-on the harsh social realities of the Depression (Munby, 40).

16. Fitzhugh Green, *The Film Finds Its Tongue* (New York: G. P. Putnam's Sons, 1929; repr., New York: Benjamin Blom, 1971), 12.

17. H. G. Knox, "Wide Range Sound: What It Is and What It Means to the Theatre," *Motion Picture Herald,* 27 Aug. 1932, Better Theatres Section, 15.

18. "Tenderloin," *Variety,* 21 March 1928, 18.

19. Alexander Bakshy, "The Shrinking of Personality," *The Nation,* 27 May 1931, 590.

20. Alfred Rushford Greason, "Vitaphone Reviews," *Variety,* 23 March 1927, 15 (This reviewer signed his name "Rush.").

21. Quoted in "Inventor Describes His Colored Picture Process," *New York Times,* 22 June 1924, sec. 7, p. 2.

22. The train reference is from Maxim Gorky, Review of the Lumière program at the Nizhni-Novgorod Fair (1896), reprinted in *Kino: A History of the Russian and Soviet Film,* ed. Jay Leyda (London: George Allen and Unwin, 1960), 408. On objects coming into the foreground in early films, see Stephen Bottomore, "The Panicking Audience? Early Cinema and the 'Train Effect,'" *Historical Journal of Film, Radio and Television* 19, no. 2 (1999): 177–216. The bush reference is from Rémy de Gourmont, "Epilogues: Cinematograph" (1907), quoted in Richard Abel, *French Film Theory and Criticism: A History/Anthology,* vol. 1, 1907–1939 (Princeton, NJ: Princeton University Press, 1988), 47. (For a different translation of the same passage, see Tsivian, *Early Cinema,* 109.) The wave reference is from *New York Dramatic Mirror,* 2 May 1896, quoted in George C. Pratt, *Spellbound in Darkness: A History of the Silent Film* (Greenwich, CT: New York Graphic Society, 1966), 16. The fingers reference is from Gorky, 408. On the medium sensitivity of early cinema viewers, see Tsivian, *Early Cinema,* 216–17; and Eileen Bowser, *The Transformation of Cinema, 1907–1915,* vol. 2 of *History of the American Cinema,* ed. Charles Harpole (Berkeley and Los Angeles: University of California Press, 1994), 92–95.

23. See, in *Early Cinema,* Tsivian's chapters "The Reception of the Moving Image" (135–61) and "The Reception of Narrative Devices" (177–215).

24. On Warner Bros. ceasing production of sound-on-disc films, see Douglas Gomery, *The Coming of Sound: A History* (New York: Routledge, 2005), 95, where he also notes that by 1933, approximately four hundred disc-only theaters were still in operation in the United States.

25. David Barrist, "The Flop of the Talking Movie," *The Exhibitor* (Philadelphia), quoted in *Harrison's Reports,* 24 Sept. 1927, 153.

26. "Facts about Talking Pictures and Instruments—No. 10," *Harrison's Reports,* 22 Dec. 1928, 201.

27. H. G. Knox, "Bewildering Problems of Sound," *New York Times,* 21 Dec. 1930, sec. 8, p. 6. Another commentator called the first Vitaphone films "a squeaky, squawky assemblage of crude noises" (Benjamin B. Hampton, *A History of the Movies* [New York: Vici Friede Publishers, 1931], 378).

28. Hampton, 385. A critic wrote, in early 1930, that "voices sound far more human than they did six months ago" ("The Talkies' Future," *The Nation,* 15 Jan. 1930, 61).

29. Crafton, 447–56.

30. Alexander Walker, *The Shattered Silents* (New York: William Morrow, 1979), 61; also see 69.

31. Mordaunt Hall, "Amazing Invention Coupling Sound with Screen Images Stirs Audiences," *New York Times,* 15 Aug. 1926, sec. 7, p. 2.

32. "Tenderloin," 18.

33. Quoted in René Clair, *Cinema Yesterday and Today,* trans. Stanley Appelbaum (New York: Dover, 1972), 128.

34. Rick Altman, "Sound Space," in *Sound Theory/Sound Practice,* ed. Altman, 47–48.

35. Myrtle Gebhart, "Voices Are Tested," *Picture Play,* July 1928, 104.

36. Chapin Hall, "Talking Films Try Movie Men's Souls," *New York Times,* 8 July 1928, sec. 3, p. 1. Similar complaints about another 1928 film are noted by Crafton (284), who also describes a film from the same year in which the "camera flits giddily through the silent scenes in Coney Island but freezes rock-steady in the talking ones, causing an abrupt change in visual style" (308). On the jarring quality of these transitions, also see John Belton, "Awkward Transitions: Hitchcock's 'Blackmail' and the Dynamics of Early Film Sound," *The Musical Quarterly* 83, no. 2 (Summer 1999): 227–28.

37. This problem is noted in "Hissing and Scratching Ended by New Process, Asserts Erpi," *Exhibitors Herald-World,* 6 Dec. 1930, 17. Examples of such noises can be heard in *Madame X* (L. Barrymore, 1929) and *Anna Christie* (Brown, 1930).

38. These difficulties included the impossibility of editing synchronized sound-on-disc film sequences, and the jumps in sound levels and ground noise that could result from editing sound-on-film sequences. Some of these problems are discussed in J. Garrick Eisenberg, "Mechanics of the Talking Movies," *Projection Engineering* 1, no. 3 (Nov. 1929): 22 and 23. In the case of sound-on-film editing, the difficulties would be substantially alleviated by the introduction of Western Electric Noiseless Recording in 1930.

39. On the higher costs of production during the period and how the studios dealt with them, see A. Walker, 93–97, who notes that Paramount's response to

the increases included setting the maximum number of takes a director could order printed to two (93).

40. On how the addition of synchronized sound resulted in a coarsening of film style, see Belton, 228–32.

41. James Lastra, *Sound Technology and the American Cinema: Perception, Representation, Modernity* (New York: Columbia University Press, 2000), 111, and see 92–122 on how the term *synchronization* has been applied in considerations of film sound-image combinations during the sound and the silent eras.

42. Sloppy postdubbing: "Warming Up," *Harrison's Reports,* 21 July 1928, 114. Dubbed-in foreign speech: Heinrich Fraenkel, "Can Industry Stay International? The Multilingual Problem and What to Do about It," *Motion Picture Herald,* 31 Jan. 1931, 58.

43. William A. Johnston, "The Public and Sound Pictures," *Journal of the Society of Motion Picture Engineers* 12, no. 35 (Sept. 1928): 615. On the novelty of early film sound, see Gorbman, 44–45.

44. Tsivian, *Early Cinema,* 153–56.

45. Eileen Creelman, *N.Y. American,* quoted in "Warner Bros. Present Vitaphone" (advt.), *Film Daily,* 17 Aug. 1926, 6.

46. Mordaunt Hall, "Vitaphone Stirs as Talking Movie," *New York Times,* 7 Aug. 1926, 6. Also suggesting an increase in screen awareness is a review of a 1923 sound film demonstration in which "conversation and music accompanying the pictures were clearly audible, and, being 'broadcast' directly from the film, synchronized with the action" ("Talking Movies Shown: Conversation and Music Accompany Pictures in Cleveland," *New York Times,* 12 Dec. 1923, 24). On the tendency to invoke radio when describing early sound films, see Crafton, 40–41.

47. Cyril Brown, "Speech to Movies by the Phonofilm," *New York Times,* 17 Aug. 1922, 6.

48. Joe W. Coffman, "Art and Science in Sound Film Production," *Journal of the Society of Motion Picture Engineers* 14, no. 2 (Feb. 1930): 176.

49. On how early sound film audiences could, by laughing, indicate that they did not know how to react to a sound film, see A. Walker, 48. Viewers would quickly adjust their faculties to accommodate the sound. As a 1930 article in *Projection Engineering* put it: "When the novelty lessens, as a result of familiarity, the theatre patron has time and opportunity to catch up, and to analyze his reactions. Given time to reason (after wonder has subsided), the theatre patron is in the mental state necessary to resume the role of critic" ("The Psychology of Sounds in Screen Presentations," *Projection Engineering* 2, no. 4 [April 1930]: 21).

50. Carlisle MacDonald, "Demand Talkies in Own Language," *New York Times,* 17 April 1930, 9.

51. Quoted in "New York Critics Like the First 'All-Talkie,'" *Film Daily,* 15 July 1928, 11.

52. Bernard Brown, *Talking Pictures* (London: Sir Isaac Pitman and Sons, 1931), 298.

53. Crafton, 490. Elsewhere he describes 1928 films that treat synchronized speech more like a special effect than like an integrated element of the mise-en-

scène (115), and notes that during the initial phase of critical consideration of the voice in relation to the image, the voice was regarded as separate from the actor's body, something with merely a surplus value (298, 447, 455–56, 460, 478, and 511). Lastra notes that "synchronization" was regarded as a kind of *performance* during both the silent and sound eras (Lastra, *Sound Technology*, 120).

54. Tom Gunning has written extensively on this sense of films during the early cinema period. See, for example, his essays "'Primitive' Cinema: A Frame-Up? Or the Trick's on Us," in *Early Cinema: Space—Frame—Narrative,* ed. Thomas Elsaesser with Adam Barker (London: British Film Institute, 1990), 95–103; "An Aesthetic of Astonishment: Early Film and the (In)Credulous Spectator," in *Viewing Positions: Ways of Seeing Film,* ed. Linda Williams (New Brunswick, NJ: Rutgers University Press, 1995), 118–19 (essay originally published in *Art and Text* 34 [Spring 1989]: 31–45); and "'Animated Pictures': Tales of Cinema's Forgotten Future, after 100 Years of Films," in *Reinventing Film Studies,* ed. Christine Gledhill and Linda Williams (London: Arnold, 2000), 318.

55. F. Green, 11.

56. Ruth Russell, "Voice Is Given to Shadows of Silver Screen," *Chicago Daily Tribune,* 16 Sept. 1926, 31 ("delicate pizacatti"); "George Bernard Shaw—Fox Movietone," 57 ("scrunch, scrunch"); the Warner anecdote is related in A. Walker, 23.

57. Lewis W. Physioc, "Technique of the Talkies," *American Cinematographer* 9, no. 5 (Aug. 1928): 24.

58. James O. Spearing, "Now the Movies Go Back to Their School Days," *New York Times* magazine section, 19 Aug. 1928, 12.

59. B. Brown, 289.

60. See for example Tsivian, *Early Cinema,* 131, 198.

61. Ibid., 198–99.

62. More evidence of the tendency to interpret a close view of a head as a view of a big head is this comment: "We hear on all sides discussions which indicate that the auditors are satisfied that synchronism is accomplished; but that there is a feeling that only at rare times does the sound seem to come from the proper source. They view a medium close-up that appears to fit the sound, there is a gasp of delight audible over the entire audience, the illusion is perfect; *then comes a large head, covering the entire screen,* the lips move in perfect synchronism with the sound, but there is a sense of disappointment in the audience" (Physioc, 25 [my italics]). Another sign is Lee DeForest's comment that "a giant face must not speak with an ordinary human voice" (Lee DeForest, "Recent Developments in 'The Phonofilm,'" *Journal of the Society of Motion Picture Engineers* 10, no. 27 [Oct. 1926]: 72).

63. On the forward-moving camera, see Tsivian, *Early Cinema,* 204–7. On perceptions of the dangerous and mysterious nature of the frame's edges, see ibid., 146–47; Tom Gunning, "An Unseen Energy Swallows Space: The Space in Early Film and Its Relation to American Avant-Garde Film," in *Film before Griffith,* ed. John Fell (Berkeley and Los Angeles: University of California Press, 1983), 363–65; and Gorky, 407, 408.

64. See for example Tsivian, *Early Cinema,* 155–56, 206.

65. Gorky, 407. One might doubt that many *general* viewing responses to

early films can be found reflected in the densely imaginative prose of this Russian Symbolist writer. Tsivian in *Early Cinema* does distinguish critical responses from ordinary ones, referring to the latter as *reactive* and the former as *reflective* (1–3). However, he also argues that Gorky's review, like other written comments dating from the period, does reveal universal tendencies in early film viewing, including that of projecting elements of cinematic discourse onto the diegesis (see, for example, 149). Gunning also believes that Gorky's response can be so generalized. (See his "Animated Pictures," 326.)

66. Hall, "Reaction of the Public," 605–6.

67. "The Jazz Singer," *Harrison's Reports,* 22 Oct. 1927, 171 ("deaf"); "Sounds in a Studio," *New York Times,* 29 June 1930, sec. 8, p. 3 ("museum"); "Phonofilm Shown in Rivoli Theatre," *New York Times,* 16 April 1923, 20 ("shops").

68. Hall, "Reaction of the Public," 607.

69. Of some human figures in a Lumière film, Gorky wrote that "their smiles are lifeless, even though their movements are full of living energy and are so swift as to be almost imperceptible" (407).

70. Hanns Eisler and Theodor Adorno, *Composing for the Films* (Freeport, NY: Books for Libraries Press, 1947; repr., 1971), 76. On Eisler and Adorno's thoughts on the ghostliness of film, see Gorbman, 39–41; Michal Grover-Friedlander, "'The Phantom of the Opera': The Lost Voice of Opera in Silent Film," *Cambridge Opera Journal* 11, no. 2 (July 1999): 182–83; and Philip Rosen, "Adorno and Film Music: Theoretical Notes and Composing for the Films," *Yale French Studies,* no. 60 (1980): 172–74. Roger Manvell and John Huntley note that music softens the "unnatural and ghostly" quality of silent film, in *The Technique of Film Music* (New York: Communication Arts Books, Hastings House, 1957), 16.

71. The opinion that nondiegetic music distracts viewers is expressed in "Playing Music While the Characters Talk," *Harrison's Reports,* 30 Nov. 1929, 192. Concerns that viewers would be wondering about the source of the music are noted by Frederick Steiner in "The Making of an American Film Composer: A Study of Alfred Newman's Music in the First Decade of the Sound Era" (Ph.D. diss., University of Southern California, 1981), 121–40. A composer who worked on early sound films recalled that when *Heaven on Earth* (Mack, 1931) "was shown in the projection room at Universal, . . . at some spots, when someone said 'how are you,' Laemmle [Jr.] said 'cut the music out under that, one has to hear the dialogue'" (Bernhard Kaun to William H. Rosar, 21 Feb. 1970, quoted in Rosar, "Music for the Monsters: Universal Pictures' Horror Film Scores of the Thirties," *Quarterly Journal of the Library of Congress* 40 [Fall 1983]: 397).

72. Hall reports that Jesse Lasky felt this way about incidental noises in relation to dialogue ("Reaction of the Public," 609). Others believed that scene transitions and important movements within the frame demanded quiet to be easily comprehendible ("The Psychology of Sounds in Screen Presentations," 21).

73. Joseph O'Sullivan, "Why Not Dramatize Sound?" *Motion Picture Herald,* 3 Sept. 1932, 17.

74. Alexander Bakshy, "With Benefit of Music," *The Nation,* 1 April 1931, 359.

75. Luigi Pirandello, "Pirandello Views the 'Talkies,'" *New York Times,* 28 July 1929, sec. 5, p. 1.

76. Gilbert Seldes, "The Movies Commit Suicide," *Harper's*, Nov. 1928, 710, quoted in Crafton, 534.

77. John Seitz, "Introduction," *Cinematographic Annual 1930* (New York: Arno Press, 1972), 17, quoted in Crafton, 249. The *Motion Picture News* editor wrote in 1928: "I believe that other important physical developments will follow now that the screen can talk. One is color and another is the third dimension effect, both designed to lend further realism to the formerly flat and silent figures of the screen" (Johnston: 618–19).

78. Alexander Bakshy, "A Year of Talkies," *The Nation*, 26 June 1929, 773.

79. André Bazin, "The Myth of Total Cinema," in *What Is Cinema?*, ed. and trans. Hugh Gray (Berkeley and Los Angeles: University of California Press, 1967), 17–22; and Noël Burch, *Life to Those Shadows*, ed. and trans. Ben Brewster (Berkeley and Los Angeles: University of California Press, 1990), 10.

80. Joseph P. Maxfield, "Some Physical Factors Affecting the Illusion in Sound Motion Pictures," *Journal of the Acoustical Society of America* 3, no. 1 (July 1931): 79. But as with synchronized sound generally, viewers also could find close-ups in sound films *enhancing* sensations of human presence. Such a view is expressed in Norbert Lusk, "Continuous Dialogue on the Screen," rev. of *Lights of New York*, *Picture Play*, Oct. 1928, 70; and Rob Wagner, "Silence Isn't Golden Any More," *Collier's*, 25 Aug. 1928, 12.

81. John L. Cass, "The Illusion of Sound and Picture," *Journal of the Society of Motion Picture Engineers* 14, no. 3 (March 1930): 325. Shots so framed could seem to leap out of a sequence and disturb a viewer's sense of a film's flow. Pirandello castigated filmmakers for "showing close-ups of the talking images, with the fine result that the scene, as a whole, is lost; that the quick succession of talking images tires the eyes; and that the dialogue loses all forcefulness. Furthermore, there is the realization that the lips of those huge images in the foreground are moving in vain because the voice does not issue from their mouths but comes out in a grotesque manner from the machine" (sec. 5, p. 2). A journalist in 1922 questioned whether close-ups should be used at all in sound films ("Talking Films Soon Will Appear Here," *New York Times*, 22 Oct. 1922, sec. 2, p. 14). And Physioc in 1928 complained that the overuse of close-ups in silent films became, in the sound era, "an even more important matter, due to the relation between the volume of sound and the size of the picture" (Physioc, 24).

82. In one article, Hall referred to "sound with shadows," "speaking likeness," and to the time when Shaw "sent his shadow and his voice over here" (Hall, "Reaction of the Public," 603, 612, and 608 respectively). Another wrote that "the irrepressible technician has at last succeeded in teaching shadows to talk" ("Hollywood Speaks," *The Nation*, 26 Sept. 1928, 285).

83. 1915 Kinetophone viewer quoted in Tsivian, *Early Cinema*, 102; Rob Wagner, "Photo-Static," *Collier's*, 23 Feb. 1929, 26 ("roared like monstrous ghosts"); Pirandello, sec. 5, p. 1–2 ("images do not talk").

84. Bakshy, "Year of Talkies," 773.

85. From an e-mail to the author by Karan Sheldon of Northeast Historic Film, who quotes an unpublished survey. The respondent's name is Neil G. Sawyer. The comment also can be found (slightly misquoted) in Crafton, 6. Also,

Fitzhugh Green described a "'hollowness' of recording" and the sometimes muffled quality of the voice (F. Green, 169–70).

86. Again Gorky supplies the central text: "It is a world without sound, without colour. Everything there—the earth, the trees, the people, the water and the air—is dipped in monotonous grey. Grey rays of the sun across the grey sky, grey eyes in grey faces, and the leaves of the trees are ashen grey. It is not life but its shadow, it is not motion but its soundless spectre" (407). Others to comment on the unrealism of film include Lotte H. Eisner, *The Haunted Screen: Expressionism in the German Cinema and the Influence of Max Reinhardt* (1952; repr., Berkeley and Los Angeles: University of California Press, 1973), 17; Gunning, "Animated Pictures," 318; and Parker Tyler, "Supernaturalism in the Movies," *Theatre Arts*, June 1945, 363.

87. See Gunning, "Animated Pictures," 316–31, especially 326, on how the addition of movement to still photographs made what was perceived to be still lacking stand out. Also see Tsivian, *Early Cinema*, 6–9, 82–83, 111, and Gunning's foreword to Tsivian's book, xxi.

88. The quoted words come from Mordaunt Hall, "The Best Ten Films," *New York Times*, 5 Jan. 1930, sec. 8, p. 6.

89. Harold B. Franklin, "Talking Pictures—The Great Internationalist," *Journal of the Society of Motion Picture Engineers* 15, no. 1 (July 1930): 18.

90. Knox, "Wide Range Sound," 15–16.

91. Gorbman, 41.

92. Tom Gunning uses the same metaphor to rework prior characterizations he has made of ambivalent responses to films during the early cinema period (Tom Gunning, "The Ghost in the Machine: Animated Pictures at the Haunted Hotel of Early Cinema," *Living Pictures* 1, no. 1 [2001]: 14–16).

93. On the audio CD of *Lugosi: Hollywood's Dracula* (Gary D. Rhodes, 2000).

94. On the stylistic particulars of these transitions, see the discussion of "audio dissolves" and "video dissolves" in Rick Altman, *The American Film Musical* (Bloomington: Indiana University Press, 1987), 62–80.

95. Altman, "Sound Space," 46–64; Lastra, *Sound Technology,* 154–79. Also see Charles O'Brien, *Cinema's Conversion to Sound: Technology and Film Style in France and the U.S.* (Bloomington: Indiana University Press, 2005), 97–102.

96. Though the foregrounded-sound approach sounds natural to us, it didn't necessarily to viewers who were unaccustomed to the convention. Two who found the effects of the technique unreal were Physioc, 25; and Gordon S. Mitchell, "The New Motion Picture and the Public," *Exhibitors Herald-World,* 22 Nov. 1930, Better Theatres Section, 11 and 40. The scale-matching approach, however, could be just as bad. MGM chief transmission engineer Wesley Miller endorsed scale matching not as a solution but as the lesser of two evils: "Any combination of picture and sound must be so proportioned that *the latter sounds natural coming from the artificial person on the screen*" (Wesley C. Miller, "Sound Pictures the Successful Production of Illusion," *American Cinematographer,* Dec. 1929, 5 and 20 [my italics]). On this comment, see Lastra, 161–62.

97. Lastra, *Sound Technology,* 194.

98. See, for example, Crafton, 279, 328.

99. Numbers in Hollywood musicals tend to be separated from what precedes and follows them unambiguously, but there are exceptions. For an example, see Altman, *American Film Musical,* 67–68.

100. Katie Trumpener, "The René Clair Moment and the Overlap Films of the Early 1930s: Detlef Sierck's *April, April!*" *Film Criticism* 23, no. 2–3 (Winter/Spring 1999): 36 and 35, respectively.

101. Ibid., 39–40.

102. On the dreamlike quality of musicals, see Altman, *American Film Musical,* chap. 4, esp. 60–61, 76–77.

103. Trumpener, 40. A U.S. review of *À Nous la Liberté* (1931) that voices an observation similar to Trumpener's is Margaret Marshall, "The Art of René Clair," *The Nation,* 8 June 1932, 660.

104. Patricia Leigh, "What the Fans Think: Talking Down the Talkies," *Picture Play,* Nov. 1928, 12.

105. The perceived tempestuous character of individual films was mirrored in some impressions of the period as a whole. An industry trade journal referred in 1929 to "this present momentous and unsettled era." Fitzhugh Green wrote that "the greatest and the lowliest are still experimenting. For though their talkie of today is a marvel compared to that of six months ago, they know that the talkie of tomorrow is going to be just that much different again. There is almost no talkie made that doesn't alter their knowledge of the art." A 1930 book on sound film noted that "great progress has already been achieved in the making of pictures that have talking sequences even as compared with the crude efforts *of a few months ago!*" (Respectively: Haviland Wessells, "Sound—as the Customers Hear It," *Projection Engineering* 1, no. 3 [Nov. 1929]: 12; F. Green, 294; and Harold B. Franklin, *Sound Motion Pictures: From the Laboratory to Their Presentation* [Garden City, NY: Doubleday, Doran, 1930], 12.) Also see "Picture-Making Changed More in 3 1/2 Yrs. since 'Jazz Singer' Than in 20 since 'Birth of a Nation,'" *Variety,* 1 April 1931, 12.

106. "Director of 'The Bride of Frankenstein' Tells All," Exhibitors' Campaign for *The Bride of Frankenstein,* reproduced in Philip J. Riley, ed., *The Bride of Frankenstein,* Universal Filmscripts Series, Classic Horror Films, vol. 2 (Absecon, NJ: MagicImage Filmbooks, 1989). On the claim of researchers in paranormal phenomena that by tuning between radio stations so that all one can hear is static, one may pick up communications from the dead, see Jeffrey Sconce's excellent *Haunted Media: Electronic Presence from Telegraphy to Television* (Durham, NC: Duke University Press, 2000), 84–91.

CHAPTER 2. LUDICROUS OBJECTS, TEXTUALIZED RESPONSES

Epigraph: Sound technician Joe Coffman shared Johnston's wariness of standardization: "Just now, production is beginning to settle down to routine, and all experts are breathing easier, feeling safe in the many tricks and expedients that they have used in producing the relatively satisfactory results now being secured. But not all these tricks are necessary or even desirable. It is well to keep the art still in a plastic state and not let some of these mistakes harden into the traditions of production" (Coffman, 173).

1. "25 Per Cent Dialogue Reduction Ordered for Universal Pictures," *Motion Picture Herald,* 29 Oct. 1932, 12.

2. MacDonald, 9.

3. Hampton, 406.

4. "X-Raying the 1927–28 Product—No. 1," *Harrison's Reports,* 11 June 1927, 93.

5. Crafton writes that multiple-camera shooting was phased out by late 1930 (216). How the economic situation weighed on the industry and acted to streamline production practices is described in Fred Stanley, "Hectic Year in Studios," *Variety,* 29 Dec. 1931, 6.

6. According to Crafton, the projectionist's cue sheet was eliminated by April 1931 (223). An article in the *Journal of the Society of Motion Pictures Engineers* indicates that the industry was anticipating making this change as early as the beginning of 1930 (Coffman, 178).

7. Ralph Cokain, "Defends Moving Shots," *Motion Picture Herald,* 13 Aug. 1932, 18. A cinematographer early in 1930 was similarly glad to see "the reappearance of such truly cinematographic effects as lap-dissolves and multiple exposure work. A year ago they were regretfully dropped from the cinematic vocabulary due to the added complication of sound photography. Now they are reappearing, as cinematographers and recorders gain more assured mastery of the new medium" (William Stull, "Multiple Exposure Cinematography in Sound Pictures," *Journal of the Society of Motion Picture Engineers* 14, no. 3 [Mar. 1930]: 318).

8. A film music composer remarked in 1932, "Characteristic music well scored under dialogue can add glamour and romance to love scenes; pathos and heart-throb to tragedy; excitement, tempo and pace to tense dramatic situations" ("A New Ratio for Dialogue in Films," *Motion Picture Herald,* 5 Nov. 1932, 24).

9. Bakshy, "The 'Talkies,'" 236.

10. Alexander Bakshy, "Concerning Dialogue," *The Nation,* 17 Aug. 1932, 152. Sometimes it was hard to tell what was having the stronger effect, the waning of the novelty or the improvements in the films, as Bakshy noted: "And now we may ask what progress has been made during the year of talkies. Judging by the opinions voiced in the press the progress must have been enormous. On closer examination, however, one finds that it is usually the fickle critic's conversion to the talking picture that is announced as improvement of the pictures themselves" (Bakshy, "Year of Talkies," 773). A sign of the decline in sensitivity specifically to sound is this editorial policy change at *Harrison's Reports:* "When sound was still new and in most pictures the recording was poor, it was the policy of this paper to state in each review whether the sound was good, fair, or poor. But today the sound is in the main good. For this reason it is only when the sound is poor that the fact is mentioned in the review. When no criticism is made, it is understood that no fault has been found" ("Why Comment on Quality of Sound Is No Longer Made," *Harrison's Reports,* 7 Feb. 1931, 24).

11. Cass, 323. Crafton suggests that Cass had not long to wait, writing that by May 1931 "the dialogue film had gone from marvel to mundane in about three and a half years" (443) and that "sound film changed from being a genre in itself to being simply generic" (269).

12. Hall, "Reaction of the Public," 604. Considering the voice on film, Michel Chion writes: "From the speech act we usually retain only the signification it bears, forgetting the medium of the voice itself. Of course the voice is there to be forgotten in its materiality; only at this cost does it fill its primary function" (Chion, *The Voice in Cinema,* 1). On this idea, also see James Lastra, "Reading, Writing, and Representing Sound," in *Sound Theory/Sound Practice,* ed. Altman, 65–86.

13. Tsivian, *Early Cinema,* 153–54.

14. Ibid., 4–5; and on early films and mirrors, see Tsivian, "Portraits, Mirrors, Death: On Some Decadent Clichés in Early Russian Films," *Iris* 14–15 (Autumn 1992): 67–83. On photographs coming to life in early films, see Tom Gunning, "Phantom Images and Modern Manifestations: Spirit Photography, Magic Theater, Trick Films, and Photography's Uncanny," in *Fugitive Images: From Photography to Video,* ed. Patrice Petro (Bloomington: Indiana University Press, 1995), 62–64. A description of a film in which figures step out of posters can be found in "Moving Pictures Sound Melodrama's Knell," *New York Times* magazine section, 20 March 1910, 7.

15. "The Hollywood Revue," *Harrison's Reports,* 24 Aug. 1929, 135.

16. "Napoleon's Barber," *Photoplay,* Jan. 1929, 93.

17. Alexandre Arnoux, quoted in Clair, 128.

18. Pirandello, sec. 5, p. 2.

19. Physioc, 25.

20. Altman, "Moving Lips," 76–77. For more on the ventriloquial nature of film, and on ventriloquism films, see Steven Connor, *Dumbstruck: A Cultural History of Ventriloquism* (Oxford: Oxford University Press, 2000), 409–14.

21. On how "talker films" during the early cinema period—in which silent films were screened while hidden performers supplied the voices of the on-screen speakers—were regarded both as a new advance in realism and as an impressive feat of trickery, see Jeffrey Klenotic, "'The Sensational Acme of Realism': 'Talker' Pictures as Early Cinema Sound Practice," in *The Sounds of Early Cinema,* ed. Richard Abel and Rick Altman (Bloomington: Indiana University Press, 2001): 156–66.

22. François Truffaut with Helen G. Scott, *Hitchcock* (New York: Simon and Schuster, 1985), 64. On the controversial practice of "voice doubling" during the early sound period, see Crafton, 509–15, and 511 on this practice in relation to Lon Chaney.

23. This statement is quoted in "Lon Chaney's Five Voices," *New York Times,* 6 July 1930, sec. 8, p. 2.

24. Gaylyn Studlar, *This Mad Masquerade: Stardom and Masculinity in the Jazz Age* (New York: Columbia University Press, 1996), 243–46.

25. Mordaunt Hall, "The Ventriloquist," rev. of *The Great Gabbo, New York Times,* 13 Sept. 1929, 33.

26. Throughout this book, "shot 1.1," "shot 1.2," etc. refer to different points

in a single shot (shot 1), while "shot 1," "shot 2," etc. refer to different, consecutive shots.

27. For another analysis of this sequence, see Ellen Draper, "Zombie Women When the Gaze Is Male," *Wide Angle* 10, no. 3 (1988): 52–62.

28. The attractiveness of the oily but charming Svengali was boosted by Barrymore's (fading) matinee-idol status in 1931. On this status in the silent era, see Studlar, 90–149. *Harrison's Reports* did not find Svengali charming in any way: "Mr. Barrymore's character is anything but attractive; he wears a beard, and his general appearance is disgusting" ("Svengali," *Harrison's Reports,* 9 May 1931, 74).

29. The film's marketing campaign conveyed a similar impression when it declared that Svengali's "hypnotic spell reaches out of darkness controlling love—hate—life itself" ("Svengali" [advt.], *Picture Play,* July 1931, 7).

30. Bakshy, "Shrinking of Personality," 590.

31. By considering *Svengali* before getting to *Dracula,* I don't mean to imply a chronological development. *Svengali* was released in May 1931; *Dracula* opened in February.

CHAPTER 3. THE MYSTERY OF *DRACULA*

1. Reproduced in Philip J. Riley, ed., *Dracula (The Original 1931 Shooting Script),* Universal Filmscripts Series, Classic Horror Films, vol. 13 (Atlantic City, NJ: MagicImage Filmbooks, 1990), 7–8. A similar view was expressed in a *Saturday Evening Post* ad for *Dracula,* which promised that "in picture-form, just produced by Universal, the story is immeasurably intensified because of the limitless possibilities of the camera" (Carl Laemmle, "Watch This Column" [advt.], *Saturday Evening Post,* 14 Feb. 1931, 59).

2. Representative subsequent criticisms of the film are in Carlos Clarens, *The Illustrated History of Horror and Science-Fiction Films* (originally published as *An Illustrated History of the Horror Film,* New York: Putnam, 1967; New York: Da Capo Press, 1997), 61–62; Bruce Dettman and Michael Bedford, *The Horror Factory: The Horror Films of Universal, 1931–1955* (New York: Gordon Press, 1976), 9–13; William K. Everson, "Horror," rev. of *Dracula, Video Review,* Feb. 1981, 97; Roy Huss, "Vampire's Progress: *Dracula* from Novel to Film via Broadway," in *Focus on the Horror Film,* ed. Huss and T. J. Ross (Englewood Cliffs, NJ: Prentice-Hall, 1972), 50–57; David J. Skal, *Hollywood Gothic: The Tangled Web of* Dracula *from Novel to Stage to Screen* (New York: W. W. Norton, 1990), 130–43; and Turner, "Two Faces of Dracula," 40 (Turner also has many good things to say about the film). A notable exception to the negative trend is Joyce Carol Oates, "*Dracula* (Tod Browning, 1931): The Vampire's Secret," *Southwest Review* 76, no. 4 (Autumn 1991): 498–510. Writers to call the film theatrical include Berenstein, 103; Ivan Butler, *The Horror Film* (London: A. Zwemmer, 1967), 36–37; Donald F. Glut, *The Dracula Book* (Metuchen, NJ: Scarecrow, 1975), 113, 117–19; Huss, 50–51; Jancovich, 55; Heidi Kaye, "Gothic Film," in *Companion to the Gothic,* ed. David Punter (Malden, MA:

Blackwell, 2000), 183–84; Arthur Lennig, *The Immortal Count: The Life and Films of Bela Lugosi* (Lexington: University Press of Kentucky, 2003), 104; Joseph Maddrey, *Nightmares in Red, White and Blue: The Evolution of the American Horror Film* (Jefferson, NC: McFarland, 2004), 11; Frank McConnell, "Rough Beasts Slouching," in Huss and Ross, 26 (essay originally published in *Kenyon Review*, no. 1 [1970], 109–20, as "Rough Beast Slouching: A Note on Horror Movies"); Oates, 502; Kendall R. Phillips, *Projected Fears: Horror Films and American Culture* (Westport, CT: Praeger, 2005), 14; Skal, *Hollywood Gothic*, 135–39; and Tudor, *Monsters and Mad Scientists*, 161–62. For some of the best thinking on the theatricality of *Dracula*, see Nina Auerbach, *Our Vampires, Ourselves* (Chicago: University of Chicago Press, 1995), 114–15.

3. "Six Best Money Stars," *Variety*, 5 Jan. 1932, 14.

4. David Cheavens, "Bela Lugosi Brings Creeps," rev. of *Dracula*, *New York Telegraph*, 13 Feb. 1931 ("prestige"); "Dracula," *Harrison's Reports*, 21 Feb. 1931, 31 ("Excellently produced"); Julia Shawell, "Dracula," *New York Graphic*, 13 Feb. 1931 ("weird thrills"); Sidney Harris, "Dracula," *Billboard*, 21 Feb. 1931, 10 ("spook-thrilling"). *Film Daily* wrote there was "no denying its dramatic power and tingling thrills" ("Dracula," *Film Daily*, 15 Feb. 1931, 11).

5. Alfred Rushford Greason, "Dracula," *Variety*, 18 Feb. 1931, 14 (review signed "Rush."). More praise for the film's restraint was given by Norbert Lusk, "'Dracula' Hit on Broadway," rev. of *Dracula*, *Los Angeles Times*, 22 Feb. 1931. Also offering a view of the film as different than the play was "'Dracula' as a Picture," *New York Post*, 14 Feb. 1931; and Marquis Busby, "'Dracula' Better Film Than Stage Play, at Orpheum," *Los Angeles Examiner*, 28 March 1931. For more on the initial praise of *Dracula*, see David J. Skal and Elias Savada, *Dark Carnival: The Secret World of Tod Browning—Hollywood's Master of the Macabre* (New York: Anchor Books, 1995), 154.

6. The *Hollywood Reporter* predicted that "they will say 'good,' but they won't rave" ("'Spooky' Film Will Draw Well," rev. of *Dracula*, *Hollywood Reporter*, 24 Dec. 1930). *Billboard* found that "at times the film is faulty in photography and sound recording" (Harris, 10). Lennig quotes at length a review in the 4 April 1931 *Hollywood Filmograph* that praises Lugosi but disparages the film. This reviewer voices opinions that would characterize much later criticism, including preferring the opening to the rest of the film, believing that the film was one of missed chances, and deploring the similarities to the play (Lennig, *The Immortal Count*, 128). For more on negative initial responses to the film, see Skal, *Hollywood Gothic*, 144.

7. Cheavens.

8. Writers who call the film campy include Huss, 57; and Prawer, 40. Typically harsh criticisms of Lugosi's acting in the film are in Michael Brunas, John Brunas, and Tom Weaver, *Universal Horrors: The Studio's Classic Films, 1931–1946* (Jefferson, NC: McFarland, 1990), 13–14; and John Baxter, *Hollywood in the Thirties* (New York: A. S. Barnes, 1968; repr., New York: Paperback Library, 1970), 100.

9. Contemporaneous criticisms of Lugosi's acting were made in "A Confidential Guide to Current Releases," *Picture Play*, June 1931, 72; and "'Spooky' Film Will Draw Well."

10. "Dracula," *Film Daily*, 11 ("a convincing performance"); Harris, 10 ("brilliant portrayal"); "Dracula," *Harrison's Reports*, 31 ("extremely convincing and horrible"). More examples of high praise for Lugosi are in Cheavens; Regina Crewe, "Shivery Cinema on View at Roxy Is Capably Acted," rev. of *Dracula, New York American*, 14 Feb. 1931; Mordaunt Hall, "'Dracula' as a Film," *New York Times*, 22 Feb. 1931, sec. 8, p. 5; Greason, "Dracula," 14; Al Sherman, "Dracula," *New York Telegraph*, 15 Feb. 1931; Shawell; Irene Thirer, "Lugosi Portrays Living Dead Man in 3 Star Talkie; New Films," rev. of *Dracula, New York Daily News*, 13 Feb. 1931; and Watts, "On the Screen," rev. of *Dracula*, 20.

11. Writers who mention but do not explore the mystery of *Dracula*'s initial success include Tudor, *Monsters and Mad Scientists*, 162; and Cosimo Urbano, "'What's the Matter with Melanie?': Reflections on the Merits of Psychoanalytic Approaches to Modern Horror Cinema," in *Horror Film and Psychoanalysis: Freud's Worst Nightmare*, ed. Steven Jay Schneider (Cambridge, UK: Cambridge University Press, 2004), 27.

12. "Dracula," *The Film Spectator*, 28 March 1931, 13.

13. Rick Altman, *Film/Genre* (London: British Film Institute, 1999), 74.

14. The artwork for a newspaper contest consisted of a drawing of Dracula's head with the facial features erased. Readers were to "Fill in the Face of 'Dracula,'" an appropriate activity, the pressbook explained, given "the mystery element in the production" (Exhibitors' Campaign for *Dracula*, reproduced in Riley, *Dracula*).

15. The film was called a mystery in, for example, Crewe; and "Dracula," *Screenland*, May 1931, 6.

16. All the publicity materials referred to above come from the pressbook, which also shows a poster declaring: "He lived on the kisses of youth!" ("Here's How to Sell *Dracula*," Exhibitors' Campaign for *Dracula*). The *Exhibitors Herald-World* reported in October 1930 that "after puzzling for a week as to whether 'Dracula,' soon to be produced by Universal, should be a thriller or a romance, Carl Laemmle, Jr., and Tod Browning decided to make it both" ("Universal's 'Dracula' to Have Romance and Thrills," *Exhibitors Herald-World*, 4 Oct. 1930, 58).

17. Altman, *Film/Genre*, 59.

18. Hamilton Deane and John L. Balderston, *Dracula: The Vampire Play in Three Acts* (1927; repr., New York: Samuel French, 1933), 71.

19. Yet another was *The House of Horror* (Christensen, 1929), of which a reviewer noted "the familiar hokum of trap doors, mysterious falling objects and doors slamming" ("The House of Horror," *Harrison's Reports*, 22 June 1929, 99).

20. In the play *The Cat and the Canary*, Annabelle says: "Just as I was falling asleep—I felt an icy breath sweep over me—I opened my eyes and out of the darkness a long claw-like hand reached toward me—it came—nearer—and nearer—I was like a person in a dream—I couldn't move—it touched my throat" (John Willard, *The Cat and the Canary: A Melodrama in Three Acts* [1921; repr., New York: Samuel French, 1927], 67). In Browning's film Mina says: "And then I saw two red eyes staring at me, and a white livid face came down out of the mist. It came closer, and closer. I felt breath on my face, and then its lips . . . Oh!"

21. Thirer, "Lugosi Portrays Living Dead Man."

22. Dracula's attacks are moved off screen in a few ways: he slides himself and the flower girl behind a column before feeding on her; a scene ends with a dissolve just before he makes contact with Lucy's neck; a scene ends with a fade to black just before he makes contact with Mina's neck; and he enfolds himself and Mina in his cape. For a brief consideration of the sexual suggestiveness of these moments, see Berenstein, 85. For a view that finds Browning's film steeped in eroticism, see Auerbach, 115–16.

23. Louis Bromfield, "First Treatment of 'Dracula'" (7 Aug. 1930), scene B-6, in Riley, *Dracula,* 49. In the play, Dracula kisses Lucy just before the curtain falls at the end of act II (Deane and Balderston, *Dracula: The Vampire Play,* 56).

24. This line appeared on several posters for the film. See the Exhibitors' Campaign.

25. Norbert Lusk, "Dracula," rev. of *Dracula,* 96.

26. Exhibitors were encouraged to develop tie-ins with local booksellers and to offer copies of the book as contest prizes (Exhibitors' Campaign for *Dracula*).

27. See, for example, "'Dracula,' Greatest Film Made by Director of Chaney Pictures," Publicity Scene Cuts section, Exhibitors' Campaign for *Dracula.*

28. Sherman.

29. Lusk, "'Dracula' Hit on Broadway." The subtitle of Lusk's review was "Horror Film Impresses, but Sympathy Lack Felt." He makes a similar point in Lusk, "Dracula," rev. of *Dracula,* 96.

30. Shawell.

31. Greason, "Dracula," 14.

32. Tzvetan Todorov, *The Fantastic: A Structural Approach to a Literary Genre,* trans. Richard Howard (originally published in French as *Introduction à la littérature fantastique,* 1970; Ithaca, NY: Cornell University Press, 1975), 27. For a similar view, see Altman, *Film/Genre,* 60–61.

33. Todorov, *The Fantastic,* 41–57.

34. "Here's How to Sell *Dracula,*" Exhibitors' Campaign for *Dracula* (two-dot ellipses in original).

35. Ibid. (two-dot ellipses in original).

36. On this and other silent Universal films in relation to the studio's 1930s horror films, see Ian Conrich, "Before Sound: Universal, Silent Cinema, and the Last of the Horror-Spectaculars," in *The Horror Film,* ed. Stephen Prince (New Brunswick, NJ: Rutgers University Press, 2004), 40–57.

37. On the German Expressionist style of this Hollywood film, see Jan-Christopher Horak, "Sauerkraut and Sausages with a Little Goulash: Germans in Hollywood, 1927," *Film History* 17, nos. 2–3 (2005): 241.

38. Oscar Cooper, "The Cat and the Canary," *Motion Picture News* (undated clipping, "Cat and the Canary" clippings file, Margaret Herrick Library, Academy of Motion Picture Arts and Sciences).

39. Quoted in Hamilton Deane and John L. Balderston, *Dracula: The Ultimate, Illustrated Edition of the World-Famous Vampire Play,* ed. and annotated by David J. Skal (New York: St. Martin's, 1993), 8.

40. Quoted in ibid., 74.

41. Deane and Balderston, *Dracula: The Vampire Play,* 70.

42. Quoted in Crafton, 309.

43. Sid Silverman, "The Last Warning," *Variety,* 9 Jan. 1929, 34 (review signed "Sid.").

44. William K. Everson, "The Cat Creeps: A Lost Horror Film *Partly* Found," *Films in Review* 37, no. 5 (May 1986): 297 and 298, respectively. I have not been able to locate these recordings to listen to them myself.

45. Bromfield, scene A-8, in Riley, *Dracula,* 45. In the novel, sounds issuing from unseen places accompany the first appearance of the vampire. These include footsteps, rattling chains, clanking bolts, and a key turning loudly (Bram Stoker, *Dracula* [1897], in *Dracula: Authoritative Text, Contexts, Reviews and Reactions, Dramatic and Film Variations, Criticism,* ed. Nina Auerbach and David J. Skal [New York: W. W. Norton, 1997], 21).

46. Bromfield, scene C-23, in Riley, *Dracula,* 54.

47. Tod Browning and Garrett Fort, "Dracula" (26 Sept. 1930 Shooting Script), shot G-66, in Riley, *Dracula.*

48. Hall, "'Dracula' as a Film," sec. 8, p. 5.

49. This anecdote of early cinema history is explored in depth in Bottomore, 177–216.

50. A sign that the editors were working without sound is that instead of noting the dialogue spoken, they wrote, for example: "CLOSE UP OF THE PROPRIETOR / Facing camera—talking—/ CLOSE UP EXT INN / Two disc.—Proprietor talking—Renfield speaks" (Continuity for "Dracula" [Picture #109-1, Browning (sound)], Box 13, Folder 3274, Part 1, shots 19 and 20 [Cinema-Television Library, University of Southern California]).

51. Ibid., Part 7, shot 37.

52. Ibid., Part 3, shot 27.

53. Tod Browning and Garrett Fort, "Dracula" (26 Sept. 1930 Shooting Script), shot B-16, in Riley, *Dracula.*

54. Dialogue 'Dracula' (Picture #109-1, Browning [sound]), Box 13, Folder 3274, 4 (Cinema-Television Library, University of Southern California).

55. Continuity for "Dracula" (Picture #109-1, Browning [sound]), Part 3, shot 21.

56. Hollywood studios produced foreign-language versions of films until dubbing became more feasible (Crafton, 436–38).

57. Continuity for "Dracula" (Picture #109-4, Melford [sound]), Box 13, Folder 3275, Part 3, shot 36 (Cinema-Television Library, University of Southern California).

CHAPTER 4. *DRACULA* AS UNCANNY THEATER

1. Quoted in Jones, 18–19.

2. See Stoker, 23–24; and Bromfield, scene A-8, in Riley, *Dracula,* 45. A comparison of the Browning and Melford versions finds in the Spanish count "an animalistic passion totally unlike Lugosi's squinting deviousness" (Lyndon W. Joslin, *Count Dracula Goes to the Movies: Stoker's Novel Adapted, 1922–1995* [Jefferson, NC: McFarland, 1995], 37).

3. A moment that hints at this former status is described in the shooting script when Dracula, waking in his coffin, looks like "a heavy sleeper aroused from a restful dream. Lethargic at first, his expression becomes singularly alive— his eyes light up in anticipation of the period of freedom before him" (Tod Browning and Garrett Fort, "Dracula" [26 Sept. 1930 Shooting Script], shot E-17, in Riley, *Dracula*). One has to look hard at Browning's film to find on Lugosi's face any signs of lethargy or excited anticipation. In the film, Dracula arguably shows some human regret at what he has become when he says, "To die, to be really dead. That must be glorious." The shooting script indicates that the character is to say this line "half-dreamily, a deeply tragic note underlying his words" (Tod Browning and Garrett Fort, "Dracula" [26 Sept. 1930 Shooting Script], shot C-18). It is debatable whether Lugosi hits this note at this or any other moment in the film. As James Curtis writes, "Lugosi's suave count was as evil and as single-minded as possible. At no time did one sense the horror of the eternal trap in which the vampire found himself" (James Curtis, *James Whale: A New World of Gods and Monsters* [Boston: Faber and Faber, 1998], 3).

4. For Dracula appearing younger, see Stoker, 155; and Bromfield, scene B-2, in Riley, *Dracula*, 47. Auerbach writes that "Lugosi's Dracula is so singular that he is impossible to emulate; the transformations he induces are muted and muddled compared to their kaleidoscopic prominence in Stoker's novel" (Auerbach, 116).

5. Other texts depicting the figure's immateriality include Bromfield's (Bromfield, scene C-15, in Riley, *Dracula*, 52). Browning resists making even the moment of the vampire's destruction a show of insubstantiality, and in this way he handles the moment differently than Stoker, Murnau, Bromfield, Frederick Stephani (author of another treatment for Universal), and Deane and Balderston (respectively: Stoker, 325; Bromfield, Sequence D, in Riley, *Dracula*, 54; [Frederick] Stephani, "'Dracula' [A Treatment]" [June 1930], in Riley, *Dracula*, 40 [the text as reproduced in Riley gives the author's name as "Fritz Stephani"]; and Deane and Balderston, *Dracula: The Vampire Play*, 74). In this way the Browning vampire's demise contrasts with that of Marguerite Chopin in *Vampyr*, in which, through a superimposition effect, she disappears, leaving behind her skeleton. (Also in this film, supernatural beings take the forms of detached reflections and shadows.) Lastly, in Browning's *London After Midnight*, a housekeeper recounts, and the film shows (though her story is later revealed to be a fabrication), a keyhole through which mist pours and then solidifies into that film's vampire figure (Philip J. Riley, ed., *London After Midnight* [New York: Cornwall Books, 1985], contains the 1927 script "The Hypnotist" by Tod Browning. On p. 52 the housekeeper recounts the incident, which is revealed to be a fabrication on p. 70. Photos depicting the incident are on pp. 129–31). The Browning Dracula, staked off-screen, remains sufficiently intact to reappear (in the form of a dummy) in *Dracula's Daughter* (Hillyer, 1936).

6. Auerbach, 115.

7. "Feet First," *Exhibitors Herald-World*, 18 Oct. 1930, 44.

8. Respectively: Prawer, 133; Crafton, 371; Daniels, 130; and Auerbach, 113.

9. Cecelia Ager, "Going Places," *Variety*, 18 Feb. 1931, 54.

10. Others to compare the two performances on the basis of the slowness of the characters' speech are Auerbach, 116; and Brunas, Brunas, and Weaver, 15.

11. A similar point is made in Gregory A. Waller, *The Living and the Undead: From Stoker's* Dracula *to Romero's* Dawn of the Dead (Urbana: University of Illinois Press, 1986), 90. In Deane and Balderston's play, the character is referred to as "this Dutch Sherlock Holmes with the X-ray eyes" (Deane and Balderston, *Dracula: The Vampire Play*, 35). Finally, to viewers who find the character's grounding in scientific ideas and methods called into question by his faith in wolfbane and crucifixes, the film offers this line, spoken by Van Helsing to an incredulous Seward: "I may be able to bring you proof that the superstition of yesterday can become the scientific reality of today."

12. Turner, "Two Faces of Dracula," 41. The speech in its presentation resembled one the same actor makes at the start of *Frankenstein*, in which he plays a similar character.

13. Turner claims that this speech was delivered in the play by Dracula (Turner, "Two Faces of Dracula," 40). In the currently available Samuel French edition and in the one edited by Skal, the speech is delivered by Van Helsing (Deane and Balderston, *Dracula: The Vampire Play*, 74; Deane and Balderston, *Dracula: The Ultimate, Illustrated Edition*, 150).

14. Dialogue 'Dracula' (Picture #109-1, Browning [sound]), 21.

15. Quoted in Arthur Lennig, *The Count: The Life and Films of Bela "Dracula" Lugosi* (New York: G. P. Putman's Sons, 1974), 73.

16. McConnell, 27. Oates finds Dracula's movement as "premeditated as a dancer's" (499).

17. Lennig, *The Count*, 98.

18. Auerbach seems to be describing the vampire's "time-sense" where she writes that "his stately, hypnotic cadences, the long close-ups that make him seem more statuesque than alive, the old-fashioned theatricality with which he confronts shrill American actors, differentiate him absolutely from his human company" (117).

19. On the character's silence and immobility in the England sequences, see Auerbach, 77.

20. The shooting script indicates that Dracula can communicate telepathically. (See Tod Browning and Garrett Fort, "Dracula" [26 Sept. 1930 Shooting Script], shots G-15, G-17, and H-34.)

21. See, for example, Lennig, *The Immortal Count*, 116–17.

22. During Renfield's similar speech in the novel, Dracula does not appear (Stoker, 244–45). Renfield makes no similar speech in either version of the play.

23. Tod Browning and Garrett Fort, "Dracula" (26 Sept. 1930 Shooting Script), shot A-12.

24. Bordwell, Staiger, and Thompson, 63.

25. Tsivian, *Early Cinema in Russia*, 206.

26. "Emotional memory" is Tsivian's term. See, for example, ibid., 139.

27. *Hollywood Filmograph*, 4 April 1931, quoted in Lennig, *The Immortal Count*, 128.

28. Shots beginning this way are indicated in the continuity documents with

"disc." This sense of being "discovered" in a shot relates to the theater technique of bringing up the lights on an onstage figure.

29. The film does not employ this technique when, in the castle, the drugged Renfield swoons and Dracula walks into view through a doorway.

30. Viewers of *The Return of the Vampire* (Landers, 1943) and *Bud Abbott and Lou Costello Meet Frankenstein* (Barton, 1948), both with Lugosi playing the vampire, would not be spared this undignified sight.

31. A cheap trick is what the same event, handled the same way, turns out to be in Browning's 1935 *London After Midnight* remake, *Mark of the Vampire*, with Lugosi playing the phony vampire.

32. These techniques resemble ones Hitchcock would use to make the sinister housekeeper Mrs. Danvers, in *Rebecca* (1940), seem omnipresent. See Truffaut with Scott, 129–30.

33. Oates, 503. Others who like the handling of Dracula's risings include Auerbach, 119; and Lawrence Contratti, "A Reconstruction of Tod Browning's *Dracula* as a Transitional Sound Film," *Classic Film Collector*, no. 43 (Summer 1974): 29.

34. Subsequent critics who praise the film's quiet include Contratti, 27, 28, 29; and Oates, 498, 499.

35. Crafton, 354. (Crafton also notes that the films of the 1931 season display a wide range of approaches to sound [360].) Contributing to the quiet of the season's films was the large number of musicals that flopped at around this time—to which producers reacted by drastically scaling back musical film production. (See Ted Taylor, "1930 in the Land of Nod," *Variety*, 31 Dec. 1930, 20; Sid Silverman, "U.S. Film Field for 1930," *Variety*, 31 Dec. 1930, 7; "Inside Stuff—Pictures," *Variety*, 31 Dec. 1930, 39; and Crafton, 269, 316, 357–60.) The situation abruptly changed from one in which, as Crafton notes, it had been hard to find a film that did not contain at least one musical number to one in which music in all its forms was being minimized or eliminated in a large number of films (315–16).

36. See Tsivian, *Early Cinema in Russia*, 82 for the first quote, 83 for the second and third.

37. Rose Pelswick, "Hair-Raising Tale Better on Screen Than on Stage," rev. of *Dracula, New York Journal*, 13 Feb. 1931. The quiet of the film also reflected the studio's desire to avoid offending local censorship boards, feedback from which underscored the studio's need to take special care with regard to the gruesomeness, loudness, and number of sound effects heard in the film. The studio's cautiousness in this regard is evident in the death groans Dracula makes when Van Helsing is staking him. The shooting script indicates that viewers are to hear "a loud and shuddering groan" followed by a "last agonizing groan" (Tod Browning and Garrett Fort, "Dracula" [26 Sept. 1930 Shooting Script], shots H-54 and H-55, respectively). The groans heard in the film are quite subdued, and even these displeased some censor boards. Chicago's, for example, instructed Universal to "cut Dracula's death groans as Doctor drives spike through his heart" (and to cut "Dracula choking man on stairs and man screaming") (Jason Joy, 17 April 1931 report of rejections made to *Dracula* by the Chicago Censor Board, 1931,

"Dracula" folder, Production Code Files, Margaret Herrick Library, Academy of Motion Picture Arts and Sciences). The studio deleted the groans, which, according to Skal, were restored for the film's laser disc release. (See his running commentary on the 1999 DVD issue of *Dracula*.)

38. Nondiegetic music is heard on three occasions when the Spanish Dracula is seen rising from his coffin. Also, the music that in Browning's film confines itself to the opening credits drifts, in this version, into the first shots of Renfield's carriage on the Borgo pass. And, while at the end of Browning's film, Mina and John exit the abbey to the accompaniment of chiming church bells that sound diegetic, in the Spanish-language film Eva (Lupita Tovar) and Juan (Barry Norton) exit to swelling nondiegetic music that continues over the end title screen. Also, many diegetic sounds heard in the Spanish version are louder than the ones heard at corresponding moments in Browning's film. These sounds include creaking doors, the howling that prompts the "children of the night" line, and the laughter of the two Renfields.

39. Bakshy, "The 'Talkies,'" 236.

40. On the modulated sound track and early sound films, see Crafton, esp. 360–73 and 378–80.

41. Everson, "Horror," 97.

42. Writers who find *Dracula*'s narrative unclear in spots include Lennig, *The Count*, 86; and Skal and Savada, *Dark Carnival*, 153.

43. Stephani, in Riley, *Dracula*, 40. (Skal mentions a third treatment, by Louis Stevens, in *Hollywood Gothic*, 113.)

44. Stoker, 200; Deane and Balderston, *Dracula: The Vampire Play*, 42. In Stephani's treatment, Dracula takes seven coffins (Stephani, in Riley, *Dracula*, 39). A comparison of the novel with the play and Browning's film is in Waller, 79–93.

45. Bordwell compares *Vampyr*'s and *Dracula*'s narratives in *The Films of Carl-Theodor Dreyer* (Berkeley and Los Angeles: University of California Press, 1981), 94–95, 112. Regarding the slow pace of the film, Lennig notes that when the action moves to the sanitarium scenes, the cutting rate plummets (Lennig, *The Immortal Count*, 118).

46. On how Universal obtained a print of *Nosferatu* to study as it planned its production of *Dracula*, see Skal, *Hollywood Gothic*, 108–9.

47. Lennig writes that this line combines two from the play (*The Immortal Count*, 114–15). See Deane and Balderston, *Dracula: The Vampire Play*, 24 and 25, for the two lines. The parallel between the locations is asserted even more baldly in the silent version of Browning's film (adapted from the sound version and produced for theaters not yet wired for sound) when, following none of the talk about repairs that precedes the line in the sound film, Dracula says: "Carfax Abbey reminds me of my own castle in Transylvania" (Continuity and Subtitles for "Dracula" [Picture #109-2, Browning (silent)], Box 13, Folder 3273, Part 3, shot 31 [Cinema-Television Library, University of Southern California]).

48. "Massive Settings in 'Dracula' Film," Publicity Scene Cuts section, Exhibitors' Campaign for *Dracula*. The *Exhibitors Herald-World* noted that the "Count takes up his abode in a deserted abbey, the one place in the country which most resembles his castle in Transylvania" ("Most Unusual Sets in U History Used to Film 'Dracula,'" *Exhibitors Herald-World*, 29 Nov. 1931, 37).

49. Edward Churchill, "Dracula," *Motion Picture Herald,* 3 Jan. 1931, 74.

50. Jack Alicoate, ed., *The 1931 Film Daily Yearbook* (New York: Film Daily, 1931), 694. The *Universal Weekly,* the studio's bulletin to exhibitors, described a promotional display for *The Cat and the Canary* involving "a cut out of a mysterious house similar to the one shown in the opening of the picture. This cut out was placed in front of the theatre and was large enough and unique enough in design to attract much attention. Waxed paper windows with a light and a shadowgraph back of them made the house spooky" ("Mysterious House and Ushers Boom 'Cat and Canary' in Seattle," *Universal Weekly,* 5 Nov. 1927), 260.

51. Oates, 507–8.

52. McConnell, 26, 31. On the power of the film's narrative simplicity, see also Leonard Wolf, *A Dream of Dracula: In Search of the Living Dead* (Boston: Little, Brown, 1972), 286.

53. On *Vampyr*'s bewildering spatiality, see Bordwell, *Films of Carl-Theodor Dreyer,* 97–109, where he contrasts Dreyer's film with the straightforward narrative spaces of *Dracula* (105–6).

54. McConnell, 32.

55. An exception is a crane shot that carries us nearly through the gateway of Seward's Sanitarium; then, following a dissolve, a moving camera shot that meanders over the sanitarium grounds until it stops on Renfield's window.

56. Skal, *Hollywood Gothic,* 160.

57. Turner, "Two Faces of Dracula," 39.

58. Alain Silver and James Ursini, *The Vampire Film: From Nosferatu to Interview with the Vampire* (New York: Limelight Editions, 1997), 67 ("greater focal length"); Skal and Savada, *Dark Carnival,* 154 ("flat, stagebound mise-en-scène").

59. Turner, "Two Faces of Dracula," 40. Skal calls the Spanish film "an almost shot-by-shot scathing critique of the Browning version" (Skal, *Hollywood Gothic,* 160).

60. Bromfield, scene A-12, in Riley, *Dracula,* 46.

61. Stephani, in Riley, *Dracula,* 36 ("(sic)" is in Riley).

62. For a brief but provocative reflection on *Nosferatu*'s arches, see Gilberto Perez, *The Material Ghost: Films and Their Medium* (Baltimore: Johns Hopkins University Press, 1998), 129.

63. Quoted in Philip J. Riley and George Turner, "Production Background," in Riley, *Dracula,* 56. This script version was by Bromfield and Dudley Murphy.

64. On the tightening of production budgets, including *Dracula*'s, at Universal, see Richard Koszarski, *Universal Pictures: 65 Years* (New York: Museum of Modern Art, 1977), 13; Thomas Schatz, *The Genius of the System: Hollywood Filmmaking in the Studio Era* (New York: Pantheon, 1988), 86–91; and Skal, *Hollywood Gothic,* 113–14, 131.

65. Quoted in Riley and Turner, "Production Background," in Riley, *Dracula,* 56.

66. Tod Browning and Garrett Fort, "Dracula" (26 Sept. 1930 Shooting Script), shot A-30. A further sign of the studio's skittishness about producing too "German" a film is this quote from the *Motion Picture Magazine,* in the *Universal Weekly,* regarding *The Cat and the Canary:* "The management of light

and shadow is effectively used to enhance the dramatic quality of each scene, but no scene is kept too dark for the full benefit of the action to be appreciated by the audience. Many things are done for 'effect,' but, since the effect accomplishes its purpose, we can't quarrel over that" ("The Cat and the Canary," *Motion Picture Magazine*, excerpted in the *Universal Weekly*, 23 April 1927, 33). It's not hard to guess, based on the studio's renewed emphasis on cost cutting and on its fear of overloading the film with Expressionistic touches, how it reacted to Bromfield's description of "a crazy stairway leading to the rooms above. The whole room is distorted like something seen in a dream" (Bromfield, scene A-3, in Riley, *Dracula*, 43).

67. "The Cat and the Canary," *Motion Picture Magazine*, in *Universal Weekly*, 33.

68. George C. Warren, "The Cat and the Canary," *San Francisco Chronicle*, quoted in *Universal Weekly*, 8 Oct. 1927, 32. More examples of the tendency to catalogue elements of the film are in "The Cat and the Canary," *Film Daily*, 15 May 1927, 7; "The Cat and the Canary," *Harrison's Reports*, 28 May 1927, 86; and Norbert Lusk, "The Screen in Review," rev. of *The Cat and the Canary*, *Picture Play*, Dec. 1927, 60.

69. Cooper.

70. William A. Johnston, editor of the *Motion Picture News*, quoted in "Paul Leni Assigned to Direct Hugo's 'The Man Who Laughs,'" *Universal Weekly*, 30 April 1927, 10.

71. Mordaunt Hall, "The Haunted House," rev. of *The Cat and the Canary*, *New York Times*, 10 Sept. 1927, 9.

72. None of this is to say that attending so closely to visualizing and complicating the interior spaces of a film necessarily serves a narrative that is itself very complicated or even interesting. Lusk wrote of *The Cat and the Canary* that, "curiously enough, the proceedings seem real, probably because interest is kept at such a high pitch that there is scant opportunity to sink back and analyze the rather conventional labyrinth of the story" (Lusk, "Screen in Review," 60).

73. Similar to the suspiciously plentiful claims about talking furniture were ones about Leni's camera making viewers feel as though they are actually inside the mansion or characters in the film. Examples include John S. Cohen, "The Cat and the Canary," *New York Sun*, quoted in the *Universal Weekly*, 24 Sept. 1927, 33; Lusk, "Screen in Review," 60; and Hall, "The Haunted House," 9.

74. Bordwell, Staiger, and Thompson, 37.

75. James Price, "The Dark House," *The London Magazine* (Aug. 1963): 70–71.

76. This is not to suggest that the coming of sound *mandated* such a transformation. Sound old-dark-house films that emphasize their spaces in ways similar to *The Cat and the Canary* include *The Cat Creeps*, the "continuity and subtitles" production document for which describes, for example, a "TRAVELING SHOT IN HALL" in which a character is "walking through hall—walks around— camera is drawn up disclosing the stairs and floor in hall below"; *The Bat Whispers*, which prompted a reviewer to note "sliding pictures, and hidden panels, and moving fireplaces, and what not. There's a murder and a scramble for the blueprints which reveal the secret room"; and Whale's *The Old Dark House*

(1932), about which one reviewer wrote: "I am always a little amazed by the intrepidity of those persons stranded of a night in strange circumstances. Those five good souls in 'The Old Dark House,' for instance—how they wander about the long corridors of the building, and pry and probe into every nook and cranny!" (Respectively: Continuity and Subtitles for "The Cat Creeps" [Picture #107-2, Julian (silent)], Box 13, Folder 2843, Part 3, shot 61 [Cinema-Television Library, University of Southern California]; "The Bat Whispers," *Modern Screen,* Feb. 1931, 100; and J. C. M., "The Current Cinema: Creeps and Shudders," rev. of *The Old Dark House, The New Yorker,* 5 Nov. 1932, 77.)

77. Charles Wolfe, "Vitaphone Shorts and *The Jazz Singer,*" *Wide Angle* 12, no. 3 (July 1990): 63.

78. Perez, 83.

79. See, for example, Noël Carroll, "Film, Emotion, and Genre," in *Passionate Views: Film, Cognition, and Emotion,* ed. Carl Plantinga and Greg M. Smith (Baltimore: Johns Hopkins University Press, 1999), 39–42; Judith Halberstam, *Skin Shows: Gothic Horror and the Technology of Monsters* (Durham, NC: Duke University Press, 1995), 27; and Jeffrey Jerome Cohen, "Monster Culture (Seven Theses)," in *Monster Theory: Reading Culture,* ed. Cohen (Minneapolis: University of Minnesota Press, 1996), 6–7.

80. Critics I am thinking of are those interested in how the cinema is different than other media and who locate the cinema's aesthetic value there. A film that hews closely to a play would likely fail to qualify as "cinematic." Rudolf Arnheim has been the most influential exponent of this view (see Rudolf Arnheim, *Film as Art* [Berkeley and Los Angeles: University of California Press, 1957]).

81. In an essay whose title inspired the title of my chapter, William Paul describes productions of the late 1910s and early 1920s in which live performance combined with projected film, creating a juxtaposition that foregrounded the uncanny and disembodied nature of the on-screen figures (William Paul, "Uncanny Theater: The Twin Inheritances of the Movies," *Paradoxa* 3, nos. 3–4 [Fall 1997]: 339–40).

CHAPTER 5. *FRANKENSTEIN* AND THE VATS OF HOLLYWOOD

1. *Frankenstein* was among the top-grossing films in 1932 ("Biggest Money Pictures," *Variety,* 21 June 1932, 62). For more on the initial box-office success of the film, see Curtis, 155–59; Tino Balio, *Grand Design: Hollywood as a Modern Business Enterprise, 1930–1939,* History of the American Cinema, ed. Charles Harpole, vol. 5 (New York: Charles Scribner's Sons, 1993), 301; and Paul M. Jensen, *The Men Who Made the Monsters* (New York: Twayne, 1996), 23. The film also made the *New York Times* "ten best" list for 1931 (Mordaunt Hall, "Blue-Ribbon Pictures of 1931," *New York Times,* 3 Jan. 1932, sec. 8, p. 5). Examples of initial high praise for the film are in William Boehnel, "Dramatic Terrors of 'Frankenstein' Splendidly Filmed," *New York World Telegram,* 5 Dec. 1931; "Frankenstein," *Film Daily,* 6 Dec. 1931, 10; "Frankenstein," *New York*

Morning Telegraph, 6 Dec. 1931; Mordaunt Hall, "The Screen," rev. of *Frankenstein, New York Times,* 5 Dec. 1931, 21; Norbert Lusk, "Frankenstein," *Picture Play,* March 1932, 47; Rose Pelswick, "'Frankenstein' a Thriller; 'Cuban Love Song' and 'His Woman' Also Reviewed," *New York Journal,* 5 Dec. 1931; and Alfred Rushford Greason, "Frankenstein," *Variety,* 8 Dec. 1931, 14 (review signed "Rush.").

2. Reviewers who called the film superior to *Dracula* include Lusk, "Frankenstein," 47; Greason, "Frankenstein," 14; and Hall, "The Screen," 21. Universal was happy to encourage such comparisons. See, for example, "For the Program," Publicity Scene Cuts section, Exhibitors' Campaign for *Frankenstein,* reproduced in Philip J. Riley, ed., *Frankenstein,* Universal Filmscripts Series, Classic Horror Films, vol. 1 (Absecon, NJ: MagicImage Filmbooks, 1989); and Carl Laemmle, "Watch This Column: Universal's Weekly Chat" (advt.), *Saturday Evening Post,* 12 Dec. 1931, 70.

3. "Old Horror Tale Full of Thrills," rev. of *Frankenstein, Hollywood Reporter,* 3 Nov. 1931.

4. H. M., "Frankenstein," *Bioscope,* 27 Jan. 1932, 20. Others who did not find the creature sympathetic include Richard Watts Jr., "On the Screen," rev. of *Frankenstein, New York Herald-Tribune,* 5 Dec. 1931; Hall, "The Screen," 21; and Laemmle, "Watch This Column: Universal's Weekly Chat" (advt.), *Saturday Evening Post,* 5 Dec. 1931, 67. Initial commentators who did find the figure sympathetic include "Frankenstein," *Harrison's Reports,* 12 Dec. 1931, 198; and Rob Reel, "Boris Karloff, Colin Clive Deliver Fine Acting in State-Lake Thriller," rev. of *Frankenstein, Chicago American,* 4 Dec. 1931; and, in the pressbook, Het Manheim, "What Does a Monster Think About?" Publicity Scene Cuts section, Exhibitors' Campaign for *Frankenstein.* This ambivalent sense of the monster appears to have been Whale's aim. (See Curtis, 133.) Sample subsequent reflections on the sympathetic nature of the monster are in Curtis, 3; Dettman and Bedford, 16; Raymond Durgnat, "The Subconscious: From Pleasure Castle to Libido Motel" (1962), in *Horror Film Reader,* ed. Alain Silver and James Ursini (New York: Limelight Editions, 2000), 39; Donald F. Glut, *The Frankenstein Legend: A Tribute to Mary Shelley and Boris Karloff* (Metuchen, NJ: Scarecrow Press, 1973), 118; Hutchings, 162–64; Kaye, 184; Schatz, 94; Kevin Thomas, "'Frankenstein' and 'Dracula' Reissued," *Los Angeles Times,* 21 Nov. 1968; Tudor, *Monsters and Mad Scientists,* 118; and George E. Turner, "*Frankenstein,* the Monster Classic," in *The Cinema of Adventure, Romance and Terror,* ed. Turner (Hollywood: ASC Press, 1989), 98.

5. Hall, "The Screen," 21 ("audience laughed"). More nervous laughter is reported in Pelswick, "'Frankenstein' a Thriller." "Strong Men Gasp and Women Scream," *New York World Telegram,* 16 Dec. 1931 ("gasping males and screaming females"). Another reviewer reported a "round of real applause from Mayfair audiences as the curtain rings down on the fadeout" (Irene Thirer, "'Frankenstein' Weird Chiller," *New York Daily News,* 5 Dec. 1931, 28). "'Frankenstein' Editors Experimenting with Thrills," Publicity Scene Cuts section, Exhibitors' Campaign for *Frankenstein* ("strong meat and monster food").

6. Curtis, 152.

7. Forrest J. Ackerman, "Foreword," in Riley, *Frankenstein,* 8. Other claims

about the initial power of this moment in the film are in Peter Underwood, *Karloff: The Life of Boris Karloff* (New York: Drake, 1972), 69; and David Zinman, "Horrors! Frankenstein Is 40," *New York Newsday,* 3 Dec. 1971, 7A. A claim that the moment "still manages to shock" is in Butler, 41.

8. Writers who have compared the two films, with *Frankenstein* coming out ahead, include Brunas, Brunas, and Weaver, 27; Curtis, 3; Dettman and Bedford, 19; Phillips, 14; and Tudor, *Monsters and Mad Scientists,* 161–62. Writers who call the film timeless include Dettman and Bedford, 9; Thomas; and Gregory William Mank, *It's Alive! The Classic Cinema Saga of Frankenstein* (San Diego: A. S. Barnes, 1981), 39. Another writes that the film "wears remarkably well" (Underwood, 70). On the ubiquity of the monster in popular culture, see Susan E. Lederer, *Frankenstein: Penetrating the Secrets of Nature* (New Brunswick, NJ: Rutgers University Press, 2002), 46–51.

9. James A. W. Heffernan, "Looking at the Monster: *Frankenstein* and Film," *Critical Inquiry,* no. 24 (Autumn 1997): 158. More reflections on the iconic status of the monster are in Curtis, 142; and Dettman and Bedford, 16–17.

10. Stefan Kanfer, "*Frankenstein* at Sixty," *Connoisseur,* Jan. 1991, 44 ("most recognizable black-and-white character"); Zinman, 7A ("face is unforgettable"); F. S. N., "At the Roxy," rev. of *The Bride of Frankenstein, New York Times,* 11 May 1935, 21 ("so vividly are etched").

11. Comments anticipating the fascination of the monster are in "'Frankenstein' Editors Experimenting with Thrills," Publicity Scene Cuts section, Exhibitors' Campaign for *Frankenstein;* and "'Frankenstein' Finished," *New York Telegraph,* 11 Oct. 1931. Reviewers who found Karloff outstanding include "Frankenstein," *Harrison's Reports,* 198; "Frankenstein," *Modern Screen,* Feb. 1932, 57; Pelswick, "'Frankenstein' a Thriller"; Reel; Greason, "Frankenstein," 14; and Thirer, "'Frankenstein' Weird Chiller." Comments praising the makeup include those in J. C. M., "The Current Cinema: Gallipoli—Thrills by Mrs. Percy B. Shelley," rev. of *Frankenstein, The New Yorker,* 12 Dec. 1931, 96; Lusk, "Frankenstein," 47; and Reel.

12. Exhibitors' Campaign for *Frankenstein.* The pressbook for the sequel reminded exhibitors that "the monster's face made a fortune for you!" and told them to "FEATURE MONSTER'S FAMOUS FACE OUT FRONT" (Exhibitors' Campaign for *The Bride of Frankenstein*). The booklet goes on to outline strategies for executing this campaign, including working "a cut-out of Karloff's head into a front for the box-office! Put dimmers or red and green blinkers behind the eyes for extra effect."

13. "Henger's Weird Trailer Proved Effective!" *Motion Picture Herald,* 23 Jan. 1932, 60. Other promotional gimmicks featuring the monster's head are described in the Exhibitors' Campaign for *Frankenstein;* and "Cassady's Attractive Poster Work," *Motion Picture Herald,* 13 Feb. 1932, 54.

14. Exhibitors' Campaign for *Frankenstein.*

15. Carl Laemmle, "Watch This Column: Universal's Weekly Chat" (advt.), *Saturday Evening Post,* 21 Nov. 1931, 38. Mary Shelley's *Frankenstein* was, in 1931, a little-read novel compared to Stoker's *Dracula.*

16. "U Has Horror Cycle All to Self," *Variety,* 8 April 1931, 2.

17. To take a reflexive turn when approaching Whale's film is nothing new.

A reviewer in 1931 wrote that "the camera has afforded almost frankenstein opportunities of emphasizing all the deadly horror of this unique piece of literature," and noted that screenwriters "Garrett Fort and Francis Edward [sic] Faragoh have considered their medium well in developing the screen treatment" (Leo Meehan, "Frankenstein," *Motion Picture Herald,* 14 Nov. 1931, 40). A month later, Whale described a scene in the film in which Frankenstein "is now in a state of feverish excitement calculated to carry both the spectators in the windmill and the spectators in the theatre with him" ("James Whale and 'Frankenstein,'" *New York Times,* 20 Dec. 1931, sec. 8, p. 4). Recent years have seen more rigorous attempts to mount metacinematic readings of the film. See, for example, Scott J. Juengel, "Face, Figure, Physiognomics: Mary Shelley's *Frankenstein* and the Moving Image," *Novel: A Forum on Fiction* 33, no. 3 (Summer 2000): 354; Heffernan; William Nestrick, "Coming to Life: *Frankenstein* and the Nature of Film Narrative," in *The Endurance of Frankenstein: Essays on Mary Shelley's Novel,* ed. George Levine and U. C. Knoepflmacher (Berkeley and Los Angeles: University of California Press, 1979), 290–315; and Marc Redfield, "*Frankenstein's* Cinematic Dream," in *Frankenstein's Dream: A Romantic Circles Praxis Volume,* ed. Jerrold E. Hogle (Feb. 2003). www.rc.umd.edu/praxis/frankenstein/redfield/redfield.html.

18. Crafton, 61.

19. Hall, "Reaction of the Public," 607.

20. From the Exhibitors' Campaign.

21. "Make Your Posters Come to Life!" (advt. for the Cutawl), *Motion Picture Herald,* 16 Jan. 1932, 37.

22. See, for example, Turner, "*Frankenstein,* the Monster Classic," 93; and Skal, *The Monster Show,* 135. Curtis says the microphone was in the grave, not the coffin (Curtis, 152).

23. Greason, "Frankenstein," 14.

24. While I found no indications in the reviews that these footstep sounds were initially impressive, George Turner told me they "got people."

25. F. C. Schmid and S. K. Wolf, "The New Importance of Acoustics to Natural Sound," *Motion Picture Herald,* 7 May 1932, 23.

26. In a 1930 unproduced play by John Balderston, from which ideas for the film were taken, the monster talks, but in a primitive manner that anticipates his speech in *The Bride of Frankenstein.* (The text of the play is in Steven Earl Forry, *Hideous Progenies: Dramatizations of* Frankenstein *from Mary Shelley to the Present* [Philadelphia: University of Pennsylvania Press, 1990], 251–86; samples of the monster's speech in this play are on 262.) In the play by Peggy Webling, which Balderston adapted into his version, the monster speaks as well (Curtis, 130). The first adaptation of Shelley's novel to strip the monster of his capacity to speak was an 1823 theatrical adaptation by Richard Brinsley Peake titled *Presumption; or, The Fate of Frankenstein* (Lederer, 32).

27. The mooing reference is from Hall, "The Screen," 21, where he also writes that "the sounds of the cries of the pursuers and the strange noises made by the monster add to the disturbing nature of the scenes," and that at the climax, "from the screen comes the sound of the crackling of the blazing woodwork, the hue and cry of the frightened and the queer sounds of the dying monster." The bark-

ing reference is from *Film Weekly,* a British publication, quoted in Riley, *Frankenstein,* 32. Others to describe the monster's weird vocalizations include H. M., "Frankenstein," 20; Thirer, "'Frankenstein' Weird Chiller," 28; and Thornton Delahanty, "The New Films," rev. of *Frankenstein, New York Post,* 7 Dec. 1931.

28. Curtis, 138. Also see Turner, "*Frankenstein,* the Monster Classic," 92.

29. Some report that green-tinted prints were screened at selected theaters on the film's first release. (See Ackerman, "Foreword," 8; and Underwood, 69.)

30. Garrett Fort and Francis Edwards Faragoh, "Frankenstein, Screen Play," shot E-3, in Riley, *Frankenstein.* The creature's status as something neither quite alive nor fully dead was played up in the film's promotion. One theater display featured a likeness of the monster with the eyes cut out and with "red lights behind, a flasher being used to give a 'dead and alive' effect" ("Cassady's Attractive Poster Work," 54). A fan magazine reported to readers that Karloff was blind for three weeks following completion of shooting, "the after-effect of a powerful drug used to paralyze an optic nerve and hold one eye in a fixed position throughout the picture" ("Death before Surrender," *Picture Play,* Feb. 1933, 66). And an article by Pierce in *American Cinematographer,* appearing a few months after the film's release, noted that the monster's eyes "were exact duplicates of the dead eyes of a 2800-year-old Egyptian corpse!" (Jack Pierce, "Character Make-up," *American Cinematographer* 13, no. 1 [May 1932]: 9).

31. Mary Shelley, *Frankenstein; or, The Modern Prometheus* (1818), in *Frankenstein,* ed. J. Paul Hunter (New York: W. W. Norton, 1996), 34.

32. Tsivian, *Early Cinema in Russia,* 9 (ellipsis original). The writer is Zinaida Gippius.

33. On the creature's mix of human and monstrous qualities, see Clarens, 64; Heffernan, 145; Juengel, 354; and R. H. W. Dillard, *Horror Films* (New York: Simon and Schuster, 1976), 13.

34. Robert Florey, Shooting Script for the lost Lugosi test footage, shot D-49, reproduced in appendix A of Riley, *Frankenstein.*

35. Greason, "Frankenstein," 14.

36. Boehnel ("more regard for individual scenes"); H. M., "Frankenstein," 19 ("crudely constructed blood-curdler"); John S. Cohen, "The Talking Pictures," *New York Sun,* 7 Dec. 1931 ("tired of aggressive prettiness"), quoted in "Studio Should Be Proud: Sherwood; Season Not Bad: John S. Cohen, Jr.," *Motion Picture Herald,* 2 Jan. 1932, 20.

37. An aspect of the narrative also arguably contributes in a minor way to impressions of the film as rough surfaced. This is a trace of an earlier script version in which the creation of the monster takes place in a windmill, not the watch tower where it happens in the film. In the film, as Turner notes, Henry's father, the baron (Frederick Kerr), asks about his son, "Why does he go messing around in an old ruined windmill?" (Turner, "*Frankenstein,* the Monster Classic," 87). Henry will be tossed by the monster from a windmill at the climax, but viewers have not yet glimpsed this location when the baron says this line.

38. Rosar notes that Universal announced to the trade press in September 1931 that two of its upcoming films, *Heaven on Earth* and *Frankenstein,* would feature "complete musical scores" (Rosar, 395; he is referring to "Complete Film Scores," *Variety,* 8 Sept. 1931, 116). This plan was not carried out for either film.

39. H. M., "Frankenstein," 20 ("creased backcloth is unmistakable"). Ivan Butler calls these "mountain passes and ridges patently studio-made" (Butler, 43). Thirer, "'Frankenstein' Weird Chiller," 28 ("papier mache"). William K. Everson, *Classics of the Horror Film* (New York: Citadel, 1974), 37 ("rough hewn realism").

40. Brian Taves, "Universal's Horror Tradition," *American Cinematographer* (April 1987): 47.

41. There are other mismatching match-on-action cuts, but these are the most glaring.

42. J. C. M., "Creeps and Shudders," 77 ("smoothness here"); and Philip K. Scheuer, "Mystery Film Opens Run at Hillstreet," rev. of *The Old Dark House*, *Los Angeles Times*, 19 Nov. 1932, sec. A, p. 7 ("Whale, improving").

43. "Waterloo Bridge," *Picture Play,* Dec. 1931, 41.

44. On both films the cinematographer was Arthur Edeson, the supervising film editor was Maurice Pivar, and the editor was Clarence Kolster. My thanks to Turner Classic Movies for making it possible for me to view *Waterloo Bridge.*

45. Curtis, 150.

46. Nestrick, 303; Heffernan, 139.

47. Ibid., 144. *Harrison's Reports,* impressed by this stroke of originality, wrote that "the body is supposed to have been made up of parts of different dead bodies and one can see the seams where these parts have been sewed together" ("Frankenstein," *Harrison's Reports,* 198).

48. McConnell, 28.

49. The mechanics of the sequence as it plays out in the film are not spelled out in the shooting script, which indicates only, following a talky "med. close shot" of the two men, a cut to a "medium shot": "THE CAMERA, CHANGING ITS ANGLE, now takes in the door, keeping Waldman and Frankenstein in the foreground. Both have now turned to the door, which slowly opens, revealing the Monster in the frame" (Garrett Fort and Francis Edwards Faragoh, "Frankenstein, Screen Play," shot E-3).

50. Price, 70.

51. Curtis notes that the low angle also makes the monster look more massive and imposing (Curtis, 150).

52. On the emergence of this prohibition, see Bowser, 89–92.

53. On the thirty-degree rule, see Ira Konigsberg, *The Complete Film Dictionary,* 2nd ed. (New York: Penguin, 1997), 418. For a consideration of "shock cuts" and horror films that includes thoughts on axial cutting, see David Scott Diffrient, "A Film Is Being Beaten: Notes on the Shock Cut and the Material Violence of Horror," in *Horror: Creating and Marketing Fear,* ed. Steffen Hantke (Jackson: University Press of Mississippi, 2004), 52–81, esp. 78–79.

54. David Bordwell, *Figures Traced in Light: On Cinematic Staging* (Berkeley and Los Angeles: University of California Press, 2005), 129.

55. Curtis, 212.

56. Jesse L. Lasky, "Production More Exacting and More Exact," *Motion Picture Herald,* 3 Jan. 1931, 60.

57. Others who see Karloff's monster evoking silent cinema include Auerbach, 118; McConnell, 28; Nestrick, 296; and Turner, "*Frankenstein,* the Monster Classic," 98.

58. Chion, 95 (ellipsis original).

59. Ibid., 97.

60. A letter Whale reportedly wrote to Clive when the film was in its planning stages explicitly mentions *Caligari* as a source of inspiration ("'Frankenstein' Finished"). Initial reviews identifying *Caligari* as a reference point for Whale's film include Boehnel; "Strong Men Gasp"; and Watts, "On the Screen," rev. of *Frankenstein*.

61. *Frankenstein*'s shooting script includes descriptions of angular sets and props "tilted at crazy angles" that call *Caligari* to mind (Garrett Fort and Francis Edwards Faragoh, "Frankenstein, Screen Play," shot A-1). On narrative and thematic similarities between *Frankenstein* and *Caligari,* see Prawer, 38–39. On narrative and thematic similarities between *Frankenstein* and *The Golem* (Wegener and Boese, 1920), see Reed Ellis, *A Journey into Darkness: The Art of James Whale's Horror Films* (New York: Arno Press, 1980), 33–34.

62. A reviewer who noted similarities between the monster and Cesare was Watts, "On the Screen," rev. of *Frankenstein*.

63. On Expressionist acting, including its minimalism and extremity of bodily movements and facial expressions, see Eisner, 137–49.

64. Gomery reports that in 1930, a quarter of all theaters in the United States were showing only silent films, and that in January 1933, 2.6 percent were showing only silent films (Gomery, *Coming of Sound: A History,* 92).

65. Eisner, 140.

66. John D. Barlow, *German Expressionist Film* (Boston: Twayne, 1982), 54–55.

67. Doane, 162.

68. Mordaunt Hall, "A British Talker," rev. of *White Cargo, New York Times,* 24 Feb. 1930, 23 ("old-time silent film"); A. Walker, 106 ("overdone and intrusive"); "The Chinese Parrot," *Harrison's Reports,* 7 Jan. 1928, 2 ("permits the old style").

69. Kristin Thompson and David Bordwell, *Film History: An Introduction* (New York: McGraw-Hill, 1994), 112.

70. Paul Rotha, *The Film till Now: A Survey of World Cinema* (1930; repr. with a section by Richard Griffith, New York: Funk and Wagnalls, 1949), 97.

71. On the decision to shoot all Vitaphone films using panchromatic stock, see J. Douglas Gomery, "The Coming of Sound to the American Cinema: A History of the Transformation of an Industry" (Ph.D. dissertation, University of Wisconsin–Madison, 1975), 164. Kristin Thompson writes that panchromatic stock became the industry standard around 1927 (Bordwell, Staiger, and Thompson, 281).

72. Bordwell, Staiger, and Thompson, 281–83.

73. My sense that *Frankenstein* is still scary in a way that *Dracula* is not is based in part on my daughter Nora's reactions to both films. When she was five, she sat through the worst of Browning's film without so much as flinching, but when she wandered one day into my office and caught the moment of the Frankenstein monster's first appearance, she hid behind my desk chair and then promptly exited the room.

74. "They Always Gasp When They Meet Bela Lugosi, Star of 'Dracula,'" Publicity Scene Cuts section, Exhibitors' Campaign for *Dracula*.

75. Gladys Hall, "The Feminine Love of Horror," *Motion Picture Classic*, Jan. 1931, 33.

76. "Actor Should Create His Own Conception of Role," Publicity Scene Cuts section, Exhibitors' Campaign for *Dracula*.

77. "Bela Lugosi, Famous Actor, Tells of Terrible Experience with Actual Human Vampire," Publicity Scene Cuts section, Exhibitors' Campaign for *Dracula*. Another report of Lugosi's past experiences with vampires is in J. Eugene Chrisman, "Bela Lugosi Is Haunted by the Mysterious Woman with Yellow Eyes," *Modern Screen*, April 1932, 83–84, 124.

78. "A Picture No Artist Ever Dared to Paint," Publicity Scene Cuts section, Exhibitors' Campaign for *Frankenstein* ("bottled Karloff up"); Het Manheim, "What Does a Monster Think About?" ("softest and best bred voices").

79. J. Eugene Chrisman, "It's More Than Curious That Boris Karloff Should Be the Successor to Lon Chaney," *Modern Screen*, April 1932, 121. The same article reports that while Karloff was shooting the film, "he didn't like the part—it was too gruesome" (82). More claims about how different Karloff was from the monster are in "The Monster Has A Heart," Feature Stories section, Exhibitors' Campaign for *The Bride of Frankenstein*; and Walter Ramsey, "The Strange History of 'Frankenstein' Karloff," *Modern Screen*, Feb. 1933, 43–45.

80. Examples of the studio's misleading claims on this point are in "Monster in Make-up Hall of Fame," Publicity Scene Cuts section, Exhibitors' Campaign for *Frankenstein*. Examples of suggestions made by reviewers on the same point are in Lusk, "Frankenstein," 47; Meehan, 40; and Boehnel. The practice of assigning credit to Karloff for his makeup continued with *The Old Dark House* and *The Mummy*. (See, for example, "The Great Pyramids Move to Hollywood and an Egyptian Mummy Comes to Life!" *Photoplay*, Dec. 1932, 49; Norbert Lusk, "The Mummy," *Picture Play*, April 1933, 53; "The Making of a Mummy," Publicity Scene Cuts section, Exhibitor's Campaign for *The Mummy*, reproduced in Philip J. Riley, ed., *The Mummy*, Universal Filmscripts Series, Classic Horror Films, vol. 7 [Absecon, NJ: MagicImage Filmbooks, 1989]; and "The Mummy" [advt.], *Universal Weekly*, 31 Dec. 1932, 21.) By 1935 the studio had dropped this deception. (See "Seven Hours to Make-Up a Monster," Current Publicity section, Exhibitor's Campaign for *The Bride of Frankenstein*; F. S. N., "At the Roxy," 21; and "Vampires, Monsters, Horrors!" *New York Times*, 1 March 1936, sec. 9, p. 4.)

81. See, for example, "Boris Karloff Succeeds Chaney," Publicity Scene Cuts section, Exhibitors' Campaign for *Frankenstein*; and "Karloff Grows in the Horror Scale," *Universal Weekly*, 19 Nov. 1932, 6. The press picked up on this idea. See, for example, "Frankenstein," *New York Morning Telegraph*; and John Scott, "'Mummy' Unusual Film," *Los Angeles Times*, 23 Jan. 1933, sec. 2, p. 11.

82. "The Making of a Mummy," Publicity Scene Cuts section, Exhibitor's Campaign for *The Mummy*. The claim was repeated in Chrisman, "It's More Than Curious," 82, where Chrisman also relates an anecdote in which Karloff, leaving after a day of studio extra work, picks up a hitchhiker who turns out to be none other than Chaney.

83. Ramsey, 45.

CONCLUSION

1. The *BFI Companion to Horror* calls this film "an alien-on-Earth film in the expressionist tradition of Universal, with a torch-bearing Scots mob and a ruined castle" (entry for Edgar G. Ulmer in Kim Newman, ed., *The BFI Companion to Horror* [London: British Film Institute, 1996], 318).

2. W. B. Seabrook, *The Magic Island* (New York: The Literary Guild of America, 1929); Kenneth Webb, "Zombie: A Play in Three Acts," 1931 (Manuscript Division, Library of Congress). Play first performed in 1932.

3. Gilbert W. Gabriel, "Dead Pans," rev. of "Zombie," *New York American,* 2 Feb. 1932.

4. "Madge Bellamy Comes Back after Absence of Two Years," Publicity Section, *White Zombie* Exhibitors' Campaign, 1932 (Lincoln Center branch of the New York Public Library).

5. Madge Bellamy, *Madge Bellamy: A Darling of the Twenties* (Vestal, NY: Vestal Press, 1989), 149.

6. For a description of Freund's film as "a massive memorial to the silent cinema," see Antonia Lant, "Haptical Cinema," *October* 74 (Autumn 1995): 66–67. On the tendency during the silent era and afterwards to associate silent films with ancient Egypt, see Lant, "The Curse of the Pharaoh, or How Cinema Contracted Egyptomania," *October* 59 (Winter 1992): 86–112.

7. This setup is explicitly noted in the shooting script. (See Shot A-3 in John L. Balderston, "Im-Ho-Tep," Shooting script dated 12 Sept. 1932, reproduced in Riley, *The Mummy.*)

Bibliography

"25 Per Cent Dialogue Reduction Ordered for Universal Pictures." *Motion Picture Herald*, 29 Oct. 1932, 12.

Abel, Richard. *French Film Theory and Criticism: A History/Anthology*. Vol. 1: 1907–1939. Princeton, NJ: Princeton University Press, 1988.

Ager, Cecelia. "Going Places." *Variety*, 18 Feb. 1931, 54.

Alicoate, Jack, ed. *The 1931 Film Daily Yearbook*. New York: Film Daily, 1931.

"All Quiet on the Western Front." *Film Daily*, 27 April 1930, 12.

Altman, Rick. *The American Film Musical*. Bloomington: Indiana University Press, 1987.

———. "The Evolution of Sound Technology" (1980). In *Film Sound: Theory and Practice*, edited by Elisabeth Weis and John Belton, 44–53. New York: Columbia University Press, 1985.

———. *Film/Genre*. London: British Film Institute, 1999.

———. "General Introduction: Cinema as Event." In *Sound Theory/Sound Practice*, edited by Altman, 1–14. New York: Routledge, 1992.

———. "Moving Lips: Cinema as Ventriloquism." *Yale French Studies*, no. 60 (1980): 67–79.

———. "Sound Space." In *Sound Theory/Sound Practice*, edited by Altman, 46–64. New York: Routledge, 1992.

Altman, Rick, editor. *Sound Theory/Sound Practice*. New York: Routledge, 1992.

Arnheim, Rudolf. *Film as Art*. Berkeley and Los Angeles: University of California Press, 1957.

———. "A New Laocoön: Artistic Composites and the Talking Film" (1938). In *Film Sound: Theory and Practice*, edited by Elisabeth Weis and John Belton, 112–15. New York: Columbia University Press, 1985.

Auerbach, Nina. *Our Vampires, Ourselves.* Chicago: University of Chicago Press, 1995.

Bakshy, Alexander. "Concerning Dialogue." *The Nation,* 17 Aug. 1932, 151–52.

———. "Hollywood Tries 'Ideas.'" *The Nation,* 22 June 1932, 708.

———. "The Movie Scene: Notes on Sound and Silence." *Theatre Arts Monthly* (Feb. 1929): 97–107.

———. "The Shrinking of Personality." *The Nation,* 27 May 1931, 590.

———. "The 'Talkies.'" *The Nation,* 20 Feb. 1929, 236+.

———. "With Benefit of Music." *The Nation,* 1 April 1931, 359–60.

———. "A Year of Talkies." *The Nation,* 26 June 1929, 772–73.

Balazs, Bela. "Theory of the Film: Sound" (1945). In *Film Sound: Theory and Practice,* edited by Elisabeth Weis and John Belton, 116–25. New York: Columbia University Press, 1985.

Balio, Tino. *Grand Design: Hollywood as a Modern Business Enterprise, 1930–1939.* History of the American Cinema, vol. 5, edited by Charles Harpole. New York: Charles Scribner's Sons, 1993.

Barber, X. Theodore, "Phantasmagorical Wonders: The Magic Lantern Ghost Show in Nineteenth-Century America." *Film History* 3, no. 2 (1989): 73–86.

Barlow, John D. *German Expressionist Film.* Boston: Twayne, 1982.

Barrist, David. "The Flop of the Talking Movie." *The Exhibitor* of Philadelphia, quoted in *Harrison's Reports,* 24 Sept. 1927, 153.

"The Bat Whispers." *Modern Screen,* Feb. 1931, 100.

Baxter, John. *Hollywood in the Thirties.* New York: A. S. Barnes, 1968. Reprint, New York: Paperback Library, 1970.

Bazin, André. "The Myth of Total Cinema." In *What Is Cinema?* Edited and translated by Hugh Gray. Berkeley and Los Angeles: University of California Press, 1967. 1:17–22.

Bellamy, Madge. *Madge Bellamy: A Darling of the Twenties.* Vestal, NY: Vestal Press, 1989.

Belton, John. "Awkward Transitions: Hitchcock's 'Blackmail' and the Dynamics of Early Film Sound." *Musical Quarterly* 83, no. 2 (Summer 1999): 227–46.

Berenstein, Rhona J. *Attack of the Leading Ladies: Gender, Sexuality, and Spectatorship in Classic Horror Cinema.* New York: Columbia University Press, 1996.

"Biggest Money Pictures." *Variety,* 21 June 1932, 1+.

Boehnel, William. "Dramatic Terrors of 'Frankenstein' Splendidly Filmed." *New York World Telegram,* 5 Dec. 1931.

Bordwell, David. *Figures Traced in Light: On Cinematic Staging.* Berkeley and Los Angeles: University of California Press, 2005.

———. *The Films of Carl-Theodor Dreyer.* Berkeley and Los Angeles: University of California Press, 1981.

Bordwell, David, Janet Staiger, and Kristin Thompson. *The Classical Hollywood Cinema: Film Style and Mode of Production to 1960.* New York: Columbia University Press, 1985.

Bottomore, Stephen. "The Panicking Audience? Early Cinema and the 'Train Effect.'" *Historical Journal of Film, Radio and Television* 19, no. 2 (1999): 177–216.

Bowser, Eileen. *The Transformation of Cinema, 1907–1915.* History of the American Cinema, vol. 2, edited by Charles Harpole. Berkeley and Los Angeles: University of California Press, 1990.

Brown, Bernard. *Talking Pictures.* London: Sir Isaac Pitman and Sons, 1931.

Brown, Cyril. "Speech to Movies by the Phonofilm." *New York Times,* 17 Aug. 1922, 6.

Brunas, Michael, John Brunas, and Tom Weaver. *Universal Horrors: The Studio's Classic Films, 1931–1946.* Jefferson, NC: McFarland, 1990.

Burch, Noël. *Life to Those Shadows.* Edited and translated by Ben Brewster. Berkeley and Los Angeles: University of California Press, 1990.

Busby, Marquis. "'Dracula' Better Film Than Stage Play, at Orpheum." *Los Angeles Examiner,* 28 March 1931.

Butler, Ivan. *The Horror Film.* London: A. Zwemmer, 1967.

Carroll, Noël. "Film, Emotion, and Genre." In *Passionate Views: Film, Cognition, and Emotion,* edited by Carl Plantinga and Greg M. Smith, 21–47. Baltimore: Johns Hopkins University Press, 1999.

———. *The Philosophy of Horror or Paradoxes of the Heart.* New York: Routledge, 1990.

Cass, John L. "The Illusion of Sound and Picture." *Journal of the Society of Motion Picture Engineers* 14, no. 3 (March 1930): 323–26.

"Cassady's Attractive Poster Work." *Motion Picture Herald,* 13 Feb. 1932, 54.

Castle, Terry. *The Female Thermometer: Eighteenth-Century Culture and the Invention of the Uncanny.* New York: Oxford University Press, 1995.

"The Cat and the Canary." (Excerpted from *Motion Picture Magazine.*) *Universal Weekly,* 23 April 1927, 33.

"The Cat and the Canary." *Film Daily,* 15 May 1927, 7.

"The Cat and the Canary." *Harrison's Reports,* 28 May 1927, 86.

Cheavens, David. "Bela Lugosi Brings Creeps." Rev. of *Dracula. New York Telegraph,* 13 Feb. 1931.

"The Chinese Parrot." *Harrison's Reports,* 7 Jan. 1928, 2.

Chion, Michel. *The Voice in Cinema.* Translated by Claudia Gorbman. French-language edition, 1982. New York: Columbia University Press, 1999.

———. "Wasted Words." In *Sound Theory/Sound Practice,* edited by Rick Altman, 104–10. New York: Routledge, 1992.

Chrisman, J. Eugene. "Bela Lugosi Is Haunted by the Mysterious Woman with Yellow Eyes." *Modern Screen,* April 1932, 83+.

———. "It's More Than Curious That Boris Karloff Should Be the Successor to Lon Chaney." *Modern Screen,* April 1932, 82+.

Churchill, Edward. "Dracula." *Motion Picture Herald,* 3 Jan. 1931, 71, 74.

Cixous, Hélène. "Fiction and Its Phantoms: A Reading of Freud's *Das Unheimliche* (The 'Uncanny')." *New Literary History* 7, no. 3 (Spring 1976): 525–48.

Clair, René. *Cinema Yesterday and Today.* Translated by Stanley Appelbaum. New York: Dover, 1972.

Clarens, Carlos. *The Illustrated History of Horror and Science-Fiction Films.* New York: Da Capo Press, 1997. Originally published as *An Illustrated History of the Horror Film.* New York: Putnam, 1967.

Coffman, Joe, W. "Art and Science in Sound Film Production." *Journal of the Society of Motion Picture Engineers* 14, no. 2 (Feb. 1930): 172–79.

Cohen, Jeffrey Jerome. "Monster Culture (Seven Theses)." In *Monster Theory: Reading Culture,* edited by Jeffrey Jerome Cohen, 3–25. Minneapolis: University of Minnesota Press, 1996.

Cohen, John S. "The Cat and the Canary." (Reprinted from the *New York Sun.*) *Universal Weekly,* 24 Sept. 1927, 33.

Cokain, Ralph. "Defends Moving Shots." *Motion Picture Herald,* 13 Aug. 1932, 18.

"Complete Film Scores." *Variety,* 8 Sept. 1931, 116.

"A Confidential Guide to Current Releases." *Picture Play,* June 1931, 72+.

Connor, Steven. *Dumbstruck: A Cultural History of Ventriloquism.* Oxford: Oxford University Press, 2000.

Conrich, Ian. "Before Sound: Universal, Silent Cinema, and the Last of the Horror-Spectaculars." In *The Horror Film,* edited by Stephen Prince, 40–57. New Brunswick, NJ: Rutgers University Press, 2004.

Continuity for "Dracula" (Picture #109-1, Browning [sound]). Box 13, Folder 3275. Cinema-Television Library, University of Southern California.

Continuity for "Dracula" (Picture #109-4, Melford [sound]). Box 13, Folder 3275. Cinema-Television Library, University of Southern California.

Continuity and Subtitles for "The Cat Creeps" (Picture #107-2, Julian [silent]). Box 13, Folder 2843. Cinema-Television Library, University of Southern California.

Continuity and Subtitles for "Dracula" (Picture #109-2, Browning [silent]). Box 13, Folder 3273. Cinema-Television Library, University of Southern California.

Contratti, Lawrence. "A Reconstruction of Tod Browning's *Dracula* as a Transitional Sound Film." *Classic Film Collector,* no. 43 (Summer 1974): 27–30.

Cooper, Oscar. "The Cat and the Canary." *Motion Picture News.* Undated clipping, "Cat and the Canary" clippings file. Margaret Herrick Library, Academy of Motion Picture Arts and Sciences.

Crafton, Donald. *The Talkies: American Cinema's Transition to Sound, 1926–1931.* History of the American Cinema, vol. 4, edited by Charles Harpole. New York: Charles Scribner's Sons, 1997.

Crewe, Regina. "Shivery Cinema on View at Roxy Is Capably Acted." Rev. of *Dracula. New York American,* 14 Feb. 1931.

Curtis, James. *James Whale: A New World of Gods and Monsters.* Boston: Faber and Faber, 1998.

Daniels, Les. *Living in Fear: A History of Horror in the Mass Media.* New York: Charles Scribner's Sons, 1975.

Deane, Hamilton, and John L. Balderston. *Dracula: The Ultimate, Illustrated Edition of the World-Famous Vampire Play.* Edited and annotated by David J. Skal. New York: St. Martin's, 1993.

———. *Dracula: The Vampire Play in Three Acts.* 1927. Reprint, New York: Samuel French, 1933.

"Death before Surrender." *Picture Play,* Feb. 1933, 22+.

DeForest, Lee. "Recent Developments in 'The Phonofilm.'" *Journal of the Society of Motion Picture Engineers* 10, no. 27 (Oct. 1926): 64–76.

Delahanty, Thornton. "The New Films." Rev. of *Frankenstein. New York Post,* 7 Dec. 1931.

Dettman, Bruce, and Michael Bedford. *The Horror Factory: The Horror Films of Universal, 1931–1955*. New York: Gordon Press, 1976.

Dialogue 'Dracula' (Picture #109-1, Browning [sound]). Box 13, Folder 3274, 1–21. Cinema-Television Library, University of Southern California.

Diffrient, David Scott. "A Film Is Being Beaten: Notes on the Shock Cut and the Material Violence of Horror." In *Horror: Creating and Marketing Fear,* edited by Steffen Hantke, 52–81. Jackson: University Press of Mississippi, 2004.

Dillard, R. H. W. *Horror Films*. New York: Simon and Schuster, 1976.

Doane, Mary Ann. "The Voice in the Cinema: The Articulation of Body and Space" (1980). In *Film Sound: Theory and Practice,* edited by Elisabeth Weis and John Belton, 162–76. New York: Columbia University Press, 1985.

"Dracula." *Film Daily,* 15 Feb. 1931, 11.

"Dracula." *The Film Spectator,* 28 March 1931, 13.

"Dracula." *Harrison's Reports,* 21 Feb. 1931, 31.

"Dracula." *Screenland,* May 1931, 6.

"'Dracula' as a Picture." *New York Post,* 14 Feb. 1931.

Draper, Ellen. "Zombie Women When the Gaze is Male." *Wide Angle* 10, no. 3 (1988): 52–62.

Du Maurier, George. *Trilby.* 1895. Reprint, New York: Dover, 1994.

Durgnat, Raymond. "The Subconscious: From Pleasure Castle to Libido Motel" (1962). In *Horror Film Reader,* edited by Alain Silver and James Ursini, 39–49. New York: Limelight Editions, 2000.

Eisenberg, J. Garrick. "Mechanics of the Talking Movies." *Projection Engineering* 1, no. 3 (Nov. 1929): 22–24.

Eisler, Hanns, and Theodor Adorno. *Composing for the Films.* Freeport, NY: Books for Libraries Press, 1947. Reprint, 1971.

Eisner, Lotte H. *The Haunted Screen: Expressionism in the German Cinema and the Influence of Max Reinhardt.* 1952. Reprint, Berkeley and Los Angeles: University of California Press, 1973.

Ellis, Reed. *A Journey into Darkness: The Art of James Whale's Horror Films.* New York: Arno Press, 1980.

Evans, Delight. "Strange Interlude." *Screenland,* Sept. 1932, 60.

Everson, William K. "The Cat Creeps: A Lost Horror Film *Partly* Found." *Films In Review* 37, no. 5 (May 1986): 297+.

———. *Classics of the Horror Film.* New York: Citadel, 1974.

———. "Horror." Rev. of *Dracula. Video Review* (Feb. 1981): 97+.

"Facts about Talking Pictures and Instruments—No. 4." *Harrison's Reports,* 8 Sept. 1928, 141+.

"Facts about Talking Pictures and Instruments—No. 10." *Harrison's Reports,* 22 Dec. 1928, 201+.

"Feet First." *Exhibitors Herald-World,* 18 Oct. 1930, 44.

Forry, Steven Earl. *Hideous Progenies: Dramatizations of Frankenstein from Mary Shelley to the Present.* Philadelphia: University of Pennsylvania Press, 1990.

Fraenkel, Heinrich. "Can Industry Stay International? The Multilingual Problem and What to Do about It." *Motion Picture Herald,* 31 Jan. 1931, 58+.

"Frankenstein." *Film Daily,* 6 Dec. 1931, 10.

"Frankenstein." *Harrison's Reports,* 12 Dec. 1931, 198.

"Frankenstein." *Modern Screen*, Feb. 1932, 57.

"Frankenstein." *New York Morning Telegraph*, 6 Dec. 1931.

"'Frankenstein' Finished." *New York Telegraph*, 11 Oct. 1931.

Franklin, Harold B. *Sound Motion Pictures: From the Laboratory to Their Presentation*. Garden City, NY: Doubleday, Doran, 1930.

———. "Talking Pictures—The Great Internationalist." *Journal of the Society of Motion Picture Engineers* 15, no. 1 (July 1930): 17–19.

Freud, Sigmund. "The 'Uncanny'" (1919). In *The Standard Edition of the Complete Psychological Works of Sigmund Freud*, 219–56. Vol. 17. London: Hogarth Press and the Institute of Psycho-Analysis, 1955.

Gabriel, Gilbert W. "Dead Pans." Rev. of "Zombie." *New York American*, 2 Feb. 1932.

Gebhart, Myrtle. "Voices Are Tested." *Picture Play*, July 1928, 58+.

"George Bernard Shaw—Fox Movietone." *Photoplay*, Sept. 1928, 57.

Giles, Dennis. "Conditions of Pleasure in Horror Cinema." In *Planks of Reason: Essays on the Horror Film*, edited by Barry Keith Grant, 38–52. Lanham, MD: Scarecrow, 1984.

Glut, Donald F. *The Dracula Book*. Metuchen, NJ: Scarecrow, 1975.

———. *The Frankenstein Legend: A Tribute to Mary Shelley and Boris Karloff*. Metuchen, NJ: Scarecrow Press, 1973.

Gomery, Douglas. *The Coming of Sound: A History*. New York: Routledge, 2005.

Gomery, J. Douglas. "The Coming of Sound to the American Cinema: A History of the Transformation of an Industry." Ph.D. dissertation, University of Wisconsin–Madison, 1975.

Gorbman, Claudia. *Unheard Melodies: Narrative Film Music*. Bloomington: Indiana University Press, 1987.

Gorky, Maxim. Review of the Lumière program at the Nizhni-Novgorod Fair (1896). Reprinted in *Kino: A History of the Russian and Soviet Film*, edited by Jay Leyda, 407–9. London: George Allen and Unwin, 1960.

Graves, Todd. "Fed Up on Gangsters." *Picture Play*, Dec. 1931, 73.

Greason, Alfred Rushford (signed "Rush."). "Dracula." *Variety*, 18 Feb. 1931, 14.

———. "Frankenstein." *Variety*, 8 Dec. 1931, 14.

———. "Vitaphone Reviews." *Variety*, 23 March 1927, 14+.

"The Great Pyramids Move to Hollywood and an Egyptian Mummy Comes to Life!" *Photoplay*, Dec. 1932, 48–49.

Green, Abel (signed "Abel."). "Strange Interlude." *Variety*, 6 Sept. 1932, 15.

Green, Fitzhugh. *The Film Finds Its Tongue*. New York: G. P. Putnam's Sons, 1929. Reprint, New York: Benjamin Blom, 1971.

Grover-Friedlander, Michal. "'The Phantom of the Opera': The Lost Voice of Opera in Silent Film." *Cambridge Opera Journal* 11, no. 2 (July 1999): 179–92.

Gunning, Tom. "An Aesthetic of Astonishment: Early Film and the (In)Credulous Spectator." In *Viewing Positions: Ways of Seeing Film*, edited by Linda Williams, 114–33. New Brunswick, NJ: Rutgers University Press, 1995. Originally published in *Art and Text* 34 (Spring 1989): 31–45.

———. "'Animated Pictures': Tales of Cinema's Forgotten Future, after 100 Years of Films." In *Reinventing Film Studies*, edited by Christine Gledhill and Linda Williams, 316–31. London: Arnold, 2000.

————. "The Ghost in the Machine: Animated Pictures at the Haunted Hotel of Early Cinema." *Living Pictures* 1, no. 1 (2001): 3–17.

————. "Phantom Images and Modern Manifestations: Spirit Photography, Magic Theater, Trick Films, and Photography's Uncanny." In *Fugitive Images: From Photography to Video,* edited by Patrice Petro, 42–71. Bloomington: Indiana University Press, 1995.

————. "'Primitive' Cinema: A Frame-Up? Or the Trick's on Us." In *Early Cinema: Space—Frame—Narrative,* edited by Thomas Elsaesser with Adam Barker, 95–103. London: British Film Institute, 1990.

————. "'Those Drawn with a Very Fine Camel's Hair Brush': The Origins of Film Genres." *Iris* 20 (Autumn 1995): 49–60.

————. "An Unseen Energy Swallows Space: The Space in Early Film and Its Relation to American Avant-Garde Film." In *Film before Griffith,* edited by John Fell, 355–66. Berkeley and Los Angeles: University of California Press, 1983.

Halberstam, Judith. *Skin Shows: Gothic Horror and the Technology of Monsters.* Durham: Duke University Press, 1995.

Hall, Chapin. "Talking Films Try Movie Men's Souls." *New York Times,* 8 July 1928, sec. 3, p. 1+.

Hall, Gladys. "The Feminine Love of Horror." *Motion Picture Classic,* Jan. 1931, 33+.

Hall, Hal. "Some Talkie Observations" (interview of William A. Seiter). *American Cinematographer* 11, no. 2 (June 1930): 19.

Hall, Mordaunt. "Amazing Invention Coupling Sound with Screen Images Stirs Audiences." *New York Times,* 15 Aug. 1926, sec. 7, p. 2.

————. "The Best Ten Films." *New York Times,* 5 Jan. 1930, sec. 8, p. 6.

————. "Blue-Ribbon Pictures of 1931." *New York Times,* 3 Jan. 1932, sec. 8, p. 5.

————. "A British Talker." Rev. of *White Cargo. New York Times,* 24 Feb. 1930, 23.

————. "'Dracula' as a Film." *New York Times,* 22 Feb. 1931, sec. 8, p. 5.

————. "The Haunted House." Rev. of *The Cat and the Canary. New York Times,* 10 Sept. 1927, 9.

————. "The Mystery of the Wax Museum." *New York Times,* 18 Feb. 1933, 13.

————. "The Reaction of the Public to Motion Pictures with Sound." *Journal of the Society of Motion Picture Engineers* 12, no. 35 (Sept. 1928): 603–13.

————. "The Screen." Rev. of *Frankenstein. New York Times,* 5 Dec. 1931, 21.

————. "The Ventriloquist." Rev. of *The Great Gabbo. New York Times,* 13 Sept. 1929, 33.

————. "Vitaphone Stirs as Talking Movie." *New York Times,* 7 Aug. 1926, 6.

Hampton, Benjamin B. *A History of the Movies.* New York: Vici Friede, 1931.

Harrington, Curtis. "Ghoulies and Ghosties." *Sight and Sound* (April–June 1952): 157–61.

Harris, Sidney. "Dracula." *Billboard,* 21 Feb. 1931, 10.

Heffernan, James A. W. "Looking at the Monster: *Frankenstein* and Film." *Critical Inquiry,* no. 24 (Autumn 1997): 133–58.

"Henger's Weird Trailer Proved Effective!" *Motion Picture Herald,* 23 Jan. 1932, 60.

"Hissing and Scratching Ended by New Process, Asserts Erpi." *Exhibitors Herald-World*, 6 Dec. 1930, 17.

"The Hollywood Revue." *Harrison's Reports*, 24 Aug. 1929, 135.

"Hollywood Speaks." *The Nation*, 26 Sept. 1928, 285–86.

Horak, Jan-Christopher. "Sauerkraut and Sausages with a Little Goulash: Germans in Hollywood, 1927." *Film History* 17, nos. 2–3 (2005): 241–60.

"The House of Horror." *Harrison's Reports*, 22 June 1929, 99.

Huss, Roy. "Vampire's Progress: *Dracula* from Novel to Film via Broadway." In *Focus on the Horror Film*, edited by Roy Huss and T. J. Ross, 50–57. Englewood Cliffs, NJ: Prentice-Hall, 1972.

Hutchings, Peter. *The Horror Film*. Harlow, UK: Longman, 2004.

"I Am a Fugitive from a Chain Gang." *Motion Picture Herald*, 22 Oct. 1932, 31.

"Inside Stuff—Pictures." *Variety*, 31 Dec. 1930, 39.

"Inventor Describes His Colored Picture Process." *New York Times*, 22 June 1924, sec. 7, p. 2.

"James Whale and 'Frankenstein.'" *New York Times*, 20 Dec. 1931, sec. 8, p. 4.

Jancovich, Mark. *Horror*. London: B. T. Batsford, 1992.

"The Jazz Singer." *Harrison's Reports*, 22 Oct. 1927, 171.

Jensen, Paul M. *The Men Who Made the Monsters*. New York: Twayne, 1996.

Jentsch, Ernst. "On the Psychology of the Uncanny" (1906). Translated by Roy Sellars. *Angelaki* 2, no. 1 (1995): 7–16.

Johnston, William A. "The Public and Sound Pictures." *Journal of the Society of Motion Picture Engineers* 12, no. 35 (Sept. 1928): 614–19.

Jones, Ernest. *On the Nightmare*. 1931. Reprint, London: Hogarth Press, 1949.

Joslin, Lyndon W. *Count Dracula Goes to the Movies: Stoker's Novel Adapted, 1922–1995*. Jefferson, NC: McFarland, 1995.

Joy, Jason. 17 April 1931 report of rejections made to *Dracula* by the Chicago Censor Board, 1931. "Dracula" folder, Production Code Files. Margaret Herrick Library, Academy of Motion Picture Arts and Sciences.

Juengel, Scott J. "Face, Figure, Physiognomics: Mary Shelley's *Frankenstein* and the Moving Image." *Novel: A Forum on Fiction* 33, no. 3 (Summer 2000): 353–76.

"Kameradschaft." *Film Daily*, 10 Nov. 1932, 6.

"Kameradschaft." *Motion Picture Herald*, 10 Dec. 1932, 50.

Kanfer, Stefan. "*Frankenstein* at Sixty." *Connoisseur*, Jan. 1991, 41–47.

"Karloff Grows in the Horror Scale." *Universal Weekly*, 19 Nov. 1932, 6.

Kaye, Heidi. "Gothic Film." In *Companion to the Gothic*, edited by David Punter, 180–92. Malden, MA: Blackwell, 2000.

Klenotic, Jeffrey. "'The Sensational Acme of Realism': 'Talker' Pictures as Early Cinema Sound Practice." In *The Sounds of Early Cinema*, edited by Richard Abel and Rick Altman, 156–66. Bloomington: Indiana University Press, 2001.

Knox, H. G. "Bewildering Problems of Sound." *New York Times*, 21 Dec. 1930, sec. 8, p. 6.

———. "Wide Range Sound: What It Is and What It Means to the Theatre." *Motion Picture Herald*, 27 Aug. 1932, Better Theatres Section, 15–16.

Konigsberg, Ira. *The Complete Film Dictionary*. 2nd ed. New York: Penguin, 1997.

Koszarski, Richard. *Universal Pictures: 65 Years.* New York: Museum of Modern Art, 1977.

Laemmle, Carl. "Watch This Column: Universal's Weekly Chat" (advt.). *Saturday Evening Post,* 14 Feb. 1931, 59.

———. "Watch This Column: Universal's Weekly Chat" (advt.). *Saturday Evening Post,* 21 Nov. 1931, 38.

———. "Watch This Column: Universal's Weekly Chat" (advt.). *Saturday Evening Post,* 5 Dec. 1931, 67.

———. "Watch This Column: Universal's Weekly Chat" (advt.). *Saturday Evening Post,* 12 Dec. 1931, 70.

Lant, Antonia. "The Curse of the Pharaoh, or How Cinema Contracted Egyptomania." *October* 59 (Winter 1992): 86–112.

———. "Haptical Cinema." *October* 74 (Autumn 1995): 45–73.

Lasky, Jesse. "Production More Exacting and More Exact." *Motion Picture Herald,* 3 Jan. 1931, 60–61.

Lastra, James. "Reading, Writing, and Representing Sound." In *Sound Theory/Sound Practice,* edited by Rick Altman, 65–86. New York: Routledge, 1992.

———. *Sound Technology and the American Cinema: Perception, Representation, Modernity.* New York: Columbia University Press, 2000.

Lederer, Susan E. *Frankenstein: Penetrating the Secrets of Nature.* New Brunswick, NJ: Rutgers University Press, 2002.

Leigh, Patricia. "What the Fans Think: Talking Down the Talkies." *Picture Play,* Nov. 1928, 8, 12.

Lennig, Arthur. *The Count: The Life and Films of Bela "Dracula" Lugosi.* New York: G. P. Putnam's Sons, 1974.

———. *The Immortal Count: The Life and Films of Bela Lugosi.* Lexington: University Press of Kentucky, 2003.

"Lon Chaney's Five Voices." *New York Times,* 6 July 1930, sec. 8, p. 2.

Lovecraft, H. P. "The Horror at Red Hook." *Weird Stories,* Jan. 1927. Republished in Lovecraft, *The Dreams in the Witch House and Other Weird Tales.* Edited and with an introduction by S. T. Joshi, 116–37. New York: Penguin Books, 2004.

Lugosi: Hollywood's Dracula. Directed by Gary D. Rhodes, 2000. DVD with audio CD.

Lusk, Norbert. "Continuous Dialogue on the Screen." Rev. of *Lights of New York. Picture Play,* Oct. 1928, 70–71.

———. "Dracula." Rev. of *Dracula. Picture Play,* May 1931, 71, 96.

———. "'Dracula' Hit on Broadway." Rev. of *Dracula. Los Angeles Times,* 22 Feb. 1931.

———. "Frankenstein." *Picture Play,* March 1932, 46–47.

———. "The Mummy." *Picture Play,* April 1933, 53.

———. "The Public Enemy." *Picture Play,* Aug. 1931, 56.

———. "The Screen in Review." Rev. of *The Cat and the Canary. Picture Play,* Dec. 1927, 60.

M., H. "Frankenstein." *Bioscope,* 27 Jan. 1932, 19–20.

M., J. C. "The Current Cinema: Creeps and Shudders." Rev. of *The Old Dark House. The New Yorker,* 5 Nov. 1932, 77–78.

———. "The Current Cinema: Gallipoli—Thrills by Mrs. Percy B. Shelley." Rev. of *Frankenstein. The New Yorker,* 12 Dec. 1931, 95–96.

———. "The Current Cinema: Silk-Shirt World—The Lockstep with Music—Robinson Becomes a Type." *The New Yorker,* 28 May 1932, 51–52.

MacDonald, Carlisle. "Demand Talkies in Own Language." *New York Times,* 17 April 1930, 9.

Maddrey, Joseph. *Nightmares in Red, White and Blue: The Evolution of the American Horror Film.* Jefferson, NC: McFarland, 2004.

"Make Your Posters Come to Life!" (advt. for the "Cutawl"). *Motion Picture Herald,* 16 Jan. 1932, 37.

Maltby, Richard. "'Grief in the Limelight': Al Capone, Howard Hughes, the Hays Code, and the Politics of the Unstable Text." In *Movies and Politics: The Dynamic Relationship,* edited by James Combs, 133–81. New York: Garland, 1993.

Mank, Gregory William. *It's Alive! The Classic Cinema Saga of Frankenstein.* San Diego: A. S. Barnes, 1981.

Manvell Roger and John Huntley. *The Technique of Film Music.* New York: Communication Arts Books, Hastings House, 1957.

Marshall, Margaret. "The Art of René Clair." *The Nation,* 8 June 1932, 659–60.

———. "'Spectacle' vs. Story." *The Nation,* 20 Jan. 1932, 82.

Maxfield, Joseph P. "Some Physical Factors Affecting the Illusion in Sound Motion Pictures." *Journal of the Acoustical Society of America* 3, no. 1 (July 1931): 69–80.

McConnell, Frank. "Rough Beasts Slouching." In *Focus on the Horror Film,* edited by Roy Huss and T. J. Ross, 24–35. Englewood Cliffs, NJ: Prentice-Hall, 1972. Originally published in *Kenyon Review,* no. 1 (1970), 109–20, as "Rough Beast Slouching: A Note on Horror Movies."

Meehan, Leo. "Frankenstein." *Motion Picture Herald,* 14 Nov. 1931, 40+.

Miller, Wesley C. "Sound Pictures the Successful Production of Illusion." *American Cinematographer,* Dec. 1929, 5+.

Mitchell, Gordon S. "The New Motion Picture and the Public." *Exhibitors Herald-World,* 22 Nov. 1930, Better Theatres Section, 11+.

"Modern Methods by Undertakers, with Actors as Demonstrators." *Variety,* 21 Jan. 1931, 1+.

"Most Unusual Sets in U History Used to Film 'Dracula.'" *Exhibitors Herald-World,* 29 Nov. 1931, 37.

"Motion and Sound." *Harrison's Reports,* 14 July 1928, 109+.

"Moving Pictures Sound Melodrama's Knell." *New York Times* magazine section, 20 March 1910, 7.

"The Moving World: A Review of New and Important Motion Pictures." *Independent,* 27 April 1914, 165.

"The Mummy" (advt.). *Universal Weekly,* 31 Dec. 1932, 20–21.

Munby, Jonathan. *Public Enemies, Public Heroes: Screening the Gangster Film from* Little Caesar *to* Touch of Evil. Chicago: University of Chicago Press, 1999.

"Mysterious House and Ushers Boom 'Cat and Canary' in Seattle." *Universal Weekly,* 5 Nov. 1927, 26.

N., F. S. "At the Roxy." Rev. of *The Bride of Frankenstein. New York Times,* 11 May 1935, 21.

"Napoleon's Barber." *Photoplay,* Jan. 1929, 93.

Nestrick, William. "Coming to Life: *Frankenstein* and the Nature of Film Narrative." In *The Endurance of Frankenstein: Essays on Mary Shelley's Novel,* edited by George Levine and U. C. Knoepflmacher, 290–315. Berkeley and Los Angeles: University of California Press, 1979.

Newman, Kim, Ed. *The BFI Companion to Horror.* London: British Film Institute, 1996.

"A New Ratio for Dialogue in Films." *Motion Picture Herald,* 5 Nov. 1932, 24.

"New York Critics Like the First 'All-Talkie.'" *Film Daily,* 15 July 1928, 11.

Oates, Joyce Carol. "*Dracula* (Tod Browning, 1931): The Vampire's Secret." *Southwest Review* 76, no. 4 (Autumn 1991): 498–510.

O'Brien, Charles. *Cinema's Conversion to Sound: Technology and Film Style in France and the U.S.* Bloomington: Indiana University Press, 2005.

O'Flinn, Paul. "Production and Reproduction: The Case of *Frankenstein*" (1986). In *The Horror Reader,* edited by Ken Gelder, 114–27. London: Routledge, 2000.

"Old Horror Tale Full of Thrills." Rev. of *Frankenstein. Hollywood Reporter,* 3 Nov. 1931.

O'Sullivan, Joseph. "Why Not Dramatize Sound?" *Motion Picture Herald,* 3 Sept. 1932, 17.

"Paul Leni Assigned to Direct Hugo's 'The Man Who Laughs.'" *Universal Weekly,* 30 April 1927, 10+.

Paul, William. "Uncanny Theater: The Twin Inheritances of the Movies." *Paradoxa* 3, no. 3–4 (Fall 1997): 321–47.

Pelswick, Rose. "'Frankenstein' a Thriller; 'Cuban Love Song' and 'His Woman' Also Reviewed." *New York Journal,* 5 Dec. 1931.

———. "Hair-Raising Tale Better on Screen Than on Stage." Rev. of *Dracula. New York Journal,* 13 Feb. 1931.

Perez, Gilberto. *The Material Ghost: Films and Their Medium.* Baltimore: Johns Hopkins University Press, 1998.

Phillips, Kendall R. *Projected Fears: Horror Films and American Culture.* Westport, CT: Praeger, 2005.

"Phonofilm Shown in Rivoli Theatre." *New York Times,* 16 April 1923, 20.

Physioc, Lewis W. "Technique of the Talkies." *American Cinematographer* 9, no. 5 (Aug. 1928): 24–25.

"Picture-Making Changed More in 3 1/2 Yrs. Since 'Jazz Singer' Than in 20 since 'Birth of a Nation.'" *Variety,* 1 April 1931, 12.

Pierce, Jack. "Character Make-up." *American Cinematographer* 13, no. 1 (May 1932): 8+.

Pirandello, Luigi. "Pirandello Views the 'Talkies.'" *New York Times,* 28 July 1929, sec. 5, p. 1+.

"Playing Music While the Characters Talk." *Harrison's Reports,* 30 Nov. 1929, 192.

Pratt, George C. *Spellbound in Darkness: A History of the Silent Film.* Greenwich, CT: New York Graphic Society, 1966.

Prawer, S. S. *Caligari's Children: The Film as Tale of Terror.* New York: Da Capo Press, 1980.

Price, James. "The Dark House." *The London Magazine* (Aug. 1963): 67–71.

"The Psychology of Sounds in Screen Presentations." *Projection Engineering* 2, no. 4 (April 1930): 21+.

"The Public Enemy." *Screenland,* June 1931, 84.

Ramsey, Walter. "The Strange History of 'Frankenstein' Karloff." *Modern Screen,* Feb. 1933, 42+.

Redfield, Marc. "*Frankenstein*'s Cinematic Dream." In *Frankenstein's Dream: A Romantic Circles Praxis Volume.* Edited by Jerrold E. Hogle. Feb. 2003. www.rc.umd.edu/praxis/frankenstein/redfield/redfield.html.

Reel, Rob. "Boris Karloff, Colin Clive Deliver Fine Acting in State-Lake Thriller." Rev. of *Frankenstein. Chicago American,* 4 Dec. 1931.

Richardson, F. H. "New Sound System." *Motion Picture Herald,* 17 Jan. 1931, 65.

Riley, Philip J., ed. *The Bride of Frankenstein.* Universal Filmscripts Series, Classic Horror Films, vol. 2. Absecon, NJ: MagicImage Filmbooks, 1989.

———, ed. *Dracula (The Original 1931 Shooting Script).* Universal Filmscripts Series, Classic Horror Films, vol. 13. Atlantic City, NJ: MagicImage Filmbooks, 1990.

———, ed. *Frankenstein.* Universal Filmscripts Series, Classic Horror Films, vol. 1. Absecon, NJ: MagicImage Filmbooks, 1989.

———, ed. *London After Midnight.* New York: Cornwall Books, 1985.

———, ed. *The Mummy.* Universal Filmscripts Series, Classic Horror Films, vol. 7. Absecon, NJ: MagicImage Filmbooks, 1989.

Rosar, William H. "Music for the Monsters: Universal Pictures' Horror Film Scores of the Thirties." *Quarterly Journal of the Library of Congress* 40 (Fall 1983): 391–421.

Rosen, Philip. "Adorno and Film Music: Theoretical Notes on Composing for the Films," *Yale French Studies,* no. 60 (1980): 157–82.

Rotha, Paul. *The Film till Now: A Survey of World Cinema.* 1930. Reprint, with a section by Richard Griffith, New York: Funk and Wagnalls, 1949.

Royle, Nicholas. *The Uncanny.* New York: Routledge, 2003.

Russell, Ruth. "Voice Is Given to Shadows of Silver Screen." *Chicago Daily Tribune,* 16 Sept. 1926, 31.

Schatz, Thomas. *The Genius of the System: Hollywood Filmmaking in the Studio Era.* New York: Pantheon, 1988.

Scheuer, Philip K. "Mystery Film Opens Run at Hillstreet." Rev. of *The Old Dark House. Los Angeles Times,* 19 Nov. 1932, sec. A, p. 7.

Schmid, F. C., and S. K. Wolf. "The New Importance of Acoustics to Natural Sound." *Motion Picture Herald,* 7 May 1932, 23+.

Sconce, Jeffrey. *Haunted Media: Electronic Presence from Telegraphy to Television.* Durham, NC: Duke University Press, 2000.

Scott, John. "'Mummy' Unusual Film." *Los Angeles Times,* 23 Jan. 1933, sec. 2, p. 11.

Seabrook, W. B. *The Magic Island.* New York: Literary Guild of America, 1929.

Shawell, Julia. "Dracula." *New York Graphic,* 13 Feb. 1931.

Shelley, Mary. *Frankenstein; or, The Modern Prometheus* (1818). In *Frankenstein*, edited by J. Paul Hunter. New York: W. W. Norton, 1996.

Sherman, Al. "Dracula." *New York Telegraph*, 15 Feb. 1931.

Silver, Alain, and James Ursini. *The Vampire Film: From* Nosferatu *to* Interview with the Vampire. New York: Limelight Editions, 1997.

Silverman, Sid (signed "Sid."). "The Last Warning." *Variety*, 9 Jan. 1929, 34.

———. "The Public Enemy." *Variety*, 29 April 1931, 12+.

———. "U.S. Film Field for 1930." *Variety*, 31 Dec. 1930, 7+.

"Six Best Money Stars." *Variety*, 5 Jan. 1932, 1+.

Skal, David J. Commentary track. *Dracula*. Directed by Tod Browning, 1931. DVD, Universal, 1999.

———. *Hollywood Gothic: The Tangled Web of* Dracula *from Novel to Stage to Screen*. New York: W. W. Norton, 1990.

———. *The Monster Show: A Cultural History of Horror*. New York: W. W. Norton, 1993.

Skal, David J., and Elias Savada. *Dark Carnival: The Secret World of Tod Browning—Hollywood's Master of the Macabre*. New York: Anchor Books, 1995.

"Sounds in a Studio." *New York Times*, 29 June 1930, sec. 8, p. 3.

Spadoni, Robert. "The Uncanny Body of Early Sound Film." *The Velvet Light Trap*, no. 51 (Spring 2003): 4–16.

Spearing, James O. "Now the Movies Go Back to Their School Days." *New York Times* magazine section, 19 Aug. 1928, 12–13.

"'Spooky' Film Will Draw Well." Rev. of *Dracula*. *Hollywood Reporter*, 24 Dec. 1930.

Stanley, Fred. "Hectic Year in Studios." *Variety*, 29 Dec. 1931, 6.

Steiner, Frederick. "The Making of an American Film Composer: A Study of Alfred Newman's Music in the First Decade of the Sound Era." Ph.D. dissertation, University of Southern California, 1981.

Stoker, Bram. *Dracula* (1897). In *Dracula: Authoritative Text, Contexts, Reviews and Reactions, Dramatic and Film Variations, Criticism*, edited by Nina Auerbach and David J. Skal. New York: W. W. Norton, 1997.

"Strange Interlude." *Film Daily*, 8 July 1932, 22.

"Strong Men Gasp and Women Scream." *New York World Telegram*, 16 Dec. 1931.

"Studio Should Be Proud: Sherwood; Season Not Bad: John S. Cohen, Jr." *Motion Picture Herald*, 2 Jan. 1932, 20.

Studlar, Gaylyn. *This Mad Masquerade: Stardom and Masculinity in the Jazz Age*. New York: Columbia University Press, 1996.

Stull, William. "Multiple Exposure Cinematography in Sound Pictures." *Journal of the Society of Motion Picture Engineers* 14, no. 3 (March 1930): 318–22.

"Svengali" (advt.). *Picture Play*, July 1931, 7.

"Svengali." *Harrison's Reports*, 9 May 1931, 74.

"The Talkies' Future." *The Nation*, 15 Jan. 1930, 61–62.

"Talking Films Soon Will Appear Here." *New York Times*, 22 Oct. 1922, sec. 2, p. 14.

"Talking Movies Shown: Conversation and Music Accompany Pictures in Cleveland." *New York Times*, 12 Dec. 1923, 24.

Taves, Brian. "Universal's Horror Tradition." *American Cinematographer* (April 1987): 36–48.

Taylor, Ted. "1930 in the Land of Nod." *Variety,* 31 Dec. 1930, 9+.

"Tenderloin." *Variety,* 21 March 1928, 18.

Thirer, Irene. "'Frankenstein' Weird Chiller." *New York Daily News,* 5 Dec. 1931, 28.

———. "Lugosi Portrays Living Dead Man in 3 Star Talkie; New Films." Rev. of *Dracula. New York Daily News,* 13 Feb. 1931.

Thomas, Kevin. "'Frankenstein' and 'Dracula' Reissued." *Los Angeles Times,* 21 Nov. 1968.

Thompson, Kristin, and David Bordwell. *Film History: An Introduction.* New York: McGraw-Hill, 1994.

Todorov, Tzvetan. *The Fantastic: A Structural Approach to a Literary Genre.* Translated by Richard Howard. Originally published in French as *Introduction à la littérature fantastique,* 1970. Ithaca, NY: Cornell University Press, 1975.

———. "The Origin of Genres." *New Literary History* 7, no. 1 (Autumn 1976): 159–70.

Truffaut, François, with Helen G. Scott. *Hitchcock.* Rev. ed. New York: Simon and Schuster, 1985.

Trumpener, Katie. "The René Clair Moment and the Overlap Films of the Early 1930s: Detlef Sierck's *April, April!*" *Film Criticism* 23, no. 2–3 (Winter–Spring 1999): 33–45.

Tsivian, Yuri. *Early Cinema in Russia and Its Cultural Reception.* Translated by Alan Bodger. London: Routledge, 1994.

———. "Portraits, Mirrors, Death: On Some Decadent Clichés in Early Russian Films." *Iris* 14–15 (Autumn 1992): 67–83.

Tudor, Andrew. *Monsters and Mad Scientists: A Cultural History of the Horror Movie.* Oxford: Basil Blackwell, 1989.

———. "Why Horror? The Peculiar Pleasures of a Popular Genre." *Cultural Studies* 11, no. 3 (1997): 443–63.

Turner, George. "The Two Faces of Dracula." *American Cinematographer* (May 1988): 34–42.

Turner, George E. "*Frankenstein,* the Monster Classic." In *The Cinema of Adventure, Romance and Terror,* edited by George E. Turner, 86–101. Hollywood: ASC Press, 1989.

Twitchell, James B. *Dreadful Pleasures: An Anatomy of Modern Horror.* New York: Oxford University Press, 1985.

Tyler, Parker. "Supernaturalism in the Movies." *Theatre Arts,* June 1945, 362–69.

"U Has Horror Cycle All to Self." *Variety,* 8 April 1931, 2.

Underwood, Peter. *Karloff: The Life of Boris Karloff.* New York: Drake, 1972.

"Universal's 'Dracula' to Have Romance and Thrills." *Exhibitors Herald-World,* 4 Oct. 1930, 58.

Urbano, Cosimo. "'What's the Matter with Melanie?': Reflections on the Merits of Psychoanalytic Approaches to Modern Horror Cinema." In *Horror Film and Psychoanalysis: Freud's Worst Nightmare,* edited by Steven Jay Schneider, 17–34. Cambridge, UK: Cambridge University Press, 2004.

"Vampires, Monsters, Horrors!" *New York Times*, 1 March 1936, sec. 9, p. 4.

"Vivid Pictures Startle." *New York Times*, 28 Dec. 1922, 20.

Wagner, Rob. "Photo-Static." *Collier's*, 23 Feb. 1929, 26+.

———. "Silence Isn't Golden Any More." *Collier's*, 25 Aug. 1928, 12+.

Walker, Alexander. *The Shattered Silents*. New York: William Morrow, 1979.

Walker, Mark. *Ghostmasters: A Look Back at America's Midnight Spook Shows*. Boca Raton, FL: Cool Hand Communications, 1994.

Waller, Gregory A. *The Living and the Undead: From Stoker's* Dracula *to Romero's* Dawn of the Dead. Urbana: University of Illinois Press, 1986.

"Warming Up." *Harrison's Reports*, 21 July 1928, 114.

"Warner Bros. Present Vitaphone" (advt.). *Film Daily*, 17 Aug. 1926, 5–7.

Warren, George C. "The Cat and the Canary." (Reprinted from the *San Francisco Chronicle*.) *Universal Weekly*, 8 Oct. 1927, 32.

"Waterloo Bridge." *Picture Play*, Dec. 1931.

Watts, Richard, Jr. "On the Screen." Rev. of *Dracula*. *New York Herald-Tribune*, 13 Feb. 1931, 20.

———. "On the Screen." Rev. of *Frankenstein*. *New York Herald-Tribune*, 5 Dec. 1931.

Webb, Kenneth. "Zombie: A Play in Three Acts," 1931. Manuscript Division, Library of Congress. Play first performed in 1932.

Weis, Elisabeth, and John Belton, eds. *Film Sound: Theory and Practice*. New York: Columbia University Press, 1985.

Wessells, Haviland. "Sound—As the Customers Hear It." *Projection Engineering* 1, no. 3 (Nov. 1929): 12+.

"When Movies Talk." *New York Times*, 17 May 1928, 24.

White Zombie Exhibitors' Campaign, 1932. Lincoln Center branch of the New York Public Library.

"Why Comment on Quality of Sound Is No Longer Made." *Harrison's Reports*, 7 Feb. 1931, 24.

Willard, John. *The Cat and the Canary: A Melodrama in Three Acts*. 1921. New York: Samuel French, 1927.

Wolf, Leonard. *A Dream of Dracula: In Search of the Living Dead*. Boston: Little, Brown, 1972.

Wolfe, Charles. "Vitaphone Shorts and *The Jazz Singer*." *Wide Angle* 12, no. 3 (July 1990): 58–78.

"X-Raying the 1927–28 Product—No. 1." *Harrison's Reports*, 11 June 1927, 93.

Zinman, David. "Horrors! Frankenstein Is 40." *New York Newsday*, 3 Dec. 1971, 7A+.

Films Cited

All Quiet on the Western Front (1930). U.S., Universal, d. Lewis Milestone.

Anna Christie (1930). U.S., MGM, d. Clarence Brown.

April, April! (1935). Germany, Ufa, d. Douglas Sirk (then Detlef Sierck).

The Bat (1926). U.S., Feature Productions, d. Roland West.

The Bat Whispers (1930). U.S., Art Cinema Corporation, d. Roland West.

Blackmail (1929). United Kingdom, British International Pictures, d. Alfred Hitchcock.

The Bride of Frankenstein (1935). U.S., Universal, d. James Whale.

Bud Abbott and Lou Costello Meet Frankenstein (1948). U.S., Universal-International, d. Charles Barton.

The Cabinet of Dr. Caligari/Das Cabinet des Dr. Caligari (1920). Germany, Decla Filmgesellschaft, d. Robert Wiene.

Carnival of Souls (1962). U.S., Harcourt Productions, d. Herk Harvey.

The Cat and the Canary (1927). U.S., Universal, d. Paul Leni.

The Cat Creeps (1930). U.S., Universal, d. Rupert Julian.

The Chinese Parrot (1927). U.S., Universal, d. Paul Leni.

Doctor X (1932). U.S., First National–Warner Bros., d. Michael Curtiz.

Don Juan (1926). U.S., Warner Bros., d. Alan Crosland.

Dracula (1931). U.S., Universal, d. Tod Browning.

Dracula (1931). U.S., Universal, d. George Melford. In Spanish.

Dracula's Daughter (1936). U.S., Universal, d. Lambert Hillyer.

Dr. Jekyll and Mr. Hyde (1931). U.S., Paramount, d. Rouben Mamoulian.

Feet First (1930). U.S., Harold Lloyd Corporation, d. Clyde Bruckman.

Frankenstein (1931). U.S., Universal, d. James Whale.

Frankenstein Meets the Wolf Man (1943). U.S., Universal, d. Roy William Neill.

Freaks (1932). U.S., MGM, d. Tod Browning.

The Golem/Der Golem, wie er in die Welt kam (1920). Germany, Ufa, d. Paul Wegener and Carl Boese.

The Gorilla (1927). U.S., First National, d. Alfred Santell.

The Gorilla (1930). U.S., First National, d. Bryan Foy.

The Great Gabbo (1929). U.S., James Cruze, Inc., d. James Cruze.

Heaven on Earth (1931). U.S., Universal, d. Russell Mack.

The Hollywood Revue of 1929 (1929). U.S., MGM, d. Charles Reisner and (uncredited) Christy Cabanne.

The House of Horror (1929). U.S., First National, d. Benjamin Christensen.

I Am a Fugitive from a Chain Gang (1932). U.S., Warner Bros., d. Mervyn LeRoy.

Interference (1929). U.S., Paramount, d. Lothar Mendes and Roy J. Pomeroy.

The Invisible Man (1933). U.S., Universal, d. James Whale.

Island of Lost Souls (1932). U.S., Paramount, d. Erle C. Kenton.

The Jazz Singer (1927). U.S., Warner Bros., d. Alan Crosland.

Kameradschaft (1931). Germany/France, Nero-Film/Gaumont-Franco-Film-Aubert, d. G. W. Pabst.

The Last Warning (1929). U.S., Universal, d. Paul Leni.

Last Year at Marienbad/L'Année Dernière à Marienbad (1961). France/Italy, Terra Films/Société Nouvelle des Films Comoran/Précitel/Como Films/Argos Films/Tamara Films/Cinetel Productions/Silver Films/Cineriz, d. Alain Resnais.

Lights of New York (1928). U.S., Warner Bros., d. Bryan Foy.

Little Caesar (1930). U.S., First National, d. Mervyn LeRoy.

London After Midnight (1927). U.S., MGM, d. Tod Browning.

Madame X (1929). U.S., MGM, d. Lionel Barrymore.

The Man from Planet X (1951). U.S., Mid-Century Film Productions, d. Edgar G. Ulmer.

Mark of the Vampire (1935). U.S., MGM, d. Tod Browning.

Metropolis (1927). Germany, Ufa, d. Fritz Lang.

The Monster (1925). U.S., MGM, d. Roland West.

The Mummy (1932). U.S., Universal, d. Karl Freund.

Mystery of the Wax Museum (1933). U.S., Warner Bros., d. Michael Curtiz.

Night of the Living Dead (1968). U.S., Image Ten, d. George Romero.

Nosferatu, a Symphony of Horror/Nosferatu, eine Symphonie des Grauens (1922). Germany, Prana-Film, d. F. W. Murnau.

À Nous la Liberté (1931). France, Tobis/Société des Film Sonores, d. René Clair.

The Old Dark House (1932). U.S., Universal, d. James Whale.

The Public Enemy (1931). U.S., Warner Bros., d. William Wellman.

Raskolnikow (1923). Germany, Neumann Film-Produktion, d. Robert Wiene.

Rebecca (1940). U.S., Selznick International Pictures, d. Alfred Hitchcock.

The Return of the Vampire (1943). U.S., Columbia, d. Lew Landers.

Scarface (1932). U.S., Caddo Company, d. Howard Hawks.

Son of Dracula (1943). U.S., Universal, d. Robert Siodmak.

Strange Interlude (1932). U.S., MGM, d. Robert Z. Leonard.

Strangler of the Swamp (1946). U.S., Producers Releasing Corporation, d. Frank Wisbar.

Svengali (1931). U.S., Warner Bros., d. Archie Mayo.

Tenderloin (1928). U.S., Warner Bros., d. Michael Curtiz.

The Thirteenth Chair (1929). U.S., MGM, d. Tod Browning.

The Unholy Three (1925). U.S., MGM, d. Tod Browning.

The Unholy Three (1930). U.S., MGM, d. Jack Conway.

Vampyr (1932). Germany/France, Tobis-Filmkunst/Carl Th. Dreyer Filmproduktion, d. Carl Th. Dreyer.

Waterloo Bridge (1931). U.S., Universal, d. James Whale.

White Cargo (1929). United Kingdom, Neo Art Productions, d. J. B. Williams and Arthur Barnes.

White Zombie (1932). U.S., Halperin Productions, d. Victor Halperin.

Index

Page numbers in italics indicate illustrations.

Text: 10/13 Sabon
Display: Franklin Gothic, Sabon
Compositor: Integrated Composition Systems
Printer and binder: Sheridan Books, Inc.